How to Conduct Telephone Surveys

2nd edition

THE SURVEY KIT, Second Edition

Purposes: The purposes of this 10-volume Kit are to enable readers to prepare and conduct surveys and to help readers become better users of survey results. Surveys are conducted to collect information; surveyors ask questions of people on the telephone, face-to-face, and by mail. The questions can be about attitudes, beliefs, and behavior as well as socioeconomic and health status. To do a good survey, one must know how to plan and budget for all survey tasks, how to ask questions, how to design the survey (research) project, how to sample respondents, how to collect reliable and valid information, and how to analyze and report the results.

Users: The Kit is for students in undergraduate and graduate classes in the social and health sciences and for individuals in the public and private sectors who are responsible for conducting and using surveys. Its primary goal is to enable users to prepare surveys and collect data that are accurate and useful for primarily practical purposes. Sometimes, these practical purposes overlap with the objectives of scientific research, and so survey researchers will also find the Kit useful.

Format of the Kit: All books in the series contain instructional objectives, exercises and answers, examples of surveys in use and illustrations of survey questions, guidelines for action, checklists of dos and don'ts, and annotated references.

Volumes in The Survey Kit:

1. **The Survey Handbook, 2nd**
   Arlene Fink
2. **How to Ask Survey Questions, 2nd**
   Arlene Fink
3. **How to Conduct Self-Administered and Mail Surveys, 2nd**
   Linda B. Bourque and Eve P. Fielder
4. **How to Conduct Telephone Surveys, 2nd**
   Linda B. Bourque and Eve P. Fielder
5. **How to Conduct In-Person Interviews for Surveys, 2nd**
   Sabine Mertens Oishi
6. **How to Design Survey Studies, 2nd**
   Arlene Fink
7. **How to Sample in Surveys, 2nd**
   Arlene Fink
8. **How to Assess and Interpret Survey Psychometrics, 2nd**
   Mark S. Litwin
9. **How to Manage, Analyze, and Interpret Survey Data, 2nd**
   Arlene Fink
10. **How to Report on Surveys, 2nd**
    Arlene Fink

The Survey Kit 2ed

4

Linda B. Bourque & Eve P. Fielder

How to Conduct Telephone Surveys

2nd edition

THE SURVEY KIT
TSK 2

SAGE Publications
International Educational and Professional Publisher
Thousand Oaks ▪ London ▪ New Delhi

For information:

Sage Publications, Inc.
2455 Teller Road
Thousand Oaks, California 91320
E-mail: order@sagepub.com

Sage Publications Ltd.
6 Bonhill Street
London EC2A 4PU
United Kingdom

Sage Publications India Pvt. Ltd.
M-32 Market
Greater Kailash I
New Delhi 110 048 India

Printed in the United States of America

Library of Congress Cataloging-in-Publication Data

The survey kit.—2nd ed.
    p. cm.
Includes bibliographical references.
ISBN 0-7619-2510-4 (set : pbk.)
1. Social surveys. 2. Health surveys. I. Fink, Arlene.
HN29 .S724 2002
300'.723—dc21   2002012405

This book is printed on acid-free paper.

02 03 04 05 10 9 8 7 6 5 4 3 2 1

Acquisitions Editor:	C. Deborah Laughton
Editorial Assistant:	Veronica Novak
Copy Editor:	Judy Selhorst
Production Editor:	Diane S. Foster
Typesetter:	Bramble Books
Proofreader:	Cheryl Rivard
Cover Designer:	Ravi Balasuriya
Production Designer:	Michelle Lee

Contents

Acknowledgments

We would like to thank Arlene Fink for her invitation to participate in this series and her helpful comments on earlier drafts of this manuscript. We particularly want to thank Kimberley I. Shoaf, Dr.P.H., for serving as project director on the Northridge study; Deborah Riopelle, M.S., for serving as project director on the Trinet Study; Jay Sumner, Ph.D., for assisting with Chapter 5; and Carrie Casteel, Ph.D., for creating Figure 5.4. David Watson from the Southern California Injury Prevention Center (SCIPRC) provided valuable clerical assistance in creating final copies of selected figures, the bibliography, and the text. For providing various kinds of assistance, including keeping us supplied with coffee, we thank Larry Chu, Ph.D., Marizen Ramirez, Ph.D., and Tom Rice, M.P.H., from SCIPRC; Caroline Sauter, M.P.H., from the Center for Public Health and Disasters; and Tonya Hays from the Institute for Social Science Research. Jess F. Kraus, Ph.D., director of SCIPRC, provided the senior author with space where she could hide from her obligations while this book was being written.

Data for the Loma Prieta study were collected under funds from the National Science Foundation (No. BCS-9002754). Data for the Northridge earthquake study were collected and processed with funds from the National Science Foundation (Nos. CMS-9416470 and CMS-9411982) and from the Los Angeles County Department of Health Services (Purchase Order R416470 and Award No. 953124). The Trinet Study was funded by Subcontracts G5934 from EQE International and G3068 from the California Institute of Technology.

How to Conduct Telephone Surveys: Learning Objectives

The aim of this book is to demonstrate how to develop and administer telephone **surveys**, with particular attention to paper-and-pencil administration, and prepare the results for analysis. Areas covered include the kinds of telephone surveys; the various methods of telephone data collection; the circumstances under which each method is appropriately used; the skills needed to design and administer the questionnaires used; how interviewers are selected, trained, and supervised; the ways in which samples are selected and response rates are calculated; how data are processed; how costs are estimated; and how the decisions made in the development and administration of telephone surveys are documented.

The specific objectives are as follows:

- Describe the methods by which telephone surveys are administered

- Identify the advantages and disadvantages of the use of telephone surveys

- Decide whether a telephone survey is appropriate for your research objective

- Determine the method of telephone data collection to be employed

- Determine the content of the questionnaire

- Develop questions for a user-friendly questionnaire

- Pretest, pilot-test, and revise a questionnaire

- Format a user-friendly questionnaire

- Develop procedures to motivate participation and increase response rates

- Write interviewer specifications that describe the procedures used in conducting the interviews and collecting the data

- Write research or questionnaire specifications that describe the objectives of the survey, characteristics of the sample, and the reasons for and sources of the questions used in the telephone survey

- Describe the different kinds of samples used

- Decide on a sampling strategy and calculate response rates

- Describe how to develop and produce a sample, identify potential resources for a sample, and organize the sample

- Describe how to hire, train, and supervise interviewers

- Describe the need for and use of "callbacks" and "refusal conversions," and how to monitor them

- Monitor data collection and sample utilization to inform and improve data collection

- Describe the procedures by which completed telephone interviews become an analyzable, machine-readable data file

- Describe how records are kept and their uses

- Estimate the costs of a telephone survey

- Estimate the personnel needed for a telephone survey

1 Overview of Telephone Surveys

In the United States, **telephone interviewing** has largely replaced **in-person (or face-to-face) interviewing** as the primary method of collecting research data from large probability samples of households or individuals. This has happened for a number of reasons. First, telephone interviewing is substantially cheaper to conduct than in-person interviewing. Second, surveyors can conduct telephone interviews over wide geographic areas. Third, telephone surveys can bypass the barriers created by security apartment buildings and the increasing reluctance among Americans to allow strangers into their homes. Finally, surveyors can complete telephone surveys in significantly shorter periods of time than would be needed for in-person surveys.

Unfortunately, as the use of legitimate telephone surveys has proliferated, so has the use of answering machines, caller ID, call-blocking devices, fax machines, computer modems, and cell phones among the general public. The result is that telephone surveyors are having increasing difficulty obtain-

1

ing representative samples of households and individual respondents. Simultaneously, businesses have discovered telemarketing—the use of the telephone to market products and services. In any given week, a household may receive numerous calls soliciting everything from votes in the next election to investment in a new limited partnership. This means that potential respondents frequently perceive telephone calls initiated by scientific, noncommercial researchers to be simply more solicitations from people trying to sell products. As a result, the costs of obtaining valid and reliable data from representative telephone interview samples of respondents and households have increased substantially over the past decade.

Like any research endeavor, and the use of any procedure for collecting data, the development and administration of telephone surveys require time and thought. This book outlines the circumstances under which telephone surveys are a good method for collecting information, what surveyors must consider in designing such studies, and the methods surveyors should use in administering telephone surveys in order to maximize the completeness, reliability, and validity of the data collected.

Types of Telephone Surveys

In telephone surveys, the data are collected within the context of telephone interviews. Thus, the stimulus for the respondent in a telephone survey is, almost without exception, exclusively auditory, whereas the stimulus for the **interviewer** is visual. One of the challenges for the surveyor in developing a **questionnaire** for use in a telephone survey is to make the questions and instructions as clear as possible for both the interviewer and the respondent. The introduction of an interviewer into the **data collection** process means that the process becomes a form of social interaction, and the interplay between the interviewer and the respondent can influence the **validity** and the **reliability** of the data collected. The introduction of the interviewer also means that a third party now stands between the researcher and the respondent. Because this is the case, the researcher must take care in the hiring, training, and supervision of interviewers, budgeting sufficient resources to ensure that these tasks are done consistently and appropriately.

The surveyor needs to take three dimensions into account when considering what kind of telephone survey to conduct. The first dimension is the amount of time that will be devoted to the actual collection of the data. The second dimension is the range of ways by which the people to be interviewed will be selected or sampled and the extent to which they represent larger populations. And the third dimension is the mechanism by which the interviews will be conducted. We address each of these dimensions below.

TIME DEVOTED TO DATA COLLECTION

The amount of time devoted to data collection in any given study can range from a few hours to months. The general rule regarding the time devoted to data collection is as follows: The shorter the data collection period, the less representative the sample will be of the **population** from which it was drawn; the longer the data collection period, the more representative the sample will be of the population from which it was drawn. Short-duration data collection is most appropriate, and necessary, when the surveyor's objective is to obtain a "snapshot" of a highly dynamic situation that is rapidly changing. This is frequently referred to as *polling.*

Researchers who employ polling as their primary method of data collection rely on the statistical properties of large sample sizes in evaluating their results rather than on the representativeness of their samples. Most poll results are reported to the public along with a margin of error. For example, the footnote for a data table displaying poll results might say, "Plus or minus 5%," meaning that the percentages shown for the responses reported (for example, the percentage of respondents who said that they agree with a particular government policy) could be as much as 5% higher or lower than the actual proportion of the sample who gave those responses.[1]

A pertinent example of the use of data collection through polling is found in the period following the attacks on the World Trade Center and the Pentagon on September 11, 2001. Within a span of just a few weeks, the World Trade Center and Pentagon were attacked, the federal government initiated a war against the Taliban in Afghanistan, and anthrax was discovered in letters delivered through the U.S. Postal Service. For many days after September 11, news coverage in the major electronic media was devoted exclusively to the rapidly unfolding events. For many months after September 11, both electronic and print media continued to devote substantial coverage to the proliferating events.

Researchers were interested in learning what various Americans knew about the events, what they thought about the events, and how their knowledge and opinions changed over time. Because events were unfolding rapidly and the news media's emphasis on various aspects of the events was also changing rapidly, researchers wanted to get quick, real-time snapshots of representative samples of the population. As a result, all of the telephone interviews in some surveys were conducted during single evenings. Usually in this kind of situation, a large number of interviewers simultaneously place calls to a large number of potential respondents. The pool of potential respondents is selected to be representative of geographically or politically described areas, but the actual sample of persons interviewed overrepresents those with whom it is easiest to complete interviews. That is, those interviewed are the persons who are at home on the night of the study and particularly those who arrive at home before the time frame within which the interviewing is conducted. For example, if interviews are conducted between 4:00 P.M. and 9:00 P.M. on a Monday evening, persons who are at home at 4:00 P.M. and who do not go out again during the data collection period are most likely to be interviewed. In addition, persons who do not tie up their telephone lines during that period (either by having conversations or by using fax machines or computer modems) and do not screen their calls through answering machines or other devices are more likely to be interviewed. And finally, persons who speak English are more likely to be interviewed, because the costs and time associated with translating an interview may be prohibitive for a study that is conducted within such a tight time frame.

In contrast, if we want to use a telephone survey to find out whether people have health insurance, with the objective of identifying groups in the population who do not have insurance or who are underinsured, we do not have to arrange to have all of the interviews conducted in a single evening—nor would it be advisable for us to do so. Whether or not a person or household has health insurance is a reasonably stable condition that in most cases will not change between today and next month. Furthermore, prior research has shown that persons who are unemployed or self-employed are less likely to have adequate insurance than are persons who work for *Fortune* 500 companies. If part of our objective is to identify families that might qualify for the Healthy Families program, we want our estimates to be as accurate as possible.[2] In such circumstances, data collection probably will last for a month or more, depending on the number of interviewers hired for the project.

Much of the interviewers' time in most telephone surveys is devoted to callbacks and refusal conversions. An interviewer makes a **callback** when an initial phone call does not result in contact with the eligible respondent; that is, when the interviewer gets no answer, a busy signal, or an answering machine, or makes contact with a person who is not eligible to be a respondent (e.g., a child in the household) or is not the designated respondent (e.g., the husband when the wife is the designated respondent). In such cases, the interviewer must call back at a later time on the same day, on the next day, or in the next week or month. If the interviewer is unsuccessful then, he or she may need to make repeated callbacks to attempt to contact the designated respondent. Generally, the more time and money built into the study budget for callbacks, the more representative the sample will be of the actual population with telephones, and the more likely that people who are rarely at home will be appropriately represented in the sample.

When an interviewer makes contact with the designated respondent (or someone speaking for the designated respondent) and that person initially refuses to be interviewed, the interviewer must make one or more attempts at **refusal conversion.** That is, the interviewer must try to convince or encourage the potential respondent to agree to be interviewed (thus converting a refusal to a completed interview).

BREADTH OF SAMPLE SELECTION

Surveyors who use telephone surveys have a wide range of objectives and employ a variety of sampling strategies. Perhaps the narrowest definition of a target population is the persons who belong to a particular organization or who appear on a particular list. In this case, the surveyor must already have a list of phone numbers or must create such a list before the telephone survey is conducted. A survey of members of a professional organization such as the American Dental Association (ADA) provides an example. The ADA is a national organization, so in-person interviewing would not be an efficient way to collect data from ADA members. If the organization wants to poll its members and also wants to maximize response rates, however, it might well use a telephone survey. Most professional organizations keep membership lists that include business and/or home telephone numbers for all of their members. The phone numbers a surveyor would need for a sample are available in a list that was created for another purpose, and the list is restricted to those persons who are members of the organization and who have provided phone numbers.

Random-digit dialing (RDD) represents the other end of the continuum. Here the potential population is not limited to those households or persons whose phone numbers appear on a published list. Rather, the potential population is represented by all telephone numbers that are currently active and is not limited only to the phone numbers that are listed in a telephone directory or on some other list. We discuss the creation of RDD samples in detail in Chapter 5.

METHOD OF DATA COLLECTION

Most telephone interviews are conducted using one of two methods: **paper-and-pencil administration** or **computer-assisted telephone interviewing (CATI)**. In paper-and-pencil **administration of questionnaires**, the interviewer reads instructions and questions to the respondent from a standard questionnaire formatted on paper and records the respondent's answers on the paper questionnaire. Interviewers in a study using paper-and-pencil administration may work out of a central location or conduct interviews from their home phones. Which of these options the surveyor selects has ramifications for both the cost of the interviews and the surveyor's ability to monitor the interviewers. Clearly, the surveyor can monitor the work the interviewers are doing more easily and efficiently if interviews are conducted in a central location, but this is not always possible. It may be too expensive to use a central location; for example, at some universities (such as the University of California) telephone charges are substantially higher on campus than they are elsewhere. In other cases, a convenient and inexpensive central location may be unavailable. For example, consider a survey that a local grade school PTA wants to conduct to ask parents whose children are enrolled in that school whether they support or oppose the PTA's asking parents to volunteer one afternoon a month to provide remedial literacy mentoring. It is very unlikely that interviewers for such a survey would be able to work in a central location.

Compared with computer-assisted telephone interviewing, studies conducted through paper-and-pencil administration can be developed and fielded much more quickly.

However, paper-and-pencil studies need more time than CATI studies after data collection for data cleaning and other preparation of the data for analysis. Despite the benefits of CATI in shortening the post–data collection phase, the costs of the data collection are lower for paper-and-pencil administration, and this frequently results in lower overall costs.

The first CATI systems were developed and tested at the University of California's Berkeley and Los Angeles campuses in the 1970s. (For a description of the use of this early system, see the article by Howard Freeman and Merrill Shanks [1983] listed in the "References and Suggested Readings" section at the end of this volume.) Setting up a CATI study requires substantial amounts of time and money, because the questionnaire has to be specially formatted and programmed into the computer system that is being used. The surveyor must find and hire a computer programmer who has the special skills required to do this work and keep a CATI system functioning for the duration of the study's data collection period, and such programmers are neither easily found nor inexpensive. In addition, the outlay in original costs for a CATI survey—that is, for the purchase of hardware and software—is substantial. In contrast to paper-and-pencil interviewers, CATI interviewers usually do their work in a central location, where members of the survey team can easily monitor them.

In a CATI survey, the interviewer reads the instructions and questions to the respondent from the computer monitor and enters the responses directly into the computer. Progression through the questionnaire is controlled by the computer. When the questionnaire is programmed properly, skip patterns or branching instructions are followed automatically, minimizing the likelihood that the interviewer will ask or skip any questions inappropriately. However, if a programming error results in an inappropriate skip that is not discovered during pretesting, the result may be permanently lost data. For example, in a CATI study conducted after the Northridge, California, earthquake of January 17, 1994, respondents were asked if they evacuated their homes after the earthquake. If they answered "yes, they had evacuated" for even a short time period, they were supposed to be asked a series of questions about why they evacuated, where they went, how long they were out of their homes, and so on. Unfortunately, when the questionnaire was programmed into the computer, it was set up in such a way that the interviewers were led to ask only a few of the people who left their homes any of the follow-up questions. This error was not identified until the survey team began work on the data analysis.

In CATI programming, all of the phone numbers that are potentially going to be called in the survey are entered into the computer. When an interviewer logs on to begin work, he or she is automatically provided with the next phone number to call. This system works well for moving through the sample at least on the first round of calls, and many of the CATI programs available today can be programmed to prompt callbacks to telephone numbers when earlier attempts resulted in outcomes such as busy signals, no answers, **language barriers,** and **refusals.** For example, if the original call to a number results in an outcome of no answer, the CATI program might schedule the next attempt to call that number on a different day of the week or at a different time of day. If the interviewer first calls the number at 4:00 P.M. on Wednesday, for instance, the first callback might be at 6:30 P.M. on Thursday. If the second call similarly results in no answer, the program might schedule the third call for a Saturday or Sunday. The rule (in either CATI or paper-and-pencil interviewing) is that callbacks should not be attempted at identical times on similar days. In other words, if a number is never answered between 6:00 and 8:00 P.M. on a weekday, the interviewer needs to try the number on a weekend or at a substantially different time on a weekday. In CATI, this algorithm is programmed into the computer prior to the start of data collection, taking a big burden off of the interviewing supervisors.

Also in CATI, interviewers who have shown that they have a better-than-average ability to complete interviews with hard-to-convince respondents can log on as refusal con-verters, and the program will direct them to any cases, or phone numbers, that had prior outcomes coded as refusals. Similarly, **bilingual** interviewers who are adept in the lan-guages required can identify themselves as bilingual when they log on, and the program will feed them the numbers of potential respondents whose prior outcomes were coded as incomplete because of a language barrier.

The single biggest advantage of CATI is that once the data are collected, they are quickly available for analysis and associated data processing. Because the interviewers type all answers directly into computers, there are no paper copies of questionnaires that have to be stored and from which answers must be entered into a machine-readable file. Thus, once all the interviews have been completed, the program-mer can quickly create SAS, SPSS, or other statistical analysis package files. CATI also makes it easy for the survey team to monitor characteristics of the sample. However, these advan-tages—the accessibility of the data for analysis and the ease of monitoring the sample—are so seductive that they can become disadvantages as well. Researchers using CATI are often tempted to look at distributions on variables while data collection is still in progress, and such "early results" can often be misleading. Persons who spend a lot of time at home and who answer the phone regularly are more easily interviewed and, as a result, are generally interviewed early in the data collection period. In contrast, people who spend very little time at home and are much more difficult to reach generally require more callbacks and are, as a result, more likely to be interviewed late in the data collection period. If behaviors and attitudes are associated with the tendency to be at home, the "picture" of the population that a surveyor sees when he or she looks at the data distributions early in the data collection period may be very different from the picture that will develop when data collection is completed.

Advantages of Telephone Surveys

The relative advantages and disadvantages of telephone surveys fall somewhere in between those associated with surveys using self-administered questionnaires and in-person surveys, with telephone surveys generally being more like the latter. The advantages of telephone surveys for the surveyor are related to issues of sampling, questionnaire construction, and control over who responds.

SAMPLING

The Need for Lists

Data collection for telephone surveys may or may not depend on the availability of lists. As we noted above, surveyors may use already existing lists of telephone numbers, but they may also use random-digit dialing sampling procedures. Sometimes surveyors use **dual-frame samples**; for example, they might attempt to combine the greater representativeness of an RDD sample with the greater efficiency in finding an eligible household that is characteristic of list samples. The availability of RDD is a distinct advantage for those conducting telephone surveys, and many argue that telephone interviews using RDD samples are the norm in the current survey environment. Usually, RDD samples are considered to represent the civilian noninstitutionalized population 18 years of age and older.

Geographic Coverage

When data collection is done by telephone, a surveyor can collect data over a larger geographic area than he or she could cover using in-person interviews. Although long-distance calls are more expensive than local calls, in fact, the toll charges across most large metropolitan areas are not uniform. For example, a researcher conducting a phone survey across all of Los Angeles County will find that the costs of the calls vary quite a bit. However, the additional costs associated with calling a representative sample of California residents rather than restricting the sample to Los Angeles County will be substantially less than the additional costs that would be associated with conducting in-person interviews throughout California. In addition, follow-up on "no outcome" cases is considerably cheaper when conducted by telephone. When an in-person interviewer has not been able to contact someone in a household, the surveyor must pay for the interviewer's travel time and mileage for numerous return trips to that household to determine eligibility and/or complete an interview. Although follow-up attempts made by telephone are not cost-free, they are considerably less expensive and more convenient to attempt than in-person follow-ups.

Any limitations associated with geographic coverage in telephone surveys have more to do with the capabilities of the researcher than with the cost of telephone charges. The wider the geographic area over which interviews are conducted, the more interviewers the researcher must have available; if the interviewing is conducted from a central location using CATI, the location must be equipped with sufficient numbers of computers from which the interviewers can work.

The practical upper geographic limit for telephone surveys is probably all of the United States, or perhaps the continental United States (that is, excluding Alaska and Hawaii). Many of the studies conducted by the federal government and established U.S. survey research centers collect data by telephone, at least in follow-up interviews, and they collect data from nationally representative samples. For example, follow-up interviews for the National Crime Victimization Survey and the Current Population Survey are conducted by telephone after initial in-person interviews in the respondents' homes. The University of Michigan's Survey of Consumer Attitudes is a national telephone study that has been conducted each month since 1977. In this study, data are collected exclusively by telephone from a sample drawn using random-digit dialing procedures. Initial interviews in the California Health Interview Survey are conducted by telephone, with some in-person interviews conducted in follow-ups with hard-to-reach respondents or those who do not have telephones. Researchers who want to include people from outside the United States in their studies will probably need to collaborate with researchers from other countries if they want to conduct surveys by telephone. Alternatively, they might use mail surveys (if they have lists of correct addresses available) or a mixed-mode form of data collection that combines telephone and mail procedures.

Telephone Availability

In the past, there was substantial concern among researchers that telephone surveys could not collect any data on persons living in households that do not have telephones. Today, however, the overwhelming majority of households in the United States do have telephones (and some have multiple phone lines, which complicates sampling designs). In 2000, 97.25% of all households in the United States had telephones. We know, however, that telephone availability differs by state, socioeconomic status, and other demographic characteristics. For example, 98.1% of households in California and 98.2% of households in North Dakota reported having a telephone in 2000. In contrast, only 94.1% of households in Mississippi had telephones. Clearly, in deciding whether or not a telephone survey is appropriate for a given study, the researcher needs to consider who the respondent population is and whether or not members of that population can be expected to have telephones.

In addition, the stability of telephone availability changes over time. This is associated with both mobility and the demographic characteristics of households. Low-income households often have only sporadic access to telephones or share telephones with other households. Of similar concern is the increasing use of cell phones and pagers. Today, many individuals find it more economical and efficient to use their cell phones as their primary telephones, and many have canceled their standard household telephone service. Currently, survey researchers do not interview people they reach on cell phones, because the numbers assigned to cell phones are not considered representative of households or residences. In addition, calls to cell phones, unlike calls to household phones, result in charges to the person answering as well as to the person calling. If the trend toward replacing household phones with cell phones continues to grow, however, survey researchers may be forced by their concerns about underrepresented population subgroups and declining response rates to reconsider their position.

Response Rates

Response rates for telephone surveys are consistently and significantly higher than those for mail surveys, but generally are thought to be lower than those for surveys using in-person interviews. A major complication arises when researchers attempt to compare the response rates for telephone and in-person interview survey studies because the procedures used for calculating response rates differ from study to study. In 2000, the American Association for Public Opinion Research issued recommended standard guidelines for reporting response rates, and other survey research organizations, both public and private, have been stating the need for researchers to establish comparable definitions for the past 15 years.

Types of nonresponse in telephone surveys can be divided roughly into three categories: those persons who actively refuse to be interviewed; those persons who are never successfully contacted because of repeated no answers, busy signals, or pickups by answering machines at their telephone numbers; and other noninterviews (these include a wide range of situations, but the ones most frequently listed are language barriers, the designated respondent is too ill to participate, and the interviewer has determined that the designated respondent is incapable of participating in the interview). Unfortunately, survey researchers do not consistently report how the nonresponses in their studies are distributed among these various categories. Many simply ignore numbers they never called or at which an interviewer never spoke with an actual person. As a result, they never determine (and thus never report) whether these telephone numbers are in households where potentially eligible respondents might live; whether they are in businesses, which would be ineligible for household studies; or whether they are numbers that are not in service.

There is no doubt that refusal rates decline as the numbers of attempted callbacks and refusal conversions increase. Rigorously conducted noncommercial telephone surveys have achieved response rates above 70%. In contrast, the Council for Marketing and Opinion Research, which represents many market research firms, reports that response rates for 12- to 15-minute commercial surveys are as low as 12% (suggesting that market researchers should perhaps consider using mail surveys, which would be as efficient and would possibly be a less expensive means of collecting data).

Members of the survey research community engage in substantial, ongoing discussion regarding trends in response rates over time. Certainly the proliferation of such technologies as caller ID, cellular phones, pagers, answering machines, fax machines, and computer modems, as well as the increasing ubiquity of telemarketing, has had a dampening effect on the reliability and validity of the data collected in telephone surveys. Steeh, Kirgis, Cannon, and DeWitt (2000) have suggested that increases in noncontact should be of greater concern than increases in actual refusals; they point out that "refusals are always troublesome but not as problematic as not being able to contact potential respondents to give them a chance to refuse" (p. 246). See Chapters 5 and 6 for more in-depth discussion of response rates in association with sample design issues and decisions regarding callbacks, refusal conversion, and interviewer training.

Literacy and Language

A substantial advantage of both telephone surveys and surveys using in-person interviewing is that respondents need not have a particular level of **literacy** to participate. When resources are available, surveyors can have their questionnaires translated into languages other than English, hire interviewers who are fluent in the relevant languages, and train them to conduct the interviews. In the past, the rate of adult **illiteracy** in the United States was estimated to be 20%. Data from the 2000 Census show that 17.6% of the population over 5 years of age do not speak English in the home, that 44% of this group speaks English less than "very well," and that 6.9% of the population over age 25 has completed less than 9 years of schooling. Persons with low levels of education frequently are functionally illiterate, meaning that they are unable to read comfortably. As a result, they cannot respond adequately to self-administered questionnaires.

An additional possible problem for survey researchers—particularly in large urban areas on the East and West Coasts—is the wide range of languages spoken in potential respondents' homes. For example, in Los Angeles County, 13% of the population is linguistically isolated—meaning that they speak no English—and an additional 26% report that a language other than English is the primary or only language spoken in the home, with 47.8% of this group speaking English less than "very well." When target populations include substantial proportions of respondents who do not speak English, interviews (whether conducted over the phone or in person) are far superior to self-administered questionnaires for collecting data.

Telephone surveys become substantially more expensive to conduct when the researchers must arrange for the **translation** of the questionnaires and must hire and train bilingual interviewers, but such additional costs are unavoidable if surveyors are going to obtain accurate descriptions of certain populations.

QUESTIONNAIRE CONSTRUCTION

Objective/Complexity

The presence of the interviewer in a telephone survey means that the study can have multiple objectives and that these objectives can be more complex than the objectives in self-administered questionnaires. For example, instead of asking respondents only whether they are currently employed and where they are employed, the surveyor can collect complete occupational histories from them and combine questions to ask about their satisfaction with their current work sites, their jobs, their employment benefits, and their coworkers, and how these factors correlate or interact with their lifestyles.

In addition, surveyors always want study participants to be interested in their research studies and motivated to respond. Well-trained interviewers can help respondents understand the questions and thus make it easier for the respondents to participate.

Format

Telephone surveys can be longer and more complex than mail or other self-administered questionnaires. Because an interviewer administers the questionnaire in a telephone survey, frequently using a CATI system, the questionnaire can be specifically tailored for many different subgroups in the population. In the post-earthquake surveys that we use as examples in this book, the respondents differed in many respects. Some people were in the affected area on the day of the earthquake, whereas others who lived in the area were not at home that day. Some people's homes were damaged and some were not. Some people left their homes after the earthquake; others did not. Some applied for assistance after the earthquake, and others did not. Within the structure of the questionnaires, the surveyors developed branching options with skip instructions so that respondents were asked only those questions that were relevant to their own situations and experiences during and after the earthquake.

In addition, the questionnaires used in telephone surveys can be longer than self-administered questionnaires. This means that surveyors can include more topics in telephone surveys and that they can explore each topic in greater depth than would be possible in a self-administered questionnaire.

Another advantage of telephone surveys is that they allow researchers to employ **open-ended questions** (that is, questions for which possible responses are not provided for the respondent, or at least are not read to the respondent by the interviewer). Respondents filling out self-administered questionnaires generally do not want to have to write lengthy responses to open-ended questions, but in interviews, it is the interviewers, not the respondents, who assume the burden of writing down the answers. Additionally, the responses to open-ended questions that interviewers obtain are usually more to the point and meaningful than those collected in self-administered questionnaires. For example, in a self-administered questionnaire, a respondent's written answer to the open-ended question "What do you like best about this cereal?" might be "I like the consistency." Does the respondent mean that he or she likes the fact that the cereal is thick or thin, crisp or soft, grainy or smooth? Well-trained interviewers know how to probe such responses to clarify exactly what respondents like and dislike.

Finally, unlike a self-administered questionnaire, the questionnaire in a telephone survey does not have to "stand alone." An interviewer is available to provide and clarify instructions and to give the respondent additional information if necessary to eliminate confusion. The researcher's objective in any form of data collection should be to make the process as easy and user-friendly for the respondent as possible. Researchers who design telephone surveys have the benefit of the presence of interviewers, but this does *not* mean that they should make their questionnaires needlessly complex. After all, interviewers appreciate user-friendly questionnaires as much as respondents do.

Order Effects

When questionnaires are administered by interviewers, whether over the telephone or in person, **order effects** are reduced. The interviewer (following the instructions of the surveyor) controls the order in which the questions are asked and whether or not the answer alternatives are made available to the respondent. In a telephone survey, the interviewer might or might not read the answer categories listed on the questionnaire aloud to the respondent; in an in-person interview with a literate respondent, the interviewer might or might not provide the respondent with a cue card that lists the possible alternative answers.

Researchers are often concerned about the extent to which one set of questions is likely to contaminate, bias, or influence respondents' answers to other sets of questions. For example, following the attack on the World Trade Center of September 11, 2001, and the subsequent discovery of anthrax in a number of letters sent through the U.S. mail, many health researchers were interested in knowing how much Americans know about anthrax, antibiotics, and antibiotic resistance. A team of health researchers conducting a survey on this topic might first try to assess respondents' initial state of knowledge by asking them whether they have ever heard the term *antibiotic resistance* and then using an open-ended question to ask respondents to describe what they think the term means. Later in the questionnaire, the researchers might give a standard definition of antibiotic resistance to ensure that all respondents have a "standard" basic understanding to work from in answering subsequent questions. If respondents were given this definition *before* they were asked to relate their own understanding of the term *antibiotic resistance,* their answers to that question would be biased, contaminated, or influenced by it, and most would likely present the interviewer with a description of antibiotic resistance that largely matches the definition read to them previously.

This example illustrates how researchers and interviewers control the order in which questions are asked and determine when respondents are given pertinent definitions. In the example study, the researchers learn the respondents' levels of knowledge about antibiotic resistance by having them describe what they think it is, and then later give the respondents a definition that allows them to answer subsequent questions with some minimal level of standardized knowledge. In contrast, in a survey using mailed or other self-administered questionnaires, the respondents determine the order in which they read questions and definitions. If the researchers in the above example were using a self-administered questionnaire, they would have to choose between giving the respondents a definition of antibiotic resistance to use in answering subsequent questions, while never finding out what the respondents thought it meant before being told, or *not* giving respondents a definition and running the risk that respondents would either refuse to complete the questionnaire because they do not understand the term or provide uninformed answers because they want to be cooperative and help the researchers.

The use of telephone interviews also allows the researcher to build validity checks into the questionnaire. If, for example, a surveyor is suspicious that respondents are more likely to underreport their ages when asked, "How old were you on your last birthday?" than when they are asked, "When were you born?" he or she can include both questions in the questionnaire, provided they are placed at a reasonable distance from each other and the researcher can compare the answers given without the respondent's knowing.

In addition, when interviewers control the question order, the opportunities for respondents to change their answers are significantly reduced or even eliminated. Surveyors should give interviewers instructions regarding the legitimacy of letting respondents change their answers to particular questions. The surveyor might instruct the interviewer that when a respondent wants to change an answer to give a more complete description of something (for example, of the last time he or she went to the hospital), the interviewer should allow the respondent to provide that additional information. In contrast, when it appears that the respondent wants to change an answer so that it reflects an opinion that the respondent thinks is more socially acceptable than the previous answer, the interviewer probably should not allow the change.

CONTROL OVER WHO RESPONDS

One of the biggest advantages of conducting a survey through interviews is that the researcher can **control** who responds to the interviewer and can institute controls over the interviewers to ensure that they follow directions. Sometimes the researcher only wants to make sure that the correct phone numbers are called, that the phone numbers represent households, and that in each household an adult who lives there can "speak for" the household in responding to the interview. In other situations, the researcher wants to randomize or in other ways ensure that different adults within households are selected across the sample. For example, the researcher does not want only women who live in households to respond to the interview because women's opinions, behaviors, and knowledge will then be overrepresented and men's opinions, behaviors, and knowledge will be underrepresented in the final sample. Similarly, researchers want to make sure that interviewers do not always interview the person who usually answers the phone in the households sampled. In some households, it is customary for the husband to answer the phone if he is at home; in others, it is customary for the wife to answer the phone; and in homes with an adolescent and a single phone line, you can almost guarantee that the adolescent will answer the phone.

To ensure that designated respondents are varied among the different adult (18 years and older) members of households, researchers use Kish tables, Troldahl-Carter-Bryant (TCB) tables, and the last/next birthday method to select individuals to be interviewed. We discuss the use of these methods to randomize the selection of respondents within households in Chapter 5.

Although in a telephone survey the interviewer does not have as much control over the interview situation as an interviewer who administers a questionnaire in person, the interviewer in a telephone survey can often detect whether or not a respondent is alone, whether the respondent is being hassled by hungry and tired children, or whether the respondent is having difficulty concentrating on the interview because of other interruptions. To ensure the **confidentiality** of the data collected from respondents, interviews should always be conducted under conditions that maximize privacy. When we conduct a telephone survey, we usually do not want a household's "group consensus" regarding whether or not the designated respondent voted in the last election; we do want to know if the designated respondent voted in the last election, and we probably want to know something about why he or she voted, which candidate he or she voted for, and why. To ensure that we get the designated respondent's honest responses and not responses that reflect what others in the household may think, we instruct our interviewers to reschedule interviews when they sense that others in a household can overhear or influence the interview.

Disadvantages of Telephone Surveys

COST

The single biggest disadvantage of telephone surveys, compared with mail or other self-administered surveys, is their cost. It is hard to establish exactly how much more telephone surveys cost, because expenses vary with the length of the interview, the characteristics of the sample, and how the interview is administered. The general rule of thumb is that, given questionnaires of the same length and the same objective, a completed questionnaire administered by telephone costs approximately twice as much as one administered by mail, but only half as much as one administered through an in-person interview. Given that the questionnaires used in telephone surveys are, by definition, lengthier and more complex than self-administered questionnaires, the only occasions that allow us to get even a rough idea of how the two methods compare are those in which researchers use telephone interviews as a last-resort method for obtaining data from respondents in studies where the original data collection was conducted using a mailed, self-administered questionnaire. In **How to Conduct Self-Administered and Mail Surveys** (Volume 3 in this series), we demonstrate that the cost for one completed telephone interview, when telephone interviews follow two mailings of the questionnaire and a postcard reminder, is approximately equal to the cost of a completed mailed questionnaire with two follow-ups. See Chapter 6 in this volume for some comparisons of task-specific costs for conducting telephone surveys given different objectives and organizational structures.

SAMPLING

Telephone surveys have two main disadvantages in the area of sampling; these involve geographic coverage and response rates.

Geographic Coverage

As we noted above, U.S. researchers can field telephone surveys relatively easily within the United States, but they find it more difficult to use telephone surveys when they are interested in samples outside the United States. Among the difficulties inherent in an international telephone survey are the costs associated with international telephone rates and the problems that arise when interviewers and respondents are in different time zones. Frequently, researchers use mail surveys rather than telephone surveys when some or all of their intended respondents live outside the United States. Alternatively, researchers might collaborate with research groups based in the countries of interest who have the capability of conducting telephone interviews. Of course, such collaborations raise issues of quality control; researchers who participate in them must be aware of factors that can influence the comparability of the data collected across the countries studied.

Increasingly, researchers who are interested in gathering survey data from international respondents are conducting their surveys online. Although telephone coverage is still somewhat marginal in many countries, access to the Internet may be comparable to **telephone access** in some areas. Of course, international surveys conducted by phone or via the Web represent a limited sector of the international population.

Response Rates

As we have noted above, the response rates for telephone surveys are substantially higher than those for mail surveys. However, as we have also noted, the procedures used to calculate response rates as well as the proliferation of technologies that are resulting in increases in noncontacts in telephone surveys have begun to confront survey researchers with very real challenges. In the future, telephone samples may be increasingly less representative of the general population, and the costs of telephone surveys are certain to rise.

IMPLEMENTATION

Telephone surveys are much more difficult to **implement** than surveys using self-administered questionnaires, but much easier to implement than comparable surveys using in-person interviews. First, telephone surveys employ substantially greater numbers of personnel than mail and other self-administered surveys because they require interviewers as well as individuals to hire, train, and supervise the interviewers. Second, telephone surveys are longer and more complex in structure than self-administered surveys; this means that the development, data collection, and administration of telephone surveys demand more sophistication and training on the part of the personnel involved. In telephone surveys using CATI, the up-front costs attached to purchasing hardware and software, the study-specific programming needs, and the ongoing costs associated with keeping the CATI system functioning while data are being collected are substantial.

TIMING

In most telephone surveys, data are collected over long enough periods that the researchers cannot always assume that all respondents get an absolutely identical stimulus. When we conduct telephone surveys, however, we generally assume that the stimulus is consistent over the period of time within which data collection is being conducted as long as no events occur, external to the study, that could directly affect respondents' reports of their behaviors and opinions. For example, in the community studies we conducted after California earthquakes that we use as examples throughout this book, we assumed that respondents' reports of what they did during and after an earthquake would not change while we collected the data. If, however, another substantial earthquake had occurred in California during the time that we were collecting data, we would have assumed that respondents who were interviewed *after* the new earthquake would react differently to the interview and, hence, provide data that would differ from those collected during interviews *before* the new earthquake.

In contrast, the events of September 11, 2001, were so unusual that many survey houses who were in the field collecting data at the time assumed that the events had effects on all the data collected. Whether this, in fact, turned out to be true has yet to be assessed at the time of this writing.

SENSITIVE TOPICS

Many surveyors believe that people are more likely to give complete and truthful information on **sensitive topics**, such as sexual behavior and illicit drug use, in a self-administered questionnaire than in an interview. Early methodological studies tended to support this perception, but more recent studies suggest that surveyors may collect sensitive information as effectively or with even greater accuracy through telephone and in-person interviews. The reason for the variation in findings on this topic across time and studies can probably be accounted for by the overall objectives of the survey studies examined, the environments in which they were conducted, the ability of the interviewers in the studies to establish rapport, the extent to which respondents believed that the data they provided would be either **anonymous** or confidential, changing social norms, and the ways in which both the overall questionnaires and individual questions were structured. We are of the opinion that surveyors can effectively study sensitive topics using all kinds of questionnaires.

Aquilino and colleagues have conducted research on respondents' reactions to sensitive topics in surveys. They found that respondents' admissions of alcohol, tobacco, and illicit drug use appear to be highest when the data are collected in in-person interviews in which the interviewers give the respondents brief self-administered questionnaires that allow them to answer questions on sensitive topics privately. These researchers also found that, among the studies they examined, telephone interviews resulted in the lowest reports of alcohol, tobacco, and illicit drug use by respondents; they did not make comparisons to studies where the data were collected only by self-administered questionnaires.

The problems associated with making such comparisons are multiple and difficult to solve. First, rarely does an indisputable standard (a so-called gold standard) exist against which the data collected by survey, regardless of type, can be compared. Although researchers usually assume that higher reports of sensitive behaviors are "good," it may well be that respondents overreport such behaviors in certain method-ological settings. Second, the lower response rates for self-administered surveys in general, and the inability to translate the questionnaires, often mean that the samples of respondents for self-administered surveys and interview sur-veys are not comparable. Third, the ability to include more questions, more complicated questions, and interviewer probing in studies conducted by interview may mean that the data obtained in interviews of any kind are more com-plete and therefore more valuable than the data that can be obtained using self-administered questionnaires. And fourth, although researchers often assume that the presence of an interviewer increases the respondent's suspicions that the information he or she provides will not be kept confidential, an alternative argument is that the presence of a well-trained interviewer who can explain questions and can describe how confidentiality is maintained might reduce a respondent's suspicions and, as a result, increase the respondent's willing-ness to provide sensitive information.

Telephone Surveys by Example

In the remainder of this book, we explain and describe how questionnaires for telephone surveys are developed and how telephone surveys are administered. Throughout the chap-ters that follow, we use as examples three recent studies in which we were involved as researchers; we describe these studies briefly below.

COMMUNITY SURVEYS

Since 1987, the Center for Public Health and Disasters, located in the School of Public Health at the University of

California, Los Angeles, and the Survey Research Center, located in the Institute for Social Science Research at UCLA, have conducted a series of telephone surveys following California earthquakes. Two of these studies were conducted following the Loma Prieta earthquake of October 17, 1989, and the Northridge earthquake of January 17, 1994. Both surveys were conducted by telephone using a standardized questionnaire that was largely identical for the two studies. Random-digit dialing was used to select households in both studies, and either the Kish tables (Loma Prieta) or a combination of Kish tables and the last/next birthday method within a split-ballot experiment (Northridge, Wave 1) was used to select the designated respondent within the household. The split-ballot method requires that half of the subject population experience one situation and the other half experience an alternate situation. In this case, half of the respondents were selected using the Kish selection table, and the other half were selected using the last/next birthday method. The assignment to the selection method was random.

Both the Loma Prieta study and the Northridge study collected information about the following: where the respondent was at the time of the earthquake, who he or she was with, and what he or she did during and immediately after the earthquake; whether or not the respondent or other members of the household were injured; whether the earthquake caused damage to the respondent's home and neighborhood; the extent to which the utilities in the respondent's home went out; the respondent's use of media to obtain information; the extent of the respondent's contact with officials and public and private agencies after the quakes; the respondent's adoption of earthquake-preparedness and damage-mitigation activities before and after the index quake; and standard demographic data about the respondent and the household.

The Loma Prieta and Northridge studies differed in five respects. First, obviously, the times of survey administration differed, with the Loma Prieta study fielded between April 29 and August 1, 1990, and the Northridge, Wave 1, study fielded between August 10 and December 6, 1994. Second, the locations of the respondents differed, with Loma Prieta respondents living in five counties in the San Francisco Bay Area (San Francisco, Alameda, Oakland, Santa Cruz, and San Mateo Counties) and the Northridge respondents living in Los Angeles County. Third, the Loma Prieta sample was stratified, with oversampling conducted in the two areas where shaking was most intense—namely, the northwest edge of the San Francisco peninsula and Oakland, and the Boulder Creek/Santa Cruz/Watsonville area—whereas the Northridge sample was not stratified. Fourth, the interviews following the Loma Prieta earthquake averaged 30 minutes, whereas the interviews following the Northridge earthquake averaged 48 minutes. The latter study's interviews were longer both because additional items were added to the questionnaire that was used following the Northridge earthquake and because respondents in the Northridge study reported more damage, injury, use of services, and dislocation than the respondents in the Loma Prieta study. And finally, the modes of administration were different for the two studies; the Loma Prieta data were collected using paper-and-pencil techniques, and the Northridge data were collected using computer-assisted telephone interviewing.

TRINET STUDY

The Trinet Study examined respondents' interest in "real-time" earthquake warnings. Under funding from the U.S. Geological Survey, the California Department of Mines, and the California Institute of Technology, a network of monitors has been installed throughout Southern California for the purpose of monitoring earthquake activity in the region. The objective of the Trinet telephone survey was to find out whether various institutional groups, representing education, health, emergency response, and utilities, in Southern California would be interested in using this network of monitors to obtain advance warning that an earthquake had been detected and that shaking could be expected within the next

10 to 50 seconds. Unlike the earthquake study, respondents for the Trinet Study were a **purposive** or quota sample of elite respondents for whom we had telephone numbers and addresses in advance. Data were collected using paper-and-pencil telephone interviews with a sample of 192 respondents between March 8 and September 30, 2000.

To reflect the normal progress and problems often associated with the design of questionnaires and the administration of surveys, in the following chapters, we discuss what worked, what did not work, and what could have been improved in our three studies. Although we draw most of our examples from these three studies, we also present examples from other sources and studies where appropriate.

Notes

1.   The term *polling* is also used to refer to the collection of data by having respondents call a telephone number or log on to a Web site advertised on a television show, or by having them send in questionnaires from magazines. A large number of people may respond to these "polls," but the data collected are not representative of any group except those who respond. These samples, which are not representative of a larger population, are referred to as *nonprobability convenience samples*. (For a discussion of sampling, see Chapter 5.)

2.   Healthy Families is a federal program that provides health insurance for children 18 and younger who are U.S. citizens or legal permanent residents. To qualify for Healthy Families in California, a family must have an annual income that is no more than 250% of the federal poverty level. At a cost of $4.00 to $9.00 per child per month, the program provides children with access to health care, including vision and dental care and coverage for hospitalization (Barreto, 2001).

2 Content of the Questionnaire

We begin this chapter by describing briefly the types of data surveyors can collect using questionnaires and how surveyors should make decisions regarding the appropriateness of using telephone surveys. The remainder of the chapter focuses on the development of the content of the questionnaire.

Types of Data Collected Using Questionnaires

Studies of people generally collect data in one or more of five areas: (a) personal information about respondents (or **demographic data**), (b) information about respondents' environments, (c) information about respondents' behaviors, (d) information about respondents' experiences or status, and (e) information about respondents' thoughts or feelings. Surveyors often use questionnaires to collect data on a combination of people's knowledge, attitudes, and behaviors within particular subject areas, for example, their use of health services. One of the worst things that can happen to a surveyor is to discover, in preparing to analyze the data, that the survey failed to collect an essential piece of information. Inexperienced surveyors often forget to collect data on one or more important demographic variables, such as age, gender, education, occupational status, ethnic or racial identification, religious affiliation, or marital status. (For more on demographic data, see **How to Ask Survey Questions,** Volume 2 in this series.)

The other four types of data noted above, alone or in combination, usually form the focus of the research question. In our studies of earthquakes, for example, we asked people about their behaviors (e.g., what did they do at the time of the earthquake?), their experiences during and after the earthquake (e.g., were they injured?), their opinions (e.g., did they think people were prepared for earthquakes?), and their environment (e.g., were their homes and neighborhoods damaged?). We also asked them to provide demographic information, namely, gender, age, employment status, household composition, home ownership, place of birth, and religious affiliation. We hypothesized that respondents' experiences, behaviors, and opinions would vary, both with the magnitude of shaking that respondents experienced during the earthquake and with the respondents' demographic characteristics.

Appropriateness of Using Telephone Surveys

Surveyors must evaluate three kinds of information in assessing whether or not they should attempt to collect data through telephone surveys: the availability of telephones in the targeted population, the motivation level of the targeted population, and the amenability of the research question to data collection by telephone.

TELEPHONE ACCESS

As we pointed out in Chapter 1, most households in the United States now have access to telephones. Nonetheless, some proportion of households do not have telephones. Some groups do not reside in traditional households and hence do not have telephones, and some households have only episodic access to telephones.

In the past, disaster researchers did not think that telephone surveys were viable tools for collecting data following natural disasters, because they assumed that telephone service was likely to fail during such disasters; in fact, however, that is rarely the case. Rather, during and immediately after a natural disaster, telephone lines get overloaded when great numbers of people place calls into and out of the disaster area to reach family members and friends to inquire about their well-being. As a result, telephone interviews are not a good way to collect data immediately after a disaster, but researchers can rarely get into the field immediately anyway. Telephone surveys *are* a good way to collect data in the weeks and months after a disaster.

In contrast, if the focus of a researcher's study is the homeless population and persons who live in single-room occupancy buildings (SROs), a telephone survey would not be a good way to collect data at any time, because the people in the study's target population do not have access to telephones.[1] To collect data effectively from people without phones, a researcher would need to use in-person interviews.

MOTIVATION

It is always difficult to assess the **motivation** of the members of a target population. In all studies, researchers want their respondents to be motivated. Obviously, if the leaders of a professional organization hire a researcher to conduct a study for them, the very request for the study suggests that the organization and its members have some minimal level of motivation to provide the data requested. In telephone surveys, interviewers are key in increasing the motivation of respondents to participate, and the process by which interviewers introduce themselves and the study is key to maximizing cooperation.

When researchers have access to the addresses as well as the telephone numbers for their target population, they can send an **advance letter** to each respondent to explain what the study is about, who is conducting it, and when the respondent will be called. In the Trinet Study, two advance letters were sent to encourage participation. The first letter, sent on the **letterhead** from the California Institute of Technology, explained the general objectives of the study (see Figure 2.1). A "fact sheet" about the early warning system (see Figure 2.2) was included with the Caltech letter. The second letter, printed on the UCLA letterhead, was sent from the researchers conducting the survey (see Figure 2.3).

The strength of the appeal conveyed by the interviewer during the introduction to the study and in advance letters can help motivate respondents to cooperate. We discuss the development of introductions and cover letters later in this chapter and again in Chapter 3.

AMENABILITY OF THE RESEARCH QUESTION

What characteristics of a research question make it amenable to a study using a telephone survey? First and foremost, such a research question is one for which some kind of questionnaire will have to be used to collect data because the data are not available from any other source. Researchers can collect data about people, their institutions, and their activities *directly,* using questionnaires, interviews, or direct observation, or *indirectly,* from written or electronic records and documents. The methods that researchers select are determined by the nature and content of the questions the researchers wish to answer, the resources available, and the accessibility of potential subjects. Researchers use questionnaires to collect data that are unavailable in written records or cannot be collected readily through observation.

California Institute of Technology
Seismological Laboratory, 252-21
Pasadena, CA 91125

August 2, 2000

«SALUTATION» «FNAME» «LNAME»
«TITLE»
«ORG»
«ADDRESS» «SUITE»
«CITY», «STATE» «ZIP»

Dear «SALUTATION» «LNAME»:

Please help us in a very important research study. Through the TriNet Project, Caltech and our partners, the US Geological Survey and the California Division of Mines and Geology, are building a digital seismic network in southern California. We are also looking at the possibility that this network could provide earthquake early warnings. We would like to know how useful these warnings might be to different types of organizations in southern California.

Warnings that a large earthquake has occurred and ground motion is approaching may be possible for some large earthquakes that originate in areas far from population centers. Receiving these "early warnings" might help people take action to avoid injury and protect property before damaging ground motion arrives. One objective of this study is to identify any protective actions that could be achieved in a **10-50 second warning time frame**.

The TriNet partners, together with the UCLA Center for Public Health and Disaster Relief (CPHDR) and EQE International are conducting this study. Within the next week, you will receive a letter from CPHDR explaining the study in more detail. After that, an interviewer from the UCLA Survey Research Center will call you to set a time to conduct the interview. If you agree to participate, you will be interviewed by phone.

Before the interview, please read the enclosed fact sheet and discuss with your colleagues what actions might be taken in your organization with 10-50 seconds of warning. Also think about the possible barriers and benefits associated with implementing an earthquake early warning system at your organization.

Thank you in advance for your help in this important study. If you have any questions, please feel free to contact me directly.

Sincerely,

James D. Goltz
SCAN Project Administrator

Office of Earthquake Programs   Tele (626) 395-3298   Fax (626) 584-1242

Figure 2.1.   Advance Letter From Caltech Used in the Trinet Study

THE TRINET SEISMIC COMPUTERIZED ALERT NETWORK (SCAN)
HOW AN EARTHQUAKE EARLY WARNING SYSTEM WORKS

- **An earthquake early warning (or alerting) system provides notification that an earthquake is occurring and that moderate to severe ground shaking is approaching a specific location.**

  A network of field stations equipped with strong motion instruments exists in Southern California. When they detect an earthquake, they send a signal to the network's computers. Depending on the size and location of the earthquake, the computers can then send a warning that an earthquake has begun and ground shaking may soon occur. The technical feasibility of issuing earthquake early warnings is based on the fact that a signal from field instruments arrives at a designated point, electronically, at the speed of light. The ground motion of an earthquake, however, moves relatively slowly by comparison, at about 2 miles (3.4 km) per second. For points that are far from the origin of the earthquake, this difference between signal arrival and that of ground motion represents the potential warning time.

- **Warning times may vary from <u>no warning at all</u> to <u>more than a minute</u>.**

  Early warnings cannot be issued for every earthquake that may cause damage. Warning times depend on the distance between field stations and the populated area. Large earthquakes (magnitude 7 or greater) centered some distance from population centers are considered good candidates for early warning. For example, a large San Andreas Fault generated earthquake that begins in central California or near the Salton Sea could produce a warning for Los Angeles that ground motion is approaching. However, earthquakes which occur in, or very near, populated areas are unlikely to generate warnings or would generate warnings of very brief duration.

- **Warning signals can be sent through telephone lines to computers, or other types of communication systems. The amount and type of information provided varies with warning time available and the type of system receiving the alert.**

  A warning could be sent to a computer. The computer could then either disseminate the warning and/or initiate some pre-determined emergency procedures. Warnings could also be transmitted to systems that might automatically shut down some operations or start up emergency generators. The message content could include information on size, direction, and estimated arrival time of the ground shaking.

- **The potential benefit of an early warning system is in more rapid response and hazard mitigation.**

  With an alert, very rapid mitigation measures could be taken to reduce the risks of injury and to protect property. For example, trains could slow down or remain in their stations, elevators could be programmed to stop and open their doors at the next floor and telephone calls could be rerouted around areas of impact. The primary purpose of the survey in which you are being asked to participate is to determine what your organization could do with 10 to 50 seconds of warning to reduce the risks of injuries and to protect property.

Figure 2.2.   Trinet Early Warning "Fact Sheet"

UNIVERSITY OF CALIFORNIA, LOS ANGELES UCLA

BERKELEY · DAVIS · IRVINE · LOS ANGELES · RIVERSIDE · SAN DIEGO · SAN FRANCISCO   SANTA BARBARA · SANTA CRUZ

UCLA CENTER FOR PUBLIC HEALTH AND DISASTER RELIEF
SCHOOL OF PUBLIC HEALTH
P.O. BOX 951772
LOS ANGELES, CALIFORNIA 90095-1772
TELEPHONE: (310) 794-6646
FAX: (310) 794-1805

August 2, 2000

«FNAME» «LNAME»
«TITLE»
«ORG»
«ADDRESS» «SUITE»
«CITY», «STATE» «ZIP»

Dear «SALUTATION» «LNAME»:

The UCLA Center for Public Health and Disaster Relief (CPHDR) is conducting a study about earthquake early warning systems. We are working on this study with the Trinet Project and EQE International. We want to know how organizations could use a warning system if it were implemented. We are interested specifically in organizations that provide education, health care, emergency, and other essential services such as utilities and transportation to persons living and working in Los Angeles County. We feel that in your position as «TITLE» at «ORG», you could provide us with very valuable information.

In the next week or two, an interviewer from the UCLA Survey Research Center (SRC) will be calling to schedule an interview with you. If you are willing to be interviewed, the interviewer will set up a time that is convenient for you, to interview you by phone. The interview will take about 30 minutes, depending on your answers. Your participation in this study is voluntary. If you agree to participate, you are free to withdraw from the study at any time without penalty.

The interview will cover topics related to an early warning system and your organization. Interview topics include:

    -a description of your worksite and work duties;
    -your organization's prior experience with earthquakes;
    -current emergency warning systems at your worksite;
    -what could be done at your organization with 10-50 seconds of warning;
    -potential barriers and benefits of implementing an earthquake warning system.

All information from the interviews will be confidential. Only persons from SRC and CPHDR will have access to the interview data. Reports, publications, or other materials developed from the study will not contain any information about specific individuals or organizations.

-1-

Figure 2.3a. Advance Letter From UCLA Used in the Trinet Study

If you have any questions about the study or do not wish to be contacted, please call one of the persons listed below:

Linda Bourque, PhD – Principal Investigator   Kimberley Shoaf, DrPH – Co-Principal Investigator
Center for Public Health and Disaster Relief   Center for Public Health and Disaster Relief
UCLA School of Public Health   UCLA School of Public Health
Phone: 310-825-4053   Phone: 310-794-0864

Or, you can call the UCLA Office for Protection of Research Subjects at 310-825-7122.

Your participation in this study would be very much appreciated and very helpful. We hope you will schedule an interview when you receive the call from SRC.

Thank you in advance for your time and for helping us find out more about the potential use of earthquake early warnings.

Sincerely,

Linda Bourque, Ph.D.   Kimberley Shoaf, Dr.P.H.
Associate Director   Research Director
UCLA Center for Public Health & Disaster Relief UCLA Center for Public Health & Disaster Relief

Enc.

Figure 2.3b.   Advance Letter From UCLA Used in the Trinet Study

Generally, the only way researchers can get information about people's attitudes, opinions, and knowledge, as well as their past, present, and anticipated behavior, is by using questionnaires. But researchers can successfully gather data using questionnaires only when respondents are available and willing to participate as research subjects.

If we want to examine the changing composition of households in the United States over the past 200 years, questionnaires would not be a good way to collect data. Rather, we would use data collected as part of the U.S. decennial census. If, in contrast, we want to know about how the composition of households today affects people's perceptions of what constitutes a family unit, and if we want to know about people's attitudes about families today, we need to collect data by questionnaire, probably within the context of telephone or in-person interviews. In general, collecting data by questionnaire, particularly when the questionnaire is administered in a telephone or in-person interview, is more expensive than collecting data from administrative records or other secondary sources of data such as the U.S. Census.

Second, if the research question is amenable to data collection by questionnaire but is too complex to be addressed using a mail or other self-administered questionnaire, the researcher will have to use telephone or in-person interviews. A complex research question requires a questionnaire that is structured so that all respondents are *not* asked every question. In the earthquake studies, for example, the focus of each study was on what happened to the respondent during and after the recent earthquake. To obtain a complete picture of what happened, the questionnaire had to be set up so that different respondents were asked different series of questions depending on their answers to previous questions. For example, if a respondent said that his or her home was damaged in the earthquake, the interviewer proceeded to ask a series of four questions about the type of damage, when the damage occurred, the estimated cost of the damage, and whether the respondent applied for assistance. If the respondent said that he or she applied for assistance, the interviewer asked eight questions about who the respondent applied to for assistance, the kind of assistance sought, how much assistance the respondent applied for, whether the respondent had difficulty applying, whether the respondent had received assistance by the time of the interview, and, if so, the amount the respondent received. If a respondent said that his or her home was not damaged, the questionnaire instructed the interviewer to **skip** the full set of questions about damage; if the respondent said that he or she had damage but did not apply for assistance, he or she was "skipped out" of the eight questions related to seeking assistance (see Figure 2.4). A self-administered questionnaire must be tightly focused on a single topic and structured in such a way that all questions are equally applicable to all respondents; such a questionnaire would not allow the researcher to tailor questions to identifiable subgroups of respondents as in this example. (See **How to Conduct Self-Administered and Mail Surveys**, Volume 3 in this series, for

more information on developing self-administered questionnaires.)

Figure 2.4.   Example of a Series of Partially Open Questions

---

8. Was the home you were living in damaged
   enough to need repairs, or did you have any
   other personal property or belongings damaged
   during this earthquake?

   YES . . . . .ASK A-K 1   V127

   NO . . . . .SKIP TO Q9 2

   A. What kind of damage was this?

   Damage to: **CIRCLE ALL THAT APPLY**

   PERSONAL PROPERTY BROKEN 1   V128
   ENTIRE BUILDING DESTROYED 1   V129
   FOUNDATION 1   V130
   BUILDING OFF FOUNDATION 1   V131
   HOUSE WALL(S) DAMAGED 1   V132
   HOUSE WALL(S) COLLAPSED 1   V133
   CHIMNEY COLLAPSED 1   V134
   CEILING/ROOF DAMAGED 1   V135
   CEILING/ROOF COLLAPSED 1   V136
   WATER PIPES BROKEN 1   V137
   WATER HEATER 1   V138
   GAS LINES BROKEN 1   V139
   FLOORS DAMAGED 1   V140
   FLOORS COLLAPSED 1   V141
   PATIO/PORCH DAMAGED 1   V142
   FENCES/FENCE WALL DAMAGED . . .1   V143
   DRIVEWAY DAMAGED/DESTROYED 1   V144
   GARAGE DAMAGED/DESTROYED . .1   V145
   OTHER 1   V146
   SPECIFY:_____ . .   V147

B. Was the damage caused by:

The earthquake itself on October 17,
    or 1
An aftershock? 2
OTHER 3   V148
SPECIFY:_____   V149

C. What is your estimate of the amount of damage to your home and property? (RECORD DOLLAR AMOUNT. PROBE FOR BEST ESTIMATE.)

DOLLAR AMOUNT:_____   V150(8)

D. Have you applied for disaster assistance?

YES ......ASK E 1

NO ......SKIP TO Q9 2   V151

E. Who did you apply to?

CIRCLE ALL THAT APPLY
GOVERNMENT AGENCIES 1   V152
THE RED CROSS 1   V153
OTHER VOLUNTEER
    ORGANIZATIONS 1   V154
INSURANCE COMPANIES 1   V155
OTHER 1   V156
SPECIFY:_____   V157

F. What type of assistance did you apply for?

CIRCLE ALL THAT APPLY
REPAIR OF HOME 1   V158
EMERGENCY HOUSING 1   V160
MEDICAL 1   V161

REPLACEMENT OF PROPERTY 1   V162
OTHER 1   V163
SPECIFY:_____   V164

G. How much did you apply for?

DOLLAR AMOUNT: _____   V165(8)

H. Did you have any difficulty applying
   for disaster assistance?

YES . . . . . .ASK 1

NO . . . . . .SKIP TO J 2   V166

I. What kind of difficulty did you have?

_____

_____

_____ V167

J. Have you received disaster assistance?

YES . . . . . .ASK K 1

NO . . . . . .SKIP TO Q9 2

DECLINED OFFER OF ASSISTANCE   3   V168

K. How much assistance did you receive?

DOLLAR AMOUNT: _____   V169(8)

Third, if the research question requires the researcher to obtain complex retrospective information about the respondents or information about what they anticipate doing in the future, telephone or in-person interviews are an appropriate method of data collection. Retrospective data are particularly sensitive to bias and unreliability, because they depend on respondents' accurately remembering and reporting what they did at some point in the past. In the earthquake studies, most of each interview focused on what happened during and after the index earthquake; the interviewer was, therefore, generally asking about things that were currently happening or that had happened in the recent past since the earthquake. But one set of questions asked the respondents about the earthquake-preparedness behaviors and activities they had engaged in, not only since the earthquake, but also before the earthquake (see Figure 2.5). We also wanted to know if people had done things specifically because of earthquakes or for other reasons. Did they, for example, store water? If they stored water, did they store it before October 17, the date of the Loma Prieta earthquake, after October 17, or both before and after October 17? And, finally, did they store water specifically in preparation for a future earthquake, for some other reason, or for both reasons?

Figure 2.5. Example of Complex Question Structure

---

8. Now I'm going to read you a list of preparation suggestions that have been made by various agencies and groups who are concerned with earthquake preparedness. As I read each one, please tell me if you have done this and whether you did this before October 17, 1989, or after October 17. First: FOR EACH "YES," ASK PART A. IF "NOT DONE," SKIP TO NEXT ITEM.

A. You said you had (. . .). Did you do that specifically in preparation for a future earthquake or for some other reason?

Figure 2.5.   Continued

	Q24 Done				Q24 Why?		
	Before Oct.17	Aftere Oct.17	Both	Not Done	E-Quake	Other Reason	Both
1. Store water?	1	2	3	4	1	2	3
2. Store canned or dehydrated food?	1	2	3	4	1	2	3
3. Having a working, battery operated radio?	1	2	3	4	1	2	3
4. Have a first-aid kit or medical supplies?	1	2	3	4	1	2	3
5. Etc.							

The combination of such a complex questionnaire structure and the collection of retrospective data demands the presence of an interviewer to move the respondent through the questionnaire. Imagine the questionnaire excerpt shown in Figure 2.5 as part of a self-administered questionnaire. How likely would it be that respondents could fill in the answers to such a series of questions on their own? Not only would it be extremely unlikely, but using such a format within a self-administered questionnaire would invite both refusal and outright antagonism from respondents.

In the case of the Trinet Study, respondents were asked not only what they currently did in their workplaces when earthquakes occurred, but also what they *might do* if they had a real-time, early warning system at their business or work settings. Just as with questions about events in the past, interviewers are key in helping people answer anticipatory, or future-oriented, questions accurately.

Fourth, when the research question is such that the researcher must have confidence in the statistical reliability of the data collected, a telephone survey is a more desirable method of data collection than a self-administered survey or even sometimes an in-person survey. In Chapter 1, we discussed the advantages of telephone surveys over self-administered and in-person surveys in terms of response rates, geographic coverage, and costs. If decisions of significant consequence are to be made as a result of the research, a rigorously conducted telephone survey is probably the best use of the surveyor's resources.

Fifth, if the research question requires that a survey be repeated with a sampled population over time (in a study design known as a *panel survey*), telephone interviewing is the best method of data collection. For example, say that you want to test a new product concept and want to know how a sampled group of individuals use the product over time. You might do initial or baseline telephone interviews to determine respondents' behaviors associated with your product concept, recruit respondents to try the product in their homes, and then interview them once a month to see if they are still using it, how they like it, and what differences, if any, your product has made in their behavior. If the research question involves interviewing the same individuals multiple times over a given period, a telephone survey is the most efficient and economical way to collect the data.

Sixth, telephone interviews generally are not the best way to conduct **exploratory studies**—that is, studies in which the research questions and the procedures by which those questions will be studied are still being developed. During the developmental stages of a study, the researcher should collect data in ways that maximize flexibility and the ability to pursue interesting topics that may or may not be central to the original question posed. Productive methods of collecting data in the early stages of a research project include the use of focus groups and semistructured in-person interviews, in which the researcher can ask a lot of open-ended questions and has the ability to probe respondents' answers; observation; and even the collection of certain kinds of secondary data. Once the boundaries of the research question are clearly delineated, if the objective is to obtain data from a target population that is dispersed across a wide geographic area, the researcher may decide that a telephone survey is the appropriate way to collect the data.

The final feature of the research question that a researcher needs to consider in making the decision to conduct a telephone survey, rather than collect data through a self-administered questionnaire or through in-person interviews, is the sensitivity of the topic. Numerous studies have found evidence supporting the hypothesis that telephone interviews are less threatening to respondents than in-person interviews simply because the interviewers and respondents cannot see each other, and therefore respondents feel more anonymous. Although other research has not always supported these findings, many researchers believe that telephone interviewing is a superior means of collecting information about such sensitive topics as substance abuse and sexual behaviors.

Checklist: Deciding Whether to Use a Telephone Interview

✓ Respondents have telephones.

✓ Respondents need to be motivated.
  - Through advance letters
  - By interviewers

✓ The topic is amenable to study using a telephone interview.
  - Data are not available in records or other secondary data sources.
  - Data cannot be collected through observation.
  - Different subgroups in the target population answer different combinations of questions.
  - Questions ask about the past and the future as well as the present.
  - People's opinions and attitudes are of interest.
  - The results need to be statistically defendable.
  - Data collection is to be repeated over time.
  - The topic is sensitive.
  - The study is not exploratory or in the process of being developed.

Developing the Content of the Questionnaire

Once the surveyor determines that it is appropriate to use a telephone survey to collect the data, his or her first task is to conduct a thorough search of the relevant or related literature. This **literature search** helps the surveyor refine the parameters of the data collection. What other studies have been done on this topic? How were the data collected in other studies? What was the content of the data collection instruments used in other studies of this topic? How can the surveyor learn from or build on these other research efforts? In developing our studies of California earthquakes, we reviewed studies on natural disasters and found out three things:

1. Research on both natural and human-generated disasters dates back to World War II.

2. Most studies completed up until the mid-1980s emphasized quick entry into disaster sites, where researchers conducted semistructured interviews with selected informants, collected data through observations, or examined selected secondary data.

3. The use of well-designed, standardized, population-based surveys after disasters was rare, but one research group had developed a questionnaire for use after an earthquake that had never been administered.

Knowledge of this literature and what it encompassed allowed us to define how our studies would build on or extend existing work in the area and to identify the data collection instruments that we should examine in deciding how to go about our studies. Specifically, our studies extended earlier research by demonstrating that population-based telephone surveys could be conducted after natural disasters; that respondents were not only willing but, in most cases, eager to participate; and that respondents "remembered" what happened to them for some extended period of time after the disaster. The existence of such data allowed us to examine "dose-response" relationships. In other words, did persons who had been closer to the epicenter of an earthquake (and thus experienced more shaking) have different experiences and respond in different ways from those who were further away from the epicenter?

Once we had completed the literature review, we knew which studies had used questionnaires to collect data and how the questionnaires had been administered. We then made every effort to obtain copies of all the earlier questionnaires *as they were actually administered to respondents*. We did *not* depend on the descriptions of the questionnaires that appeared in published articles or project reports. A particular advantage for our earthquake studies was the fact that through the literature review we identified a questionnaire that had been developed by Ralph Turner and associates in the 1970s. This questionnaire had been developed as part of a large study of earthquake predictions and was designed to be used if a moderate-sized earthquake occurred in the Los Angeles area during the period of that earthquake study. No earthquakes of sufficient size occurred during the period, so the questionnaire was never used.

ADOPTING STANDARD QUESTION BATTERIES

Ideally, we would have liked to find sets of questions that had already been developed and widely used and then simply **adopt** those questions as written. There are multiple advantages to this strategy of adopting **standard question batteries**. First, such batteries are usually made up of fully or partially **closed-ended questions**, and the possible answer categories have already been worked out and tested in prior studies. Second, the instructions have been developed and tested. Third, using questions *exactly* as they were used in other studies allows surveyors to compare the data they collect to the data collected in those prior studies or to a standard population. For example, many surveyors choose to ask questions about ethnicity or race exactly as they are asked in the U.S. Census form. They make this decision not because they think the U.S. Census has the "perfect" method for asking such questions, but because they want to be able to compare their own samples to the populations in particular regions. Questions 7 and 8 in Figure 2.6 show how the 2000 U.S. Census determined race and ethnicity. Using questions exactly as they were worded in the 2000 Census would allow a researcher to compare the race and ethnic distribution of his or her study sample with a "standard" population— namely, the population surveyed by the U.S. Census.

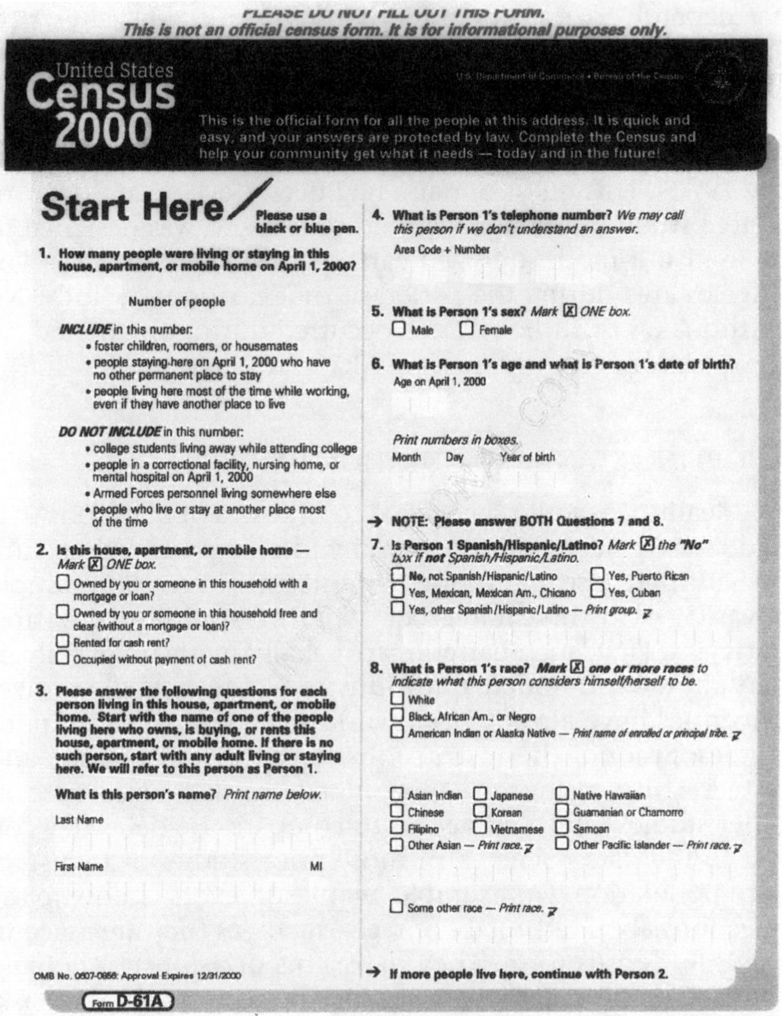

PLEASE DO NOT FILL OUT THIS FORM.
This is not an official census form. It is for informational purposes only.

United States
Census
2000

This is the official form for all the people at this address. It is quick and easy, and your answers are protected by law. Complete the Census and help your community get what it needs — today and in the future!

Start Here **Please use a black or blue pen.**

1. How many people were living or staying in this house, apartment, or mobile home on April 1, 2000?

Number of people

INCLUDE in this number:
- foster children, roomers, or housemates
- people staying here on April 1, 2000 who have no other permanent place to stay
- people living here most of the time while working, even if they have another place to live

DO NOT INCLUDE in this number:
- college students living away while attending college
- people in a correctional facility, nursing home, or mental hospital on April 1, 2000
- Armed Forces personnel living somewhere else
- people who live or stay at another place most of the time

2. Is this house, apartment, or mobile home — *Mark ☒ ONE box.*
- ☐ Owned by you or someone in this household with a mortgage or loan?
- ☐ Owned by you or someone in this household free and clear (without a mortgage or loan)?
- ☐ Rented for cash rent?
- ☐ Occupied without payment of cash rent?

3. Please answer the following questions for each person living in this house, apartment, or mobile home. Start with the name of one of the people living here who owns, is buying, or rents this house, apartment, or mobile home. If there is no such person, start with any adult living or staying here. We will refer to this person as Person 1.

What is this person's name? *Print name below.*

Last Name

First Name MI

4. What is Person 1's telephone number? *We may call this person if we don't understand an answer.*

Area Code + Number

5. What is Person 1's sex? *Mark ☒ ONE box.*
☐ Male ☐ Female

6. What is Person 1's age and what is Person 1's date of birth?

Age on April 1, 2000

Print numbers in boxes.

Month Day Year of birth

→ **NOTE: Please answer BOTH Questions 7 and 8.**

7. Is Person 1 Spanish/Hispanic/Latino? *Mark ☒ the "No" box if **not** Spanish/Hispanic/Latino.*
- ☐ **No,** not Spanish/Hispanic/Latino
- ☐ Yes, Puerto Rican
- ☐ Yes, Mexican, Mexican Am., Chicano
- ☐ Yes, Cuban
- ☐ Yes, other Spanish/Hispanic/Latino — *Print group.*

8. What is Person 1's race? ***Mark ☒ one or more races*** *to indicate what this person considers himself/herself to be.*
- ☐ White
- ☐ Black, African Am., or Negro
- ☐ American Indian or Alaska Native — *Print name of enrolled or principal tribe.*
- ☐ Asian Indian
- ☐ Japanese
- ☐ Native Hawaiian
- ☐ Chinese
- ☐ Korean
- ☐ Guamanian or Chamorro
- ☐ Filipino
- ☐ Vietnamese
- ☐ Samoan
- ☐ Other Asian — *Print race.*
- ☐ Other Pacific Islander — *Print race.*
- ☐ Some other race — *Print race.*

→ **If more people live here, continue with Person 2.**

OMB No. 0607-0856: Approval Expires 12/31/2000

Form D-61A

Figure 2.6. 2000 U.S. Census Form, Race and Ethnicity Questions

In other situations, surveyors adopt a question or set of questions because they want to compare respondents across samples. In Wave 1 of the Northridge study, we adopted, or replicated, questions exactly as they had been used in the Loma Prieta study. This allowed us to compare Los Angeles County residents after the Northridge earthquake directly with San Francisco Bay Area residents after the Loma Prieta earthquake. For example, both groups of respondents were asked the following question:

Did any of your utilities go off as a result of the earthquake?

CIRCLE ALL THAT APPLY

GAS .1
ELECTRICITY 1
WATER 1
OTHER 1
SPECIFY:_____

The most prevalent answer given in the **residual "other" category** was telephones. The inclusion of this question in both questionnaires allowed us to compare the extent to which utilities were off at least briefly after the two earthquakes. For example, San Francisco Bay Area residents were more than twice as likely as Los Angeles County residents to say that their gas was off (10% versus 4%), were just as likely to say their water was off (7% versus 8%), more likely to say their electricity went off (68% versus 52%), and less likely to say their telephones were off (21% versus 26%).

Surveyors also use existing sets of questions exactly as they have been used before for two other reasons. First, many questionnaires—particularly those developed in the psychological literature—are protected by copyright. Copyright protection assures the authors of questionnaires that others cannot use or change their instruments without their permission. In both earthquake studies, we included the Brief Symptom Inventory (BSI), an instrument that is under a formal copyright and for the use of which surveyors must pay a fee. We also included a second measure, the Civilian Mississippi Scale for Posttraumatic Stress Disorder, which we considered to be under informal copyright; that is, we did not have to pay to include the set of questions in our studies, but we were obligated to use the questions exactly as they were designed and to cite fully the researchers who developed and tested the questions. These two sets of questions also have the second characteristic that encourages surveyors to use existing questionnaires exactly as written: The validity and reliability of the items have been tested extensively over time and with different sample populations. The fact that the questions had previously been tested increased our confidence that the measures would accurately assess the range and intensity of psychological symptoms in our target populations as well as allow us to compare our community samples with other target populations.

ADAPTING SETS OF QUESTIONS

Unfortunately, many surveyors think that it is okay simply to select and use some questions from existing instruments. Neophyte surveyors and persons developing questionnaires for the first time are particularly prone to fall into this trap because of their eagerness to be able to say to potential respondents that "it will only take 5 minutes to complete this interview." There is no such thing as a telephone interview that takes only 5 minutes. It usually takes more than 5 minutes for the interviewer to introduce him- or herself, explain the purpose of the study, ascertain that he or she has dialed the correct number, confirm that the number dialed is a household, and, when necessary, determine who in the household is the designated respondent for the study.

Surveyors do sometimes **adapt** or change existing instruments for use in their questionnaires, but they must be aware that when they do this, they can no longer reference prior psychometric testing of the instruments they have adapted, nor can they make direct comparisons between their samples and those to whom the original instruments were administered.

Surveyors usually adapt existing questionnaires for one of four reasons:

- They cannot use the existing questionnaires in their entirety because they are too long.

- They are studying populations other than the populations for which the original questions were developed.

- They need to translate the existing instruments into other languages.

- They need to expand, reorder, or otherwise elaborate on items or change the procedures by which data are collected (e.g., an item written for a self-administered questionnaire may be modified for a telephone interview).

When surveyors modify existing instruments, they need to pilot-test the new versions as well as evaluate the reliability and validity of those versions.

In the earthquake studies, we adapted questions both intentionally and unintentionally. As we have noted above, the questionnaire that formed the basis of our instrument had been developed but never used. Because our studies were not part of a panel design—that is, we were not contacting people who had already been interviewed as part of a larger ongoing study—we had to change the questionnaire's introductory material. Also, because our budget only allowed for 30-minute interviews following the Loma Prieta earthquake and the original questionnaire took longer than 30 minutes to administer, we had to shorten the questionnaire.

In the case of the Brief Symptom Inventory, the set of 53 questions was originally designed to be self-administered. To use the questions instead as part of a telephone interview, we had to change, at minimum, the administrative procedures used. With that kind of change, surveyors who are adapting existing question batteries often must provide additional or different instructions on the questionnaire for the interviewer. Figure 2.7 shows how the BSI was originally formatted for self-administration and how we changed it for the telephone interview. Because the respondents would not be able to read the questions and the possible **response categories**, we had to add instructions for the interviewers to reread the response categories to the respondents periodically as they went through the 53 questions.

Figure 2.7.   Adapting a Self-Administered Questionnaire

A. Brief Symptom Inventory: Self-Administered

Brief Symptom Inventory
INSTRUCTIONS

Below is a list of problems and complaints that people sometimes have. Read each one carefully, and select one of the numbered descriptors that best describes how much discomfort that problem has caused you during the past two weeks including today. Place that number in the open block to the right of the problem. Do not skip any items, and print your number clearly. If you change your mind, erase your first number completely. Read the example below before beginning, and if you have any questions please ask the technician.

EXAMPLE   POSSIBLE RESPONSES
How much have you   0 Not at all
been bothered by   1 A little bit
body aches   2 Moderately
                                         3 Quite a bit
                                         4 Extremely

1. Nervousness or shakiness inside you . . . .

2. Faintness or dizziness . . . .

3. Etc . . . .

21. Feeling that people are unfriendly to you . . . .

22. Feeling inferior to others . . . .

B. Brief Symptom Inventory: Telephone Interview

26. Now I am going to read you a list of problems and complaints that people sometimes have. As I read each one, please tell me how much that problem has bothered or distressed you during the past two

weeks, including today. Using a scale of not at all, a little bit, moderately, quite a bit, or extremely, how much would you say you were bothered by (. . .) In the past two weeks, including today?

		Not At All	A Little Bit	Moderately	Quite A Bit	Extremely
A.	Nervousness or shakiness inside	1	2	3	4	5
B.	Faintness or dizziness	1	2	3	4	5
C.	Etc.					

When surveyors decide to adapt an existing question battery for a study they are conducting, they have certain ethical obligations. Their first step should be to contact the authors of the instrument they want to adapt and request their permission to select only certain items for use in the questionnaire. If the instrument is under copyright and the surveyors learn that the authors will not allow them to select items out of the battery to use in subsets, then the surveyors must find different measures. Even if the questionnaire the surveyors want to adapt is not under formal copyright, they have a responsibility to respect the advice of the instrument's authors. If the authors agree that the surveyors can make modifications, the surveyors have a responsibility to document carefully any changes they make and to state the reasons for the changes in any reports of their survey findings, where they must also acknowledge the source of the original questionnaire. In addition, the surveyors need to test the validity and reliability of the adapted questions.

In the case of the Civilian Mississippi Scale for Posttraumatic Stress Disorder, we *inadvertently* adapted the measure. One change was intentional, however. The original set of 35 items, which was developed in research on Vietnam veterans, was called the Mississippi Scale for Combat-Related Posttraumatic Stress Disorder. That measure was in the process of being revised for use in civilian populations when we first included it in the Loma Prieta study. Four items had been added to the original scale, and items that contained references to the Vietnam War were changed to have general referents. When we pretested the 39-item civilian version, the last item elicited laughter from respondents in telephone interviews. This item read, "If something happens that reminds me of the past, I get so anxious or panicky that my heart pounds hard; I have trouble getting my breath, I sweat, tremble, or shake; or feel dizzy, tingly, or faint." We contacted the authors of the measure and they provided us with a replacement item that read, "I feel numb."

So when we started the Loma Prieta study, we knew that we had modified our source questionnaires in four ways.

First, we had shortened and changed some of the questions in the original earthquake questionnaire designed by Turner and associates. Second, we had taken two questionnaires originally designed for self-administration, the Brief Symptom Inventory and the Mississippi Scale, and modified them for use in a telephone interview. Third, we had intentionally replaced one question in the Mississippi Scale. And finally, we had translated all of the questionnaires into Spanish. We did all four of these things with the knowledge and approval of the persons who originally designed the questionnaires that we adapted. What we did *not* know until we started to analyze the data was that we had also inadvertently changed some of the response alternatives within the Mississippi Scale. Originally, the Mississippi Scale was designed with three slightly different sets of **answer categories.** The first set was "Not at All True," "Slightly True," "Somewhat True," "Very True," and "Extremely True"; the second set was "Very Unlikely," "Unlikely," "Somewhat Unlikely," "Very Likely," and "Extremely Likely"; and the third set was "Never," "Rarely," "Sometimes," "Frequently," and "Very Frequently." In setting up the questionnaire to be used in the telephone interview, we simply did not see the different sets of response alternatives, and we set all of the 39 questions up in a three-page grid that used only the first set of five response alternatives. Figure 2.8 shows the original self-administered format and our telephone interview format.

Figure 2.8.   Inadvertent Errors in an Adapted Questionnaire

A. Mississippi Scale: Self-Administered

Please circle the number that best describes how you feel about each statement.

---

1. In the past, I had more close friends than I have
    now.

    01......02......03......04......05
    NOT AT ALL SLIGHTLY SOMEWHAT   VERY   EXTREMELY
      TRUE   TRUE   TRUE   TRUE   TRUE

2. I do not feel guilt over things that I did in the past.

    01......02.......03......04......05
    NEVER   RARELY SOMETIMES USUALLY   ALWAYS
    TRUE   TRUE   TRUE   TRUE   TRUE

3. If someone pushes me too far, I am likely to become
    violent.

    01......02......03......04......05
    VERY   UNLIKELY SOMEWHAT   VERY   EXTREMELY
    UNLIKELY   UNLIKELY LIKELY   LIKELY

B. Mississippi Scale: Telephone Interview

   27. I am going to read you a list of statements that
       people sometimes use to describe themselves. As I
       read each one, please tell me whether that state-
       ment is not at all true of you, slightly true of you,
       somewhat true of you, very true of you, or
       extremely true of you.

	Not At All True	Slightly True	Somewhat True	Very True	Extremely True
A. In the past, I had more close friends than I have now.	1	2	3	4	5
B. I do not feel guilt over things that I did in the past.	1	2	3	4	5
C. If someone pushes me too far, I am likely to become violent.	1	2	3	4	5

DESIGNING NEW QUESTIONS

Developing new questions for a study's questionnaire takes a great deal of time, and often, the questions a surveyor designs "from scratch" are not as comprehensive or as clear as questions that others have already developed, pretested, modified, and used repeatedly. The fact that Turner and his colleagues had developed a questionnaire for use after an earthquake greatly speeded up our development of a comprehensive questionnaire that was appropriate for our objectives. Because we have now conducted a series of studies following California earthquakes, we have a core questionnaire that has been tested repeatedly and in which we have confidence.

But even when they adopt questionnaires that are largely "ready to go," surveyors often need to adapt those instruments, adjusting, adding, or deleting questions in response to the unique characteristics of the situation under study. For example, we added the question about utilities described earlier to the Loma Prieta questionnaire because of something we had learned when we conducted an earlier study following the Whittier Narrows earthquake. In that earlier study, respondents were asked:

6. When the earthquake struck, did you have the radio or television on?

      YES, RADIO . . . . .SKIP TO B 1

      YES, TELEVISION . . . . .SKIP TO B 2

      NO, NEITHER . . . . ASK A 3

A. Did you turn on a TV or radio to get more information about the earthquake?

      YES . . . . . .ASK B 1

      NO . . . . . .SKIP TO Q8 2

In answering Question 6, many respondents said that they did not try to get information from radios or television sets because their electricity was out. Recognizing that lack of electricity would limit access to non-battery-operated radios and TVs, we inserted the question about utilities *right before* the question about getting information from the electronic media. When we wrote the utilities question, we were not particularly interested in respondents' experiences with their utilities, we were simply trying to "clean up" our questions about respondents' use of the electronic news media. The question subsequently turned out to be very valuable, but our original reason for adding it to the questionnaire was to make a series of existing questions clearer.

Sometimes surveyors have no alternative but to develop their questionnaires from scratch. The Trinet Study is an example; in that study, the research team had to develop the entire questionnaire. Only two prior studies had investigated real-time warning for earthquakes. One was conducted in Mexico, primarily using informants and observations; the other, which was conducted in California, used a self-administered questionnaire and had objectives that were different from those of the Trinet Study. Because we had primarily been conducting community studies following earthquakes for the prior 10 years and had a largely developed core questionnaire for those surveys, as members of the research team on the Trinet Study, we seriously underestimated the amount of time it would take to develop a completely new questionnaire.

We started by conducting focus groups with elite informants from different areas in Southern California. We then used data collected from the focus groups as the basis for developing a more structured questionnaire. The first four drafts of the questionnaire were circulated among members of the research team for suggestions about modifications. When the research team had reached some consensus about the content and structure of the questionnaire, we pretested the draft questionnaire with experienced interviewers.

We found in pretesting that the questionnaire was much too long, and many parts of it were incomprehensible to our targeted respondents. As a result, we revised and reworked the questionnaire and pretested it again. After a third round of pretesting, we had an instrument that was comprehensible to our intended respondents, met the objectives of the study, and could be completed within the average of 30 minutes budgeted for data collection. But whereas we had originally thought we would start our data collection in October 1999, the need for multiple revisions meant that we did not start until March 2000.

We recommend that, whenever possible, surveyors either adopt or adapt questions from other studies. Surveyors should take advantage of the fact that others have developed and tested questions that they can use to operationalize concepts important to their research questions. By doing so, surveyors can maximize the clarity of their questionnaires and begin their data collection sooner. When surveyors adapt or adopt questions from other sources, research ethics demand that they document where the instruments were obtained and give credit to the original designers. The following guidelines summarize the discussion above concerning whether and how surveyors should adopt or adapt questions developed by others for their own questionnaires.

Guidelines for Deciding on
the Content of the Questionnaire

✓ Conduct a literature review to define the parameters of the study, learn what others have done, and learn what others recommend.

✓ Adopt standard sets of questions because the questions and instructions have already undergone development and testing, and because using such instruments allows for comparison of the data with

---

other studies. Give proper credit to the persons who developed the questions and pay fees for permission to use the questions if required.

✓ Adapt questions from other studies if the original questionnaires are too long, the mode of administration is different, a different population is being studied, or translations must be made. Pretest or pilot-test the new version and assess its reliability and validity. Also, give credit to the sources of the questions adapted and explain the reasons for adaptation.

✓ Develop new questions when you cannot find any existing sets of questions that you can appropriately adopt or adapt for the purposes of your study. Allow sufficient time for development and repeated pretesting and modification of the questionnaire.

Note

1. SROs are buildings where individuals rent single rooms to live in by the day, week, or month. Persons who reside in SROs usually cannot afford to have their own phones.

3 User-Friendly Questionnaires and Response Categories

Surveyors should always seek to maximize the user-friendliness of their questionnaires. In the case of telephone surveys, surveyors must consider the needs of two different kinds of users—interviewers and respondents—when they are designing instruments to gather complete, valid, and reliable responses. Surveyors need to pay attention to the ways in which the questions are written, where the questions are located in the questionnaire, and how the answer categories are to be used. They also need to decide whether to use open-ended questions and, if so, how and at what points in the questionnaire. Clear and sufficient instructions need to be provided in the questionnaire for both interviewers and respondents, along with transitions between topics that will help interviewers and respondents move through the questionnaire. Finally, surveyors need to make every effort to avoid projecting their own personal biases into the wording of questions and answer categories.

Construction of Questions

SHORT-AND-SPECIFIC FORMAT

Questions should be as short as possible and specific rather than general. In creating short, specific questions, surveyors need to follow the basic rules for constructing any kind of questionnaire. For example, they should be careful to avoid **double-barreled** or triple-barreled questions—that is, questions that ask two or more things at once—such as "After the earthquake, did you evacuate your home, where did you go, and how long did you stay away?" They should also avoid using long, run-on sentences such as the following.

When you think about the events of September 11, 2001, and you think about all the people who were killed and injured and what happened to their families and friends, how much money should be given to these people?

Creating short, specific questions may mean asking multiple questions rather than a single question. For example, when we conducted a study after the Whittier Narrows earthquake in 1987, we asked the following questions about injuries.

15. In this earthquake was anyone you know injured?

      YES ......ASK A 1

      NO ......SKIP TO Q16 2

   A. Who was that?

(CIRCLE ALL THAT APPLY)

RESPONDENT 1
OTHER HOUSEHOLD MEMBERS .1
NEIGHBORS 1
RELATIVES 1
COWORKERS 1
FRIENDS 1
OTHER 1
SPECIFY:_____

B. FOR EACH "YES" IN Q.15, ASK: You said
(. . .) was injured in the earthquake. Can
you tell me about that? Who exactly
was this, and how were they injured?

_____

_____

_____

When we started to analyze the data from that study, we
realized that these questions, although short, were neither
specific nor precise. As a result, the responses we got did not
allow us to estimate the prevalence of injuries, who was
injured, and whether and where they sought care—all
important issues in public health. For the Northridge study
we modified the questions as shown in Figure 3.1 to obtain
better and more complete data.

CARE IN THE USE OF LANGUAGE

Along with developing short, precise questions, surveyors should keep the language used in questions as simple as
possible. The accepted rule is to use a sixth-grade level of
vocabulary whenever possible. This means avoiding the use
of multiple-syllable words when single-syllable words will
do. In addition to using simple words, surveyors should
write questions in active voice rather than passive voice
whenever possible and should avoid the use of dependent
clauses.

Figure 3.1. Developing Precise Questions

---

17. The next set of questions ask about physical and emotional injuries that you yourself, members of your household, or other people you know experienced either during the earthquake, during the aftershocks, during the period immediately after the earthquake, or while working in jobs related to earthquake recovery and repair.

First of all, how about you, did you have any physical injuries—even minor cuts and bruises—as a result of the earthquake?

     YES . . . . .ASK A 1

     NO . . . . . .GO TO Q18 . . .2

A. When exactly were you injured?
   Were you injured:

     During the earthquake itself, ...1
     Immediately after the earthquake, . . .2
     Within the first 48 hours after
        the earthquake, ...3
     During an aftershock, or 4
     Some other time? 5
     SPECIFY:_____

B. Can you tell me the date and time
   of the injury?

            RECORD AS GIVEN

C. Can you describe exactly what hap-
    pened to cause your (injury/injuries)?

_____

_____

RECORD AS GIVEN

D. What exactly (was/were) your (injury/injuries)?

_____

_____

RECORD AS GIVEN

E. What part(s) of your body were
    injured?

_____

_____

RECORD AS GIVEN

F. Did you seek medical care for your
    injury?

    YES 1

    NO . . . . . .GO TO Q18 . . .2

Researchers often protest when we suggest that they write simple questions using simple words, saying, "But I am interviewing doctors and they have a lot of education and understand these words!" We believe that even if a survey's target population is doctors or other professionals who have a lot of education, big vocabularies, and the ability to understand highly complex sentences, there is no reason for the researcher to make the questions more difficult than they have to be. When a researcher writes complex questions, this usually means that he or she has not thought consciously—or at least not thought sufficiently—about how to make interviews as easy as possible for *all* respondents. Obviously, the importance of using simple vocabulary and grammar is even greater when respondents have relatively little education or are functionally illiterate.

CARE IN THE USE OF VAGUE QUALIFIERS

Surveyors frequently write questions that contain **vague qualifiers**—that is, modifying terms that may be interpreted differently by different people. The following questionnaire item is an example:

Do you usually attend religious services?

YES 1

NO 2

The adverb *usually* here is a vague qualifier. To some respondents, in the context of this question, it may mean "every day," whereas to others, it may mean "once a week"; still others may take it to mean "once a year." Questions using vague qualifiers give surveyors imprecise information about respondents. In the case of the question above, the surveyor would have no way of knowing how frequently respondents who answer yes to the question actually attend religious services. A better question would ask respondents to specify the frequency or regularity with which they attend services. For example:

How frequently do you attend
religious services?

Would you say:

Once a week or more, ...1
Two or three times a month, ...2
Once a month, ...3
A few times a year or less, ...4
Only on holidays, or 5
Never? 6

All adverbs are likely to be vague qualifiers. Whenever surveyors write questions or sets of response alternatives that include adverbs such as *rarely, sometimes, occasionally,* or *possibly,* they should evaluate carefully whether the questions precisely measure the concepts under study.

CARE IN THE USE OF SLANG, ABSTRACT TERMS, AND JARGON

Surveyors should try to minimize the use of **slang, abstract terms,** and **jargon** in questionnaires, and when they feel they must use such specialized language, they need to be sure that their respondents understand it. Often, surveyors attempt to use slang because they think it will help them establish rapport with their respondents, but unfortunately, it may have just the opposite effect. Slang terms are used by the members of subgroups in the population as a way of establishing their group identity and differentiating themselves from others. Thus, adolescents develop slang terms, at least in part, to distance themselves from parents and other adults. The slang terms that are currently in use within any given group, and their meanings, change rapidly. When surveyors try to incorporate slang terms into questions in the hope that this might encourage certain respondents to participate in their studies, they may in fact find out that the slang they are using is out-of-date. A cogent example is the use of the terms *hot* and *cool.* Whether either or both of these words equate with bad or good or have some other meaning has often changed in the target population by the time a surveyor can incorporate the words into a questionnaire and field the study. The word *bad* is another example of a slang term that has had and continues to have different connotations across time and groups.

Unfortunately, many standard question batteries include slang words or phrases. For example, we worry about the inclusion of questions about "feeling blue" in psychological batteries. Such terms are particularly bothersome when instruments have to be translated into languages other than English.

Abstract terms and jargon terms that are specific to particular disciplines are similarly problematic. For example, in earthquake studies, we often want to find out whether any injuries or damage that respondents and their families have experienced occurred in the earthquake itself or as a result of aftershocks that occurred after the earthquake. The term *aftershock* originated as jargon among researchers who study earthquakes, but it has since been adopted widely by the general population. When we conduct studies about earthquakes in communities where earthquakes have recently occurred, we assume that respondents understand the term. Nonetheless, we and the interviewers working on the earthquake studies are aware that we should remain alert to the possibility that some respondents may not understand the term, and the interviewers are prepared to explain what it means.

Acronyms may be considered a form of jargon. For example, after an earthquake, we ask questions about whether respondents sought disaster assistance from groups such as HUD (Housing and Urban Development), the SBA (Small Business Administration), or FEMA (the Federal Emergency Management Agency). We recognize that our respondents may not recognize *either* the acronyms *or* the names of the agencies they stand for, so again, we prepare the interviewers for that possibility and provide them with standard descriptions or definitions and explanations.

Unfortunately, in many cases, surveyors may find that there are no synonyms they can readily use in place of jargon or abstract terms. This can become particularly problematic in health studies, where one objective of the study may be to find out whether respondents have ever had certain diseases or conditions, such as infectious mononucleosis, pneumonia, diabetes, or, increasingly, even measles. For example, some subgroups in the population refer to diabetes as *sugar, high sugar,* or *blood sugar.* Similarly, asking respondents about medications or medical treatments and different kinds of health practitioners can be problematic. For example, can respondents be expected to understand what a sigmoidoscopy, an MRI, or a nurse practitioner is? Such terms are particularly hard to translate into languages other than English. For example, the term *nurse practitioner* is often confused with the term *practical nurse* when questionnaires are translated into Spanish.

Abstract terms and jargon exist in every area of human society. Surveyors need to be sensitive to their existence, recognize them when they occur, and make an effort to avoid using such terms in their survey instruments, or, if that is impossible, give both interviewers and respondents the information they need so that respondents can answer the questions validly. As we noted in Chapter 2, when the entire focus of a study is a concept described by an abstract term such as *antibiotic resistance,* the researcher may want to start the series of questions by first asking whether or not the respondent has ever heard the term *antibiotic resistance,* then proceed to ask the respondent in a nonaccusatory fashion to describe what the term *antibiotic resistance* means to him or her, and finally give the respondent a definition in lay language.

The Trinet Study was particularly troublesome in regard to the use of abstract terms and jargon. We were interviewing people about the likelihood that they or the institutions they represented would use a system that did not exist. Although our respondents were, by definition, people who were knowledgeable about earthquakes, about what happens during an earthquake, and about what people need to do during and immediately after an earthquake, it is hard to be knowledgeable and answer questions about a system that does not exist. We started by sending respondents two advance letters and an information sheet that explained the study and the hypothetical warning system (see Figures 2.1 to 2.3 in Chapter 2). Before we asked questions about the hypothetical system in the interview, we again provided the respondent with a brief description of what the system might do. Figure 3.2 displays the long introductory statement we used, followed by questions about the hypothetical system. Generally, we try to avoid including long statements of this sort in questionnaires because respondents often lose interest while the interviewers go through such explanations. In this case, we could not avoid a long statement, but we divided the text up into short paragraphs to encourage the interviewer to pause between sentences and give the respondent time to absorb the information.

EASY-TO-DIFFICULT PROGRESSION

In designing all questionnaires, surveyors should try to start with the easiest questions and proceed to more complex or sensitive questions. Figures 3.1 and 3.2 provide examples of such a progression from easier to more difficult questions.

Figure 3.2.   Constructing and Ordering Questions From Easy to Difficult

---

Now I would like to review with you the proposed early warning system. As you may remember, we sent you an information sheet about the system.

An earthquake early warning system sends a signal telling you that an earthquake has occurred and that moderate to severe shaking may occur at your site.

Warning times can vary from no warning at all to more than a minute.

Warning signals can be sent to computers, or other communication systems. The warning time an organization receives depends on the size and location of the earthquake and the system receiving the earthquake.

16. Thinking about the existing warning or alert systems your organization has. . . what parts might be used in an earthquake early warning system? Could you use:

		NONE EXIST/			
		YES	NO	DK	NA
A.	The methods by which you alert workers that a danger exists?	1	0	8	9
B.	Manual shutdown or activation procedures?	1	0	8	9
C.	Automatic shutdown or activation procedures?	1	0	8	9

In the next set of questions, I am going to ask you about what your organization does to protect people and property when an earthquake occurs and what could be done if you had 10 or 50 seconds of warning before shaking begins.

17. First, when an earthquake begins, what does your organization or the people at your organization do now?

PROBES:

For example, what do they do to prevent injuries and save lives?

What do you do now to prevent disruption of services or key operations?

What do you do to prevent damage to equipment?

What emergency response procedures do you start?

_____

_____

_____

_____

Okay, now thinking about if you had an earthquake early warning system and you received 10 seconds of warning before the shaking began . . .

18. What could you do with that 10 seconds of warning? How could you add to or enhance what you already do when an earthquake begins?

PROBE:

What would you do differently with 10 seconds warning? Would you do more? Would you do less?

_____

_____

_____

19. Now, what if you had 50 seconds of warning before the shaking began? How could you add to or enhance what you already do or what you could do with 10 seconds? PROBE.

_____

_____

Prior to the set of questions shown in Figure 3.2, we had asked respondents about the kinds of warning or alert systems they already had in their organizations. For the sequence of questions in Figure 3.2, we first asked respondents about whether they thought that they could use any of their existing warning systems in the proposed earthquake early warning system. Here we guided respondents to particular parts of their existing warning systems, namely, those methods by which they alerted workers, manual shutdown or activation procedures, and automatic shutdown or activation procedures. We then asked them to describe what they currently do when an earthquake starts. This question was more difficult for the respondents to answer, but we gave the interviewers probes to use to help respondents think about what they do. We then asked two hypothetical questions about what the respondents' organizations might do differently if they had either 10 or 50 seconds of warning. These last two questions were both more complex than the previous questions and required more thought; as a result, they were particularly difficult questions for respondents to answer. Yet obtaining answers to these questions (and others that followed) represented the primary objectives of the study.

Similarly, the set of questions in Figure 3.1, which asked community members about whether they were injured during the Northridge earthquake, also progresses from easier questions to more difficult questions. We started by asking the respondent if he or she was injured. If the answer was yes, we then asked when the injury occurred, followed by questions about what caused the injury, what the injury was, and whether the respondent sought medical care for the injury.

LOGICAL ORDER

Questions should be asked in **logical order**. One common error that beginning surveyors make is in ordering questions according to when they think about them instead of in some logical sequence. In the most extreme case, they may even ask respondents to flip back and forth between topics. When this happens, even the most talented interviewer will have difficulty helping the respondent provide accurate information. Figure 3.3 provides an example of this kind of error. Here we have two demographic questions (Questions 1 and 3), two questions about physical activity (Questions 2 and 5), and one attitude question related to a demographic question (Question 4). If these questions were asked in logical order, related questions would be grouped together. In other words, Questions 1 and 4 would be in sequence and, along with question 3, would be placed with other demographic questions. Questions 2 and 5 would be together and placed with other questions about physical activities.

Figure 3.3.   Example of an Illogical and Poorly Ordered
              Questionnaire

---

1. Are you currently employed at a regular job?

    YES . . . . .ASK A-B 1

    NO . . . . . .GO TO Q2 2

    A. What days of the week do you
       usually work?

    _____

    RECORD AS GIVEN

    B. What hours do you usually work?

    _____

    RECORD AS GIVEN

2. About how often do you participate in sports or physical activities? Would you say:

    At least once a day, ...1
    Less than once a day but several
        times a week, ...2
    2-3 times a week, ...3
    Once a week, ...4
    Less than once a week, or 5
    Never? 6

3. How old were you on your last birthday?

    _____

    RECORD AS GIVEN

4. How do you like your job? Would you say that you are:

> Very satisfied with your job, ...1
> Somewhat satisfied
>   with your job, ...2
> Neither satisfied or unsatisfied
>   with your job 3
> Somewhat dissatisfied
>   with your job, or 4
> Very dissatisfied with your job? . .5

5. When you participate in physical activities, about how long do you participate each time?

RECORD # OF MINUTES
DO NOT PARTICIPATE. . . .999

The questions about injuries in Figure 3.1 also provide an example of putting questions in logical order. It would have made no sense for us to ask respondents about whether they sought medical care for injuries *before* we found out if they had any injuries. As Figures 3.1 and 3.2, show, questions work better when they proceed from more general topics to more specific ones.

PLACEMENT OF DEMOGRAPHIC QUESTIONS

In the preceding section, we advised surveyors to group questions by topic area. This also applies to demographic questions (questions about respondent characteristics such as age, gender, employment status, income, and marital status). Surveyors differ, however, in their opinions concerning *where* in the questionnaire demographic questions should be located. We believe that is it best to place demographic questions at the end of the questionnaire, except when surveyors must ask demographic questions to determine who is eligible for a study or when a branching series of questions is dependent on the respondent's gender.

Why Demographic Questions at the End?

We recommend putting demographic questions at the end of the questionnaire for three reasons. First, every telephone interview starts with an introductory statement that describes the subject matter of the study. Sometimes, as in the Trinet Study, a letter that explains the study is sent to each potential respondent in advance of any telephone contact. The purpose of these introductory statements is to intrigue respondents and encourage their participation in the study. If the first questions in the questionnaire are demographic ones, this tends to negate the positive influence of the introductory statements. Second, many people find demographic questions boring. By beginning with boring questions, the surveyor increases the probability that respondents will become disinterested in the study and refuse to complete the interview. Finally, many respondents consider the topics of some demographic questions, such as age and income, to be highly personal. Starting a questionnaire with questions that respondents are reluctant to answer reduces the probability that respondents will complete the interview.

Other surveyors disagree with this position and believe that it is best to ask demographic questions at the beginning of a questionnaire. They have two reasons for this position. First, demographic questions are easy for respondents to answer because they know the information being sought; if they begin an interview by answering such questions, they may be less likely to think of the interview as some kind of "test." Second, if a respondent terminates an interview before it is completed, the surveyor at least has demographic information about the respondent, and thus information about some of the characteristics of people who refuse to be interviewed.

Demographic Data for Screening Purposes

In many studies, the researchers want to interview people with certain characteristics; for example, they may want to interview only women or recent immigrants. In such cases, the questionnaire has to include some demographic questions at the beginning, so that interviewers can screen out any persons who are not eligible for the study. In the Loma Prieta study, for example, we wanted to interview only individuals who lived within the five-county area in which the study was being conducted on October 17, 1989, the day of the earthquake.

In other cases, surveyors do not want to interview the first person who answers the phone in every household. Rather, they want to make sure that people who are not always home or do not always answer the phone in their homes are represented within the final sample of respondents. In such cases, the surveyor must design a procedure for the interviewer to follow in which the interviewer first lists all the eligible people who live in the household (e.g., all adults 18 and older). The interviewer then selects the designated respondent, using either a Kish table or the last/next birthday method (we discuss the selection of respondents within households in detail in Chapter 5). Usually, when we have the interviewer list all the adults in the household before selecting the designated respondent, we go ahead and have the interviewer also find out the sex and age of each adult and each child living in the household. We call this listing a *household roster.*

Figure 3.4   Household Roster

---

2. Now I would like to make a list of the persons 18 years old or over who are members of your household. This will tell me who I am to interview. Just give me their first names.

ASK Q'S A-G FOR EACH PERSON IN HOUSEHOLD 18 AND OVER. RECORD RESPONSES IN CHART. FOLLOW INSTRUCTION FOR COLUMN G.

    A. Let's start with the oldest person in the household and work our way down to the youngest person, over 18. Starting with the oldest person, (INSERT NEXT ADULT IN HOUSEHOLD AS YOU GO DOWN THE LIST), what is his/her first name?

    B. Is this (. . .)'s permanent residence?

    C. Is (. . .) male or female?

    D. What was (. . .)'s age on his/her last birthday?

    E. What is (. . .)'s relationship to you?

    F. On the day of the Bay Area earthquake on October 17, 1989, did (. . .) live:

        At this same address, ...1
        At a different address in
          the same community, ...2
        Somewhere else in these
          five counties (Alameda,
          Santa Clara, Santa Cruz,
          San Mateo, and
          San Francisco), or 3
        Outside these five counties? 4

    G. IF RESPONSE IS CODE "1," "2," OR "3" IN F., BEGIN WITH "1" IN COLUMN G OF THE CHART AND CONTINUE NUMBERING SEQUENTIALLY ONLY FOR EACH HOUSEHOLD MEMBER WHO LIVED EITHER AT THE SAME ADDRESS OR IN ONE OF THE FIVE COUNTIES ON OCTOBER 17, 1989. IF NO ONE IN HOUSEHOLD QUALIFIES, TERMINATE.

ADULT ROSTER
FILL IN CHART BELOW FOR RESPONSES TO Q2.

	A.	B.		C.		D.	E.	F.				G.
	FIRST NAME	PERMANENT RESIDENT		SEX		AGE	RELAT. TO RESP.	ADDRESS STATUS				#
		YES	NO	M	F			SAME	DIFF	ELSE BAY	OUT BAY	1-8
1.		1	2	1	2			1	2	3	4	
2.		V12 1	2	V13 1	2	V14(2)	V15(2)	1	V16 2	3	4	V17
3.		V18 1	2	V19 1	2	V20(2)	V21(2)	1	V22 2	3	4	V23
4.		V24 1	2	V25 1	2	V26(2)	V27(2)	1	V28 2	3	4	V29
5.		V30 1	2	V31 1	2	V32(2)	V33(2)	1	V34 2	3	4	V35
6.		V36 1	2	V37 1	2	V38(2)	V39(2)	1	V40 2	3	4	V41
7.		V42 1	2	V43 1	2	V44(2)	V45(2)	1	V46 2	3	4	V47
8.		V48 1	2	V49 1	2	V50(2)	V51(2)	1	V52 2	3	4	V53
		V54		V55		V56(2)	V57(2)			V58 3		V59

83

REFER TO LABEL ON FRONT OF SCREENER TO SELECT RESPONDENT. IF SELECTED RESPONDENT IS NOT SAME AS INFORMANT, ASK TO SPEAK TO SELECTED PERSON. IF RESPONDENT IS NOT AVAILABLE, ASK FOR BEST TIME TO CALL BACK. IF SELECTED RESPONDENT IS INFORMANT, CONTINUE WITH INTERVIEW.

OFFICE USE ONLY

LINE # OF RESP: ___ TOTAL # ADULTS: ___ TOTAL # CHILDREN: ___

3. Now I would like to make a list of those persons under 18 years old who are living here as members of your household. Let's begin with the youngest person and work our way up to those who are 17 years old.

LIST THOSE 17 YEARS OLD AND UNDER. ASK Q'S A-D FOR EACH PERSON LISTED. RECORD RESPONSES IN CHART.

A. Please give me the (youngest/next) child's first name.

B. What is (. . .)'s relationship to you?

C. Is (. . .) male or female?

D. What was (. . .)'s age on (his/her) last birthday?

	A.	B.	C.		D.
	FIRST NAME	RELATIONSHIP TO RESP.	SEX		AGE
			M	F	
			1	2	
1.		V63(2)	V64		V65(2)
2.		V66(2)	V67		V68(2)
3.		V69(2)	V70		V71(2)
4.		V72(2)	V73		V74(2)
5.		V75(2)	V76		V77(2)
6.		V78(2)	V79		V80(2)
7.		V81(2)	V82		V83(2)
8.		V84(2)	V85		V86(2)

Figure 3.4 shows the household roster that we created at the beginning of the Loma Prieta study. The first two pages were printed on facing pages in a booklet format, with the questions on the left-hand page and the grid or table where the answers were to be written on the facing page. Adult household members were listed from oldest person to youngest person, with the first name recorded in the first column labeled A on the second page. The interviewer then asked four demographic questions about each adult listed: whether the person was a permanent resident of the household, his or her sex and age, and the person's relationship to the adult providing the information. For purposes of the Loma Prieta study, the interviewer asked a screening question: Did the person live in the Bay Area on October 17, 1989? Note, then, that only those adults who lived in the Bay Area on the day of the earthquake were eligible to be selected for the interview. Note also that the person the interviewer eventually selected for the interview may or may not have been the person who gave the interviewer all the household roster information. If, after filling in the roster, the interviewer found that someone else in the household qualified as the designated respondent, the interviewer had to ask to speak to that person. If the designated respondent was not available at the time, the interviewer had to arrange another time to call him or her.

As Figure 3.4 shows, the interviewer used the third page of the household roster to record the gender, age, and relationship to the designated respondent of each of the children living in the household.

Checklist for Constructing Questions

✓ Keep questions short.

✓ Make questions specific.

✓ Avoid vague qualifiers.

✓ Avoid abstract terms.

✓ Avoid jargon.

✓ Avoid slang.

✓ Start with easier questions and move to more difficult ones.

✓ Ask questions in a logical order.

✓ Decide where to place demographic questions and why you are choosing that location.

Open- Versus Closed-Ended Questions

Items in questionnaires used in interviews can be completely open-ended, open-ended as presented to the respondent but not to the interviewer, or closed-ended. Questions 16A-C in Figure 3.2 and Questions 1, 2, and 4 in Figure 3.3 are examples of completely closed-ended questions. Questions 17, 18, and 19 in Figure 3.2 and Questions 1A-B, 3, and 5 in Figure 3.3 are examples of completely open-ended questions. Completely open-ended questions have no lists of possible answers; completely closed-ended questions include lists of possible answers that, in the case of telephone interviews, the interviewer reads to the respondent and from which the respondent selects the answer or answers that best represent his or her view or situation.

Although open-ended questions are much easier to write than closed-ended items, they generally are more difficult to answer, code, and analyze. Because respondents are not provided with lists of possible answers, they must work harder in answering open-ended questions. This is where skilled interviewers are invaluable; they can help respondents explore what they know, think, or feel about the topic under study. Open-ended questions make the interviewer work harder also. The interviewer is instructed to **probe** responses as part of the process of helping respondents give complete answers. The interviewer also has the burden of recording the answers, either by writing them down or typing them into a computer. Surveyors usually want interviewers to record complete information, indicate if and when they probed any answers, and, if so, what language they used in probing. (We discuss probing in greater depth in Chapter 6.) Prior to analysis, surveyors must develop code frames or categories to organize and summarize the data collected using open-ended questions. This process is sometimes referred to as **content analysis.**

Compared with open-ended questions, closed-ended questions are much more difficult to design; however, if the researcher designs them carefully and pretests them sufficiently, closed-ended questions result in much more efficient data collection, data processing, and analysis. Closed-ended questions are much easier for the interviewer to administer as well; instead of having to write out the respondent's answers, the interviewer selects from the lists of answer categories the words, phrases, or statements that best match the respondent's answers.

PARTIALLY OPEN QUESTIONS

When data are collected in an interview, the questionnaire may include some **partially open questions** such as those shown in Figure 2.4 in Chapter 2. Look at Question 8A in Figure 2.4 in particular. Here the interviewer reads the question to the respondent but does *not* read the list of possible answers. Thus, although the question appears open-ended to the respondent, the interviewer is provided with a list of answers that the surveyor anticipates most respondents will use in describing the damage that occurred as a result of the earthquake. As the respondent describes the damage, the interviewer records the things he or she mentions by using the list rather than writing out the answers verbatim.

There are three reasons surveyors may want to design questions so that they include lists for the interviewer that are not read to the respondent. First, surveyors are always concerned about trying to obtain valid data from respondents that represent what actually happened to them, not what the surveyors think might or should have happened to them. When interviewers read answer categories to respondents, this tends to "lead" the respondents. That is, the categories suggest possible answers, and respondents, partly because they don't have to think as hard and partly because they want to please the researcher, choose from among the responses given. This tendency among respondents to want to cooperate with and please surveyors is called **acquiescence bias**.

Second, when interviewers read lists of possible responses to respondents, the likelihood that primacy effects, recency effects, or satisficing will occur increases. **Primacy effect** refers to a respondent's tendency to "hear" and select the first answer read in response to a closed-ended question rather than listening to the full list of alternatives. **Recency effect** is the reverse of primacy effect; that is, the respondent "hears" and selects only the last alternative read. **Satisficing theory** suggests that respondents answer questions by choosing the first satisfactory or acceptable response alternative offered to them rather than taking time to select an optimal answer.

Third, the existence of the list of response categories in the questionnaire means that the interviewer does not have to write down all the things the respondent says. Rather, the interviewer can use the list to record the answer. The list also provides the basis for the code frame that the surveyor will use in analyzing the data, and thus reduces the need for content analysis.

There are, however, some caveats that surveyors need to consider in creating partially open questions. For one thing, the lists of answers provided for such questions have to be clear and not too long. The list in Figure 2.4 represents about the maximum number of responses that should be provided.

If a list is too long or the alternatives provided in the list are too complex, the interviewer cannot easily use it. When a list gets too long and complex, the surveyor needs to consider other ways of recording the answers. This may mean using a completely open-ended question instead, or it may mean asking multiple questions. In the case of Question 8A in Figure 2.4, we would advocate the use of multiple questions.

When surveyors use partially open questions, they should arrange the answer categories in alphabetic order (unless the response categories are incremental) so that interviewers can more easily locate and mark respondents' answers.

Surveyors who use computer-assisted telephone interviewing to administer their questionnaires rarely use partially open questions with long lists of possible answer categories from which respondents may select anywhere from none to all of the categories, because setting up such questions requires substantial repetitive programming. Certainly, in our experience, CATI programmers have been resistant to the inclusion of such questions in questionnaires.

DECIDING WHEN TO USE OPEN-ENDED QUESTIONS

There are four situations in which the use of open-ended questions is clearly recommended. First, when the topic under study is exploratory, open-ended questions are often valuable and frequently represent the only way in which some data can be collected. By *exploratory*, we mean that the study topic has not been examined before or little is known about the topic; the Trinet Study is an example. In such instances, the surveyor does not know what the range of possible answers is or even what the logical sequence of questions might be. The surveyor thus needs to create a situation in which respondents can explore the topic and share their perceptions of what is happening, what could happen, or how they think about the topic.

Second, even after preliminary research, a surveyor may not be able to figure out how to create closed-ended response categories for some questions. Figure 3.5 provides an example. We originally asked this question as a completely open-ended question after the Whittier Narrows earthquake. After doing some content analysis of the answers obtained, we partially closed the question for the Loma Prieta study by listing responses for the interviewer to use. This proved to be premature and unworkable, however. In fact, people often do multiple things simultaneously during an earthquake. For example, they take cover at the same time they call out instructions to others. Interviewers found it impossible to record adequately the first thing each respondent said he or she did, so they simply wrote down everything the respondents said and ignored the categories. In future studies, we would continue to leave this question completely open-ended and postcode the answers using content analysis.

Figure 3.5.   Example of a Question That Was Prematurely Closed

---

3. When you felt the earthquake, what was the very first thing you did?

GOT UNDER DOORWAY/TABLE/COVER 1
FROZE/STAYED WHERE WAS 2
CAUGHT FALLING OBJECTS 3
RAN OUTSIDE 4
WENT TO CHILD 5
CALLED INSTRUCTIONS
        TO OTHERS IN AREA 6
PULLED CAR OVER 7
CONTINUED DRIVING 8
OTHER(S) 9
SPECIFY: _____

Another quite different example of the use of open-ended questions concerns questions about income. We generally provide income categories when we ask a respondent about his or her individual income or the income of the respondent's family or household. We do so because the topic of income is assumed to be sensitive, and it is true that if a respondent is going to refuse to answer a question, it is almost always going to be the question about the respondent's income. Use of categories for such a question is thought to make the question less sensitive and more impersonal. The problem comes in figuring out what the answer categories should be. How many categories should there be? How broad should each be? Should there be two categories of $30,000-34,999 and $35,000-39,999, or should there be one category of $30,000-39,999? What should be the lowest income category? What should be the highest income category?

In the Whittier Narrows earthquake study conducted in 1988, our top income category for Los Angeles County families was "over $40,000." We based our selection of categories on prior studies that had been conducted in the county, without considering whether the categories adequately represented the full range of family incomes. When we started to analyze the data, we found that 38% of our respondents reported family incomes over $40,000. As a result, we did not have a clear idea of how family income was distributed in Los Angeles County, and that significantly limited the value of the income data in our analyses.

This experience provides an example of both heaping and a ceiling effect. **Heaping** refers to the creation of response categories in such a way that most respondents end up in one category. **Floor** and **ceiling effects** can be considered special kinds of heaping in which the overused category is either the lowest or the highest category among categories that can logically be rank ordered from lowest to highest. Although it flies in the face of tradition, the lesson here is that if the surveyor is unsure about the range and composition of the income categories to be used, he or she might be better advised to use an open-ended question when asking about income.

Third, a researcher may decide to leave questions open-ended because they take up less space on the questionnaire in that form, writing down the answers will not be onerous for the interviewer because the answers will be short, and the surveyor expects to obtain data of higher quality than he or she might get otherwise. Questions 1A-B, 3, and 5 in Figure 3.3 provide examples of questions with these features. Why list age categories for a question about how old a person is? Age categories take up space, and they also give us data that are ordinal in format, rather than interval or ratio. Categorized ordinal data are more difficult to analyze because means cannot be computed.

Fourth, and finally, it is wise to end interviews with one or more **ventilation questions**—that is, questions that invite respondents to tell the surveyor what they liked about the interview, what they disliked about the interview, which questions were difficult to answer, which questions they did not understand, and what they feel the surveyor should have asked about but did not. Ventilation questions are always open-ended.

Construction of Response Categories

Clearly, if closed-ended questions are more difficult to design than open-ended questions, the task of developing the answer categories for such questions represents a major source of that difficulty. A list of response categories should have the following characteristics:

- The list should be **exhaustive** while simultaneously not being too long.

- The categories in the list should be **mutually exclusive,** and respondents and interviewers should be able to distinguish the boundaries separating the categories easily.

- The list should be set up to allow respondents to provide multiple answers when relevant.

- When appropriate, the list should include a residual "other" category.

In designing attitude and opinion questions, the surveyor must decide how many response categories to provide.

As the above discussion of partially open questions indicates, a clear advantage of interviews over self-administered questionnaires is that in interviews, respondents may or may not be exposed to response categories. A second advantage is that surveyors can make use of longer and more complex lists of answer categories, because the interviewer is available to help guide the respondent through the alternatives to select those that represent him or her.

A disadvantage of telephone interviews in particular is that respondents receive an exclusively auditory stimulus, and there is no easy way by which the auditory stimulus can be enhanced or reinforced with a visual stimulus, such as a card with alternative responses listed. Thus, when the interviewer reads the response choices to the respondent, he or she must clearly state all items on the list of alternatives and be prepared to repeat them. This means that the risk of primacy or recency effects is increased. Surveyors often try to temper these effects by training the interviewers to read all the response categories from first to last and then read them again, starting over at the top, before asking the respondent for an answer.

As we have noted above, an advantage of telephone interviews and particularly of the use of partially open questions is that respondents are more likely to volunteer answers that are not on the list. Thus, if a list does not provide an adequate description of a respondent's behavior or feelings, or if the list is not read, the respondent is more likely to ignore the list and give an answer without getting frustrated by the inadequacies of the alternatives provided. Nonetheless, if response alternatives are persistently too restrictive or too vague, respondents may become frustrated by their inability to describe themselves accurately. To the extent that respondent frustration increases, terminations increase and response rates decrease. Thus, it is extremely important that surveyors spend sufficient time developing and pretesting the response alternatives provided for each question in telephone interviews.

EASILY USED CATEGORIES

In the Loma Prieta study, we wanted to find out whether people used the electronic media (radio and television) after the earthquake to get information. Because the earthquake occurred shortly after 5:00 P.M. on the first day of the World Series, just before the scheduled start of a game between the San Francisco Giants and the Oakland Athletics, we knew that many people in the Bay Area already had their radios or TVs on. Thus, we had to allow for three possibilities: that people were already using some form of electronic media and it stayed on, that their TVs and/or radios were on and then went off, or that they tried to turn on some form of media, either successfully or unsuccessfully. The series of short questions displayed in Figure 3.6 was the best way to get this information.

On the face of it, the response list for each question in Figure 3.6 is short, exhaustive, and mutually exclusive, but in fact, neither Question 6A nor Question 6C provides an exhaustive list of responses. Shortly after beginning the data collection, interviewers told us two things. First, in answering Question 6A, many people said that media had gone off briefly and then returned to the air and stayed on. In answering Q6C, many people said that they went to their cars and turned on their car radios to find out what was happening. Although car radios are technically "battery radios," we decided that it was important to add "car radios" as a separate response alternative. For Question 6A, we added a response "Yes, briefly" to capture information about brief unavailability of radios and televisions.

Another problem involved Questions 6 and 6C. Some people had both the radio and television on at the time of the earthquake, and many people tried multiple radios and

Figure 3.6.   Easily Used, Exhaustive, and Mutually Exclusive
Answer Categories

6. When the earthquake struck, did you have the
radio or television on?

        YES, RADIO . . . . . . .ASK A 1
        YES, TELEVISION . . .ASK A 2 V119
        NO, NEITHER . . . . . .SKIP TO C . .3

A. As far as you know, did it stay on
the air for at least two hours after
the earthquake?
YES . . . . .SKIP TO E 1 V120
NO . . . . . .ASK B 2

B. Why didn't it stay on?

        POWER/ELECTRICITY WENT OUT . . .1
        RADIO/TV DAMAGED 2 V121
        OTHER 3
        SPECIFY:_____ V122

C. Did you (try to) turn on or find
(another/a) TV or radio to get more
information about the earthquake?

        YES, REGULAR TV . . . . .ASK D 1

        YES, BATTERY TV . . . . . .ASK D 2

        YES, REGULAR RADIO   ASK D 3
                                                                V123

        YES, BATTERY RADIO . . .ASK D 4

        NO . . . . .SKIP TO Q7 . .5

D. Were you able to find a station to
   listen to?

   YES . . . . .ASK E 1

   NO . . . . . .SKIP TO Q7 . . .2

E. Did they suggest any actions you
   should take?

   YES 1

   NO 2

7. You told me you were (INSERT ANSWER FROM
   Q1A OR Q2A AS APPROPRIATE) when the earthquake struck. Was there any damage in the immediate area where you were when the earthquake
   struck, that is, within five blocks in any direction,
   to major structures—such as buildings, homes,
   freeways, dams, or roads?

   YES 1

   NO 2

TVs before finding one that worked or giving up. As written,
each of these questions asked for a single response. We could
have improved both questions by providing instructions
that would allow the interviewers to use all the alternatives
to capture more exactly what respondents did.

EXHAUSTIVE LIST OF CATEGORIES

   We just saw how incomplete lists of answer categories for
two questions in Figure 3.6 forced us to add additional cate-

gories after data collection started. Earlier in this chapter, we presented an example concerning a list of answer categories for a question asking about the frequency of religious service attendance. Looking back at that list, we can see that it is technically not exhaustive. For example, we do not provide an answer for attending religious services "4-5 times a week" or "several times a year." A better list of categories might be as follows:

Nearly every day, ...1
4-5 times a week, ...2
Once a week, ...3
2-3 times a month, ...4
Once a month, ...5
Several times a year, ...6
Only on special holidays, or 7
Never? 8

Traditionally, questions on marital status provide the response alternatives of "never married," "married," "divorced," "separated," and "widowed." These alternatives, however, really represent legal statuses. With the large and increasing numbers of people living together without getting married today, and the increasing recognition of same-sex relationships, many researchers have either expanded the categories or asked a second question about "living with someone as married." According to the 2000 U.S. Census, 5.2% of households in the United States currently describe themselves as "unmarried partner households," ranging from a low of 3.2% for Puerto Rico to a high of 7.5% for both Alaska and Vermont.

MUTUALLY EXCLUSIVE CATEGORIES

We used Question 3 in Figure 3.5 to try to find out what people did first during the Loma Prieta earthquake. As we noted earlier, the list of response categories we provided was neither exhaustive nor mutually exclusive. We assumed (incorrectly) that an individual could name one "physical activity" that he or she did first during the earthquake. We found out that people both did multiple "first things," and that the things they did were not necessarily physical activities. Some people reported "first things" that were cognitive: "I prayed"; "I recognized that it was an earthquake." Other people reported doing multiple activities, such as simultaneously calling instructions to others, running to a child, and seeking cover under a door frame. In this instance, our effort to provide an exhaustive list with alternatives that were clearly mutually exclusive was so *unsuccessful* that we gave up the idea of using a closed-ended or partially open-ended question to get this information and told interviewers to handle the question as if it were completely open-ended.

MULTIPLE ANSWERS

Surveyors use two techniques in making response categories both flexible and exhaustive. The first is to set up response categories so that respondents can select more than one answer to describe themselves. In Figure 2.4, Question 8A allows respondents to select multiple answers, and that enabled us to get a complete picture of the kinds and amount of damage respondents experienced as a result of the earthquake.

When the questionnaire makes provisions for respondents to give multiple answers, the surveyor must also make provisions for the multiple answers to be efficiently and completely coded into the data set for analysis. The easiest way to do that is to create a separate variable for each response provided and set up consistent **coding** for whether a given response is or is not selected by the respondent and circled by the interviewer. In the example in Figure 2.4, we decided that circled responses would be coded 1 for "mentioned" and those not circled would be coded 2 for "not mentioned." We prefer the coding of the "not mentioned" to the alternative of coding only "mentioned" because we feel more secure when we have the interviewer verify that a response was not mentioned; we don't have to wonder if the answer is blank because the item wasn't read or because the interviewer forgot to circle the "yes" for that item. The responses to Question 8A then generate 20 variables—one for each of the 19 possible categories, including "Other," that were provided, plus an additional variable to indicate whether or not an answer was written into the "Other, specify" space.

We assigned both the code 1 for "mentioned" and the variable name before the data were collected. Contrast the codes provided for the questions in Figure 3.6 with those provided for Question 8A in Figure 2.4. Within each question in Figure 3.6, sequential numbers are assigned as codes for the alternative response categories. For example, for Question 6C, 1 for "Yes, regular TV"; 2 for "Yes, battery TV"; 3 for "Yes, regular radio"; 4 for "Yes, battery radio"; and 5 for "No." In contrast, for Question 8A in Figure 2.4, a code of 1 is provided for each alternative response category and an instruction is provided that reads "Circle All That Apply." Both the presence of the instruction and the kind of numeric codes provided indicate to the interviewer that only one answer is to be recorded for Question 6C, whereas multiple answers can be selected for Question 8A. The preassigned variable names also signal the interviewer that a single answer is to be recorded for the questions in Figure 3.6, whereas multiple answers are to be recorded for Question 8A.

Although the convention is to use a single number code, usually 1, when multiple answers can be selected, and different, sequential numbers when a single answer is to be selected, sometimes long lists of response alternatives are more easily used with sequential numbers for the responses. For example, for Question 8A in Figure 2.4, instead of having a code of 1 for each of the 19 alternatives mentioned, we might have had codes that went from 01 for "personal property broken" to 19 for "other." A surveyor might want to set up codes this way to reduce errors that interviewers might make in recording the answers during paper-and-pencil administration of the questionnaire, and also to avoid repetitive type errors that often occur in data entry when long strings of the same number are entered. It is probably easier for the interviewer to associate a unique, different number with a given alternative—for example, 07 for "chimney collapsed"—than to pick out the 1 that is associated with "chimney collapsed." The surveyor's goal should always be to make the tasks of answering questions and recording answers correctly as easy as possible for both the respondent and the interviewer.

RESIDUAL "OTHER" CATEGORY

The inclusion of a residual "other" category is another technique surveyors can use to increase flexibility in answer categories. Both Question 8A in Figure 2.4 and Question 6B in Figure 3.6 include residual "others," and we discussed earlier how Question 6C should have included a residual "other." In Question 8A, we tried to create an exhaustive list of the different kinds of damage that people might experience during an earthquake. We based our list on earlier studies that we had conducted. Because reported damage within an area can range from none to complete destruction of homes, we needed to create a list that would be as exhaustive as possible and also allow for the fact that some people only had dishes fall out of cabinets, while others had chimneys that collapsed and still others had combinations of damage that included roof damage, collapsed walls, and damaged water heaters.

In creating an exhaustive list, we did not want to create a list that was too long or *too* detailed. For example, we combined "patios" and "porches." Once we had finished our pretest and felt that our list was fairly exhaustive, we still could not be 100% sure, so we added a residual "other." Thus, if a respondent reported damage to something that we failed to include in our list, or if the interviewer was not comfortable with recording an answer in the available list, the interviewer could circle the 1 corresponding to "other" and describe the damage in the space provided.

Sometimes, interviewers are unsure about which combination of categories to use. For example, if a person said that his or her "roof collapsed, walls collapsed, floors collapsed, the house fell off its foundation, and the whole house fell down," the interviewer might not want to make a decision between selecting the single alternative "entire building destroyed" or selecting the five alternatives that correspond to each of the discrete answers given. In this case, the interviewer could circle the 1 that corresponds with "other" and write down the things the respondent said were damaged.

Once all of the interviews have been conducted, the surveyor must decide how to handle each of the residual "other" answers in data analysis. There are two choices: The surveyor can either move a volunteered answer into one of the existing variable categories or create a new (in the case of Question 8A, 20th) variable to represent the new answer. We would code the answer in the example given above into the existing categories. A number of respondents in the Loma Prieta study, however, lived in mountainous areas outside Santa Cruz, California, where many of the homes have elevated water tanks or towers on their property. Many of these water tanks collapsed or were damaged during the earthquake, and these respondents reported this damage in answering Question 8A. Because no alternative existed for these answers, the interviewers recorded them in the residual "other" category and described them in the space provided. During analysis, we created a new, 20th variable that represented destroyed or damaged water towers.

The surveyor needs to apply two general rules in deciding whether or not to create a new category or variable from an answer recorded in the residual "other" category. First, he or she needs to determine how closely the answer given in the residual "other" category relates to answer categories already specified. In the above examples, we decided that the first answer was adequately represented using existing categories, but that the water tanks required a new category or variable. Second, the surveyor needs to examine the number of respondents who give answers that interviewers decide should be recorded in the residual "other" category. If, for example, we had had a lot of respondents specify that it was the north walls of their houses that collapsed, we might have decided that the number of responses justified the creation of a category that differentiated the north wall from all other walls. Because the energy from earthquakes moves through the earth in patterns that can be discerned after the fact, it might be pertinent to differentiate damage to the north sides of buildings from damage to the other three sides of buildings. The surveyor must make decisions concerning whether or not new categories and variables should be created during data entry or analysis.

In developing answer categories, the surveyor should try to minimize the need for interviewers to mark the residual "other." If more than 10% of the answers given by respondents to a particular question have to be recorded in the residual "other" category in order to be described completely, either the surveyor has done insufficient thinking before creating the list of answer possibilities or the categories are not clear to the interviewers or respondents. If the latter is the case, it may mean that interviewer training, monitoring, and pretesting have been inadequate, but it also may mean that the surveyor did not think out the answer alternatives carefully. Furthermore, when interviewers find that the list of responses provided for a question consistently does not allow them to describe accurately what respondents say, they may begin to put responses arbitrarily into a category simply because it is there, and not because it adequately represents the answers given.

NEUTRAL RESPONSES IN ATTITUDE QUESTIONS

Many, if not most, surveyors want to find out what people think about various things. In other words, they want to find out people's attitudes and opinions. Usually, attitude questions include ranges of answers for respondents to use in answering. For example, in Figure 3.3, Question 4 asks respondents how satisfied they are with their jobs. Often, surveyors use many questions to operationalize or measure a particular concept or construct. Figure 2.7 and 2.8 in Chapter 2 show the first few questions from the Brief Symptom Inventory, which measures psychological symptomatology, and the Civilian Mississippi Scale, which measures posttraumatic stress disorder. Note that in the BSI, the same five alternative responses are provided for each question: "Not at all," "A little bit," "Moderately," Quite a bit," and "Extremely." In this example, an odd number of categories are provided, and every category is labeled.

Psychometricians (that is, people who specialize in the development of standardized scales) differ in their recommendations about how surveyors should create answer categories when they are developing multiple attitude questions. Most psychometricians recommend that researchers create a minimum of five answer categories, but they differ in whether they consider an even number or an odd number of categories to be better, and in whether or not they recommend that each category should be labeled. The discussion regarding odd or even numbers of categories revolves around the meaning or interpretation given to the middle categories in the set. For example, consider the following question:

How do you feel about congressional proposals for stimulating the economy?

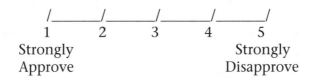

1   2   3   4   5

Strongly   Strongly
Approve   Disapprove

Here we define or provide names for the two extreme categories, but we do not provide names for the three "in-between" categories. Now consider this alternative:

How do you feel about congressional proposals
for stimulating the economy? Would you say you:

Strongly support the proposals, ...1
Generally support the proposals, ...2
Understand the proposals,
    but are undecided about them, ...3
Tend to be against the proposals, or . .4
Strongly object to the proposals? 5

Here, in contrast, we name all five of the alternatives.

What are the relative strengths and weaknesses of these two formats? We can argue that the set of answer categories in the first question acts more like an interval scale, and that the wording of the question itself, when combined with the answer categories, creates a "neutral" question, one that through its wording and format pushes the respondent to agree or disagree with the subject of the question. There are, however, two disadvantages to the format of this question. First, the middle category, or the 3, is undefined. If a respondent selects the 3, what does he or she mean to say? Does a choice of 3 mean that the respondent knows about congressional proposals but has no opinion about them, or does it mean that the respondent does not know what the question is talking about?

A second problem with the first question is particularly relevant for telephone interviewing. In order to make the alternative answers available to respondents to answer, interviewers need instructions. These instructions generally require that in-between numbers be given labels, and that reduces our ability to argue that these answer categories represent an interval variable, and we still have the problem of deciding what to label the 3. We can give it a label of "No opinion," which a respondent may interpret to mean "I don't know anything about this topic," or we can label it

"Neither agree or disagree," which tends to "push" toward an interpretation that respondents who select the 3 know something about congressional proposals but are undecided about them.

The second version of the question presents different challenges. It is better than the first version in that each answer category is labeled, and thus interviewers can read the labels to respondents. Also, the middle category is clearly stated to indicate that the respondent "knows about these proposals but has no opinion about them." But, at the same time, the labels reduce the neutrality of the stimulus that the respondent receives and create an ordinal set of categories rather than categories that we could more easily argue are interval. Neutrality is lost because the categories used— "strongly support," "generally support," "tend to be against," and "strongly object"—are not symmetrical around the central category or 3 and, because they employ vague qualifiers, their meaning and how they are interpreted may well vary from respondent to respondent. We could fix some of this by changing the wording of the labels for the last two alternatives to "generally against" and "strongly against," but we would still be left with modifying adverbs whose meanings will differ across respondents.

Another issue is whether the number of response alternatives should be odd or even. In the above examples, the number of alternatives in both cases is odd, with the result that there is an "exact middle" category, a 3. But some researchers, recognizing the difficulties associated with an exact middle category, recommend using six response categories rather than five in questions like those above to avoid those difficulties. In addition, some researchers argue that people always have opinions, and the elimination of a middle alternative forces them to reveal the direction of their opinions; without an exact middle category, a respondent cannot hide behind an answer that can be interpreted to be completely neutral.

"DON'T KNOW" CATEGORY

We do not recommend including in the ranges of alternative answers any categories for "Don't know," "Not relevant," or "Refused." The inclusion of such categories encourages interviewers to record "don't know" answers to questions when, in fact, the respondents *do* have answers. When faced with questions from interviewers, many people in the United States will preface their responses by saying, "I don't know." Most of the time, this expression simply means that the respondent is thinking about and trying to choose among the possible answers to give the answer that best represents him or her. In general, U.S. culture does not encourage silent pauses in conversation. People say "I don't know" in part because of this norm against remaining silent; during a telephone interview, the respondent may say "I don't know" as a way of acknowledging that he or she has heard the question and is still on the phone.

Similarly, the inclusion of a "refused" category encourages the interviewer to use it too quickly rather than waiting to see if the respondent has an answer or is simply unclear about what the question is asking. And there is generally no reason to include "Not applicable" in answer lists because such responses are usually handled by skip instructions and during data entry.

Checklist for Constructing Response Categories

✓ Decide when and where open-ended questions are needed.

✓ Create exhaustive lists of responses.

✓ Keep answer alternatives short and precise.

✓ Create mutually exclusive answer categories.

✓ Decide for each question whether respondents should be restricted to a single response or allowed to provide multiple responses.

✓ Decide for each question whether the response alternatives will or will not be read to respondents.

✓ Consider the need for a residual "other" answer category.

✓ For attitude and opinion questions, decide whether to provide an odd or even number of categories.

✓ For attitude and opinion questions, decide whether or not to label all answer categories.

✓ Decide whether to include "Don't know," "Not applicable," and "Refused" in question alternatives, and why.

Clear and Sufficient Instructions

Clear and sufficient instructions are important in any study and for any questionnaire. We discuss general instructions, more specific instructions, and the instructions known as research or questionnaire specifications below.

GENERAL INSTRUCTIONS

In telephone surveys, questionnaires contain **general instructions** that include information for interviewers and explanations for interviewers to read to respondents.

Explanations for Respondents

Explanations for respondents take two forms. When the surveyor has a list of respondents, households, or institutions with complete addresses, the first contact will often be in the form of an advance letter. Figures 2.1 to 2.3 in Chapter 2 display the advance letters and a flyer that we sent to potential respondents in the Trinet Study. Advance letters have two purposes: (a) to encourage the potential respondent to participate in the study and (b) to explain what the study is about. Notice in Figure 2.1 that the letter from the California Institute of Technology starts with the sentence "Please help us in a very important study." It goes on to describe who is conducting the study and the general topic of the study. We provided further information about the proposed warning system in that same mailing by enclosing the information sheet shown in Figure 2.2. Later, the UCLA Center for Public Health and Disasters sent the second advance letter shown in Figure 2.3; notice that it describes the content of the study in more detail and tells the potential respondent who will be interviewing him or her and when.

When a surveyor does not have respondents' addresses in advance, he or she must include general instructions for respondents in the questionnaire; these instructions are provided to each respondent verbally by the interviewer. The questionnaire provides a text for the interviewer to use, but the burden of motivation and explanation falls on the interviewer. The interviewer may have to repeat the introductory text multiple times with different members of the household or organization targeted for study. In the Loma Prieta study, the text for the first contact was as follows:

> Good morning/afternoon/evening. I'm (. . .) from the Survey Research Center at UCLA. We are conducting a study to find out about people's recent experiences with earthquakes. Our questions are about both the recent Bay Area earthquake and about people's experiences in other earthquakes. Findings from this study will be made available to state and local legislators, policy makers, and planners.

The trick with verbal introductions is to provide enough information so that potential respondents can make a decision about whether or not they want to participate in the study while simultaneously not burdening them with repetitive information that causes them to refuse simply out of boredom. Obviously, surveyors can provide more information in advance letters than in verbal introductions.

Interviewer Specifications

Surveyors provide interviewers with general instructions in two forms: in a general interviewing skills manual (used in training or in briefings; we discuss training in Chapter 6) and in study-specific interviewer **specifications**.

Once the surveyor has finalized the questionnaire, he or she needs to write the questionnaire specifications. This first major documentation of the study should include information on the study's objectives, who the respondents are and how they are to be selected, how contacts with respondents are to be made, how questions are to be asked, the reason each question or set of questions is included in the questionnaire, and instructions for how each question is to be administered. In a telephone survey, the surveyor must write two sets of specifications: a set to be used by the research team and a second set, usually reduced from the first, that focuses on what interviewers need to know about how they should ask questions and, when relevant, how they should probe for more information. This second set is generally referred to as *interviewer specifications.*

Interviewer specifications should include, at minimum, information about the objective of the study; the selection and **tracking** of respondents in the study; how the interviewer should approach respondents, handle questions about the study, ask and record answers for individual questions, and conduct probes; when and where the interviewer should send completed interviews (in the case of paper-and-pencil studies); and the number and timing of administrations and follow-up procedures.

Figure 3.7. Excerpts From Sample Interviewer Specifications

Study Objectives This study has multiple objectives. First, we want to find out about San Francisco Bay Area residents' experiences after the earthquake on October 17, 1989: where they were, how they reacted, where they obtained information, whether their property was damaged or they experienced injury, what agencies they were in contact with, etc. Second, this study allows us to compare Bay Area residents' earthquake-related knowledge, experience, and behaviors in 1989 with those of Los Angeles County residents following the Whittier Narrows earthquake of October 1, 1989. Of interest is the extent to which Bay Area and Southern California residents differ in their level of preparedness, exposure to earthquake predictions, and knowledge of agencies involved in post-earthquake assistance. Third, the sample design allows us to compare the experiences, behaviors, and after-effects of persons in the high-impact areas with those of other persons in the Bay Area. And, finally, this questionnaire includes standard measures of psychological distress, which allows us to find out whether the earthquake caused people to have psychological problems.

Responent Questions Purpose If the respondent questions the purpose of the study, explain that this interview asks about experiences and feelings about earthquakes and that the findings will be used to evaluate the adequacy of current efforts to improve earthquake preparedness and post-earthquake assistance procedures.

Why This Household? If you are asked why you are interviewing this particular household, explain that this happens to be one of the representative households picked by random selection from the Bay Area and that it is very important that we obtain information about the kinds of people that she/he, this household, represents.

Respondent Questions Time Required for Interview   If the respondent asks how much time is required for the interview, tell him or her that the usual length is between 20 and 30 minutes. Do not say that the interview will take only a few minutes.

Refusals   Our experience has been that few respondents actually refuse to cooperate. However, if you have difficulty in obtaining an interview, explain the purpose and importance of the survey and STRESS THE CONFIDENTIAL TREATMENT ACCORDED ALL INFORMATION FURNISHED BY THE RESPONDENT. This also should be done at any point during the interview if the respondent hesitates to answer certain questions.

Your Manner   Your greatest asset in conducting an interview efficiently is to combine a friendly attitude with a businesslike manner. If a respondent's conversation wanders away from the interview, try to cut it off tactfully—preferably by asking the next question on the questionnaire. Over-friendliness and concern on your part about the respondent's personal troubles may actually lead to your obtaining less information.

Spanish-Speaking NON-BILINGUAL INTERVIEWERS, PLEASE READ:

Respondent If the respondent is Spanish-speaking, record the telephone number and return it to the ISSR office for immediate reassignment to a Spanish-speaking interviewer.

Other Languages If the respondent speaks NEITHER English nor Spanish, find out whether there is an English-speaking resident in the household who could translate for you.

Note: Policy Don't Know Whenever the interviewer receives a "don't know" response that is not pre-coded on the questionnaire (alternative answers to questions are not followed by "DON'T KNOW" with a separate code number), the interviewer must write clearly the abbreviation "DK" in the left margin next to the response categories.

Use of Cards Cards are not used in this survey because it is a telephone survey. Therefore, alternatives must be carefully read to respondents.

Probing We have adopted standards on probing to aid our professional interviewing staff. We know this may involve some "relearning" on your part, but the result will be a much better interview (and fewer calls to you from the field office).

Unless specified, all open-ended questions require probes to get complete, clear information. Because we also want to know how you are probing, please follow the standards.

    1. NEVER USE (P), /, X, i.e., any symbols to indicate you have probed.

2. The probe "anything else" would never be used. Instead, use "what else." It is too easy for R just to say "No" in response to this probe.

3. NEVER leave an open-ended question without an ending probe (e.g., W.E.) with the verbatim answer R gives (e.g., "that's all.").

We want you to record the probe you use; there are several ways of doing this:

1. Repeat the KEYWORD, e.g., "Convenient" (convenient) near shops, schools.

2. Underline KEYWORD(S) and follow with /(slash), e.g., "Convenient"/near shops, schools."

3. Record words you use; e.g., "Convenient (mean near shops, schools," or "Convenient (how) near shops, schools."

4. Appropriate probes: MEAN, HOW, WHY, EXPLAIN, EXAMPLE, WHAT, use of KEYWORD(S). Use a probe that makes sense in the context of the questions and that will elicit clarification of what R means by phrases such as "convenient," "law and order," "inflation," etc.

5. New abbreviations:

   (W.E.) = "What else?
   (W.O.W.) = "What other ways?"
   (R.) = Repeating keyword(s)
   (R.Q.) = Repeating entire question

(EX) = Example
(EXP) = Explain

Bilingual abbreviation:
(O.C.) = "Otra cosa?"

Final Probes   Unless specified, all open-ended questions must have a final probe. This is your way of telling us R has no further information on a subject. Checking for final probes is a part of the editing process, so make sure you always use and record them.

The (W.E.) "What else can you tell me about (. . .)?" is a final probe you will probably see most often. If R gives you no new information, record his or her response to the (W.E.) verbatim, e.g., "(W.E.) I can't think of anything else."

When you have a question that asks R to list things, e.g., problems in Los Angeles and the United States, you can say, "What other problems . . . ?" and indicate this probe with (OTHER). If R has given two problems and says "Nothing else" to your (W.E.) or (OTHER) probe, record the probe and his/her answer verbatim on the next line, a line where R might have thought of another problem. This is very important because it tells us he or she could not think of any more problems, or whatever the question refers to.

Editing   Editing of interviews is done in four stages. The first edit is done by you as an interviewer. Each questionnaire should be edited carefully as soon as possible after its completion, while it is still fresh in your mind. A thorough edit on your part is essential, so that editing at other stages can proceed quickly. The interviewer edit involves the following

tasks: checking that handwriting is legible; no questions have been missed; all SKIP directions have
been followed; all information in boxes is coded;
code numbers, not letters, are circled unless otherwise specified. If you have circled the code for
"other," check that you SPECIFY exactly what
"other" is; all open-ended questions must show an
appropriate final probe (e.g., W.E.) with R's ending
statement verbatim; a check to see that you have
interviewed the proper respondent and that his/her
number is circled on the LABEL and on the adult
roster; and finally, that your name and ID number
are on the contact page. Remember, editing is more
than "tidying up" the questionnaire. It is your way
of giving us a clear picture of the interview situation
and the respondent, our way of knowing what went
on.

Figure 3.7 displays excerpts from the interviewer specifications used in the Loma Prieta study. Notice that the study
had four objectives, with Objective 2 being to compare data
collected after this earthquake with data collected after an
earlier earthquake and Objective 3 being to compare people
close to the earthquake site with those further away. By out-
lining the study objectives in the interviewer specifications,
the surveyor can help interviewers to "buy into" the study. If
interviewers do not understand what the study is about, they
are less likely to think that individual questions or sets of
questions are important. If, in contrast, they think the objectives are worthwhile, they are more likely to be able to
answer questions raised by respondents and to encourage
respondent participation.

One of the most important sections of the interviewer
specifications anticipates the kinds of questions respondents
may ask and gives the interviewer suggestions for answering

those questions. Figure 3.7 includes examples of how interviewers should handle questions about the purpose of the
interview, how respondents were selected, and the time
required for the interview; it also includes instructions for
interviewers regarding how they should handle people who
want to refuse and how interviewers should present themselves in conducting the interviews. Notice that the specifications also warn interviewers about becoming too involved
with their respondents.

Most of our studies are conducted in at least two languages—English and Spanish—and interviewers need to
know what to do if they do not speak the designated respondent's language. Sometimes we instruct the interviewer to
conduct the interview using a bilingual resident of the
household to translate for the designated respondent; this
was the method we used in the Loma Prieta study. In other
cases, we might tell the interviewer to consider the household ineligible if the designated respondent does not speak
one of the languages in which the study is being conducted.
Surveyors must tell interviewers, in the interviewer specifications, how they should handle such situations; the objective
is for all such situations to be handled in a standard fashion
by all interviewers.

If surveyors do not include "don't know" categories in
the printed answer alternatives, they must tell interviewers
what to do if a respondent really does not have an answer to
a question. Also, because interviewers cannot use cards to
prompt respondents in telephone interviews, the interviewer
specifications need to include instructions for situations in
which cards would appropriately be used in an in-person
interview.

The interviewer specifications also need to address the
very important issue of probing—that is, the things that
interviewers do to help respondents give complete answers.
Probing is used primarily, and is most important, when
open-ended questions are asked. Figure 3.7 provides examples of the kinds of instructions we give interviewers. Note
that we carefully instruct interviewers *not* to use "Anything

else?" when they probe. We do this because respondents often interpret "Anything else?" as the termination of a question. Because we want to have complete information from our respondents concerning any issue we ask about, we want to make sure that they are not cut off before they are finished answering. Often, the most important information a respondent provides is the information that it takes him or her a while to remember or think of.

Finally, our example concludes with information about the interviewer's editing of the questionnaire after the conclusion of the interview. As Figure 3.7 indicates, the interviewer should check that all the questions have been answered and that the answers are clear. If the interviewer missed any questions, he or she should call the respondent again and ask those questions. Sometimes there are discrepancies within an interview that appear inconsistent to an outsider but, in fact, make sense. For example, when an interviewer creates a full household roster and asks respondents about the number of household members who are dependent on the income coming into the household, the number of people noted on the roster as being in the household sometimes does not match the number of people dependent on the income. This can happen because a child is away at college, because a member of the household is paying alimony or child support, or for many other reasons. The interviewer must note such discrepancies during editing and make it clear to the survey staff why they are not errors but, in fact, represent what is actually happening in that household.

Finally, notice that all of the instructions in Figure 3.7 are formatted in a way that makes it easy for interviewers and other research staff to find information on particular subjects.

SPECIFIC INSTRUCTIONS

Surveyors need to provide specific instructions for the interviewer concerning particular questions and how to administer them, as well as instructions regarding transitions between sets of questions.

Instructions for Specific Questions

Some kinds of questions require detailed instructions for the interviewer. For example, as Figure 3.4 illustrates, household rosters are quite complicated, and the surveyor needs to help the interviewer collect all of the information needed for the roster through a combination of formatting and instructions. In the questionnaires we use in our studies, we differentiate instructions to the interviewer from the text that the interviewer reads to the respondent by putting instructions in ALL CAPITAL LETTERS. Thus, when an interviewer working on one of our studies sees words and sentences in all capital letters rather than in standard upper- and lowercase, she or he knows that the text in capitals is not to be read to the respondent.

In the household roster items in Figure 3.4, we first introduce the topic and then provide a general instruction for the interviewer. For each person 18 or older who lives in the household, the interviewer obtains six kinds of information. Once the interviewer has listed all of the people in the household, he or she is given a lengthy instruction about how to select the designated respondent. Once the interviewer has selected the designated respondent, he or she is provided with further instructions regarding how to contact that person. Finally, the questionnaire includes some instructions about summarizing the roster that are used by the field staff, not the interviewer. Although detailed instructions for the interviewer about filling in the household roster appear in the questionnaire, the interviewer specifications also include instructions about completing the roster; these read as follows:

> Q2   Question 2 generates a standard adult roster of the household residents. Section F is particularly important. Only adults living in five Bay Area counties (Alameda, San Francisco, San

Mateo, Santa Clara, Santa Cruz) on the day of
the Loma Prieta earthquake are eligible respondents for this study.

Most questions are less complex than a household roster.
Many questions, however, have skip instructions that interviewers must follow. Figure 3.6 shows a set of questions with
skips. For example, if the respondent answers Question 6 by
saying he or she did not have either a radio or television on
when the earthquake struck, the interviewer skips to
Question 6C. In contrast, if the respondent had a television
or radio on, the interviewer next asks Question 6A. If the
respondent answers Question 6A by saying that the radio or
television stayed on for at least two hours, the interviewer
skips to Question 6E.

Question 7 in Figure 3.6 asks about damage in the
respondent's neighborhood. This is a particularly important
question because it starts a series of questions that enable us
to find out about the prevalence and magnitude of damage
throughout the area. Notice that instructions are embedded
in the question in two ways. First, the interviewer is
instructed to insert information collected earlier (about
where people were when the earthquake struck) into the text
of the question. Second, both the interviewer and the
respondent are given a definition of "the immediate area"—
"that is, within five blocks in any direction." This instruction, which is particularly important, is emphasized in the
specifications:

Q7–Q12   These questions ask about damage and injuries
          that R might have experienced that caused
          them to need services.

Q7   Q7 begins the series of questions and asks
      about damage to structures in the immediate
      area where R was when the earthquake struck.
      A frequently used definition of neighborhood
      is used to define "immediate area" as "within
      five blocks in any direction." We are not inter-

> ested in knowing about the Bay Bridge collapse or the Marina fire <u>unless</u> R was in one of those two areas at the time of the earthquake.

Transitions

Most questionnaires include questions about a number of different topics, and surveyors need to provide **transitions** between the topics for interviewers to read to respondents. In the following example, the first part of Question 25 is a transition that tells the respondent that the topic is changing to "feelings and experiences."

> 25. Thinking back to your feelings and experiences during and immediately after the October 17, 1989, earthquake, which of the following best describes your overall feelings? Would you say you were:
>
> > Very frightened and upset, ...1
> > Somewhat frightened and upset, ...2
> > Not very frightened and upset, ...3
> > Not at all frightened and upset, or . . .4
> > Did you enjoy the experience? 5

This transition also sets a new time referent by taking the respondent back in time to "during and immediately after the earthquake." It simultaneously changes the topic and briefly resets the context. The questions that preceded Question 25 asked respondents about injuries to themselves and others and about losses that other families suffered. Such transitional instructions give respondents a chance to "catch their breath" and help them change the focus of their thinking.

The transitional instructions shown in the questionnaire excerpt in Figure 3.2, from the Trinet Study, are more elaborate. In that case, the instructions were not given simply for purposes of transition; rather, they reminded respondents that they had received information in the past and briefly repeated that information so that the respondents would be prepared for the next set of questions.

RESEARCH OR QUESTIONNAIRE SPECIFICATIONS

Novice surveyors frequently feel that once they have completed the design and administration of a study, they cannot possibly forget any detail of its creation or the decisions made during the study period, but in fact, substantial amounts of time can pass before collected data are actually analyzed or written up. Sometimes, surveyors run out of money and cannot complete their studies in a timely fashion. Sometimes, other competing activities or research projects necessitate the postponement of a study's completion. Sometimes, the people originally involved in a study leave the organization to take other jobs. We personally know of situations where it has taken as long as 10 years for a study to be completed. Even when such interruptions do not occur, it behooves the conscientious surveyor to document the decisions made during the construction and administration of the questionnaire.

Earlier, we said that two kinds of specifications are created, one set to be used by the research team and a second set for interviewers that is abstracted from the first. The set of specifications used by the research team, known as the *research specifications* or *questionnaire specifications,* includes all of the interviewer specifications as well as other important information about the research design, sample, and sources of questions. Figure 3.8 displays excerpts of the questionnaire specifications from the Loma Prieta study.

Selection of the Sample

The intended sample design is the first thing outlined in Figure 3.8. Note that this was to be a stratified RDD sample with an anticipated size of 675 persons, with 225 persons selected from the two areas where shaking was most intense and the remaining 451 persons selected from the rest of the five-county area. In fact, a total of 656 interviews were conducted, with 122 collected in the Santa Cruz area, 83 in the San Francisco/Alameda area, and 451 in the rest of the study

(text continues on page 126)

Figure 3.8.   Examples of Material Included in
Research/Questionnaire Specifications but Not in
Interviewer Specifications

Community Response to the October 17, 1989, Bay Area (Loma Prieta) Earthquake Questionnaire Specifications March 1990

This is a telephone survey of San Francisco Bay Area residents' experiences in and responses to the Loma Prieta earthquake of October 17, 1989. Between 600 and 700 adult residents of Alameda, Santa Clara, Santa Cruz, San Mateo, and San Francisco counties will be selected by random digit dialing (rdd) and interviewed by telephone for this study. Overall, 675 persons will be interviewed: 225 in the high impact areas, and 450 throughout the rest of the Bay Area. High impact areas are identified as areas that had Modified Mercalli isoseismal scores of 8 or above. Two such areas exist: the area in San Francisco and Alameda counties adjacent to the Bay Bridge and including the Marina area; and areas of Santa Clara and Santa Cruz counties, which include the towns of Boulder Creek, Santa Cruz, and Watsonville. The exact census tracts included are: 43 in San Francisco County (101-135, 177, 179, 201, 208, 226-228, and 607); 13 in Alameda County (4010-4016, 4022, 4034, 4053, 4054, 4060 and 4063); 3 in Santa Clara County (5070, 5071, 5118); and 15 in Santa Cruz County (1002, 1008, 1010, 1103, 1104, 1203, 1204, 1209-1212, 1218, 1219, and 1224). The 225 interviews in the high impact areas will be evenly divided between the San Francisco and Alameda County tracts on one hand, and the Santa Cruz and Santa Clara County tracts on the other. The remaining 450 interviews will be proportionally distributed throughout the remaining areas of San Francisco

County, Alameda County, Santa Clara County, Santa Cruz County and San Mateo County.

. . .

INTERVIEW   Many of the items in this questionnaire are identical to or minor modifications of questions used in the survey of Los Angeles County residents following the Whittier Narrows earthquake of October 1, 1987. These interviews were conducted between October 1, 1988, and May, 1989. Many of those items were, in turn, adapted from the Los Angeles Metropolitan Area Survey (LAMAS) conducted after the 1971 Sylmar earthquake, interviews conducted by Bourque in 1971 at California State University, Los Angeles, in Sylmar and under the Van Norman Dam, or by Turner as part of his study of earthquake predictions in the late 1970s. (See: Ralph H. Turner, Joanne M. Nigg, and Denise Heller Paz, *Waiting for Disaster, Earthquake Watch in California*, University of California Press, 1986; Linda Brookover Bourque, Leo G. Reeder, Andrew Cherlin, Bertram H. Raven, and D. Michael Walton (1973), *The Unpredictable Disaster in a Metropolis: Public Response to the Los Angeles Earthquake of February, 1971*. Los Angeles: Survey Research Center, University of California, Los Angeles; Linda Brookover Bourque, Andrew Cherlin, and Leo G. Reeder (1976), "Agencies and the Los Angeles Earthquake." *Mass Emergencies* 1:217-228.)

. . .

Q14-Q15   Questions 14, 15 and 28 are adapted from dimensions suggested by Fran Norris as being important in the study of Post-Traumatic Stress Disorder (PTSD). This set of questions represents material that is new to this questionnaire. It was not included in either the study of Los Angeles County residents conducted after the Whittier Narrows earthquake or in earlier studies conducted by Turner, Bourque, Reeder, or their colleagues.

Since these questions have never been used before and are adapted from theoretical suggestions made by Norris, the were both modified and reduced after pretesting. Eliminated because of time constraints were questions that asked about perceptions of life threat, responsibility and control, intrusive memories, and the number of other persons in the neighborhood who experienced damage or evacuated following the earthquake.

Q28 asks R if she/he has experienced other events within the last year that might result in symptoms of post-traumatic stress disorder. R is asked about six events: robbery, physical or sexual assault, automobile accidents, accidental deaths, homicidal or suicidal deaths, and other significant life events. If multiple events are reported, ask R about the most upsetting event. For that event, ask B-C. If R reports no events, skip to Q29. See Q28 specifications for information about the other Norris questions eliminated. (See: Fran Norris, "Screening for Traumatic Stress: A Scale for Use in the General Population," *Journal of Applied Social Psychology*, in press, 1989.)

area. The specifications also include documentation about the census tracts that represented the high-impact area.

Surveyors can use information about the intended sample, as documented in the research specifications, during data collection to monitor whether appropriate numbers of interviews are being collected in particular areas. In this study, we obtained fewer interviews than we wanted in the San Francisco/Alameda area and more than we needed in the Santa Cruz area, but almost the exact number we wanted in the rest of the area. We became aware while interviews were being conducted that we were having more difficulty contacting households in the San Francisco/Alameda area. As a result, we were able to assign more interviewers to that area to maximize our chances of obtaining a sufficient number of interviews there.

Documenting the Sources and Changes in Questions

The rest of Figure 3.8 shows examples of the documentation necessary for individual questions. In an overview, the specifications state that large parts of the questionnaire are identical to or modifications of questionnaires used in three prior studies, and full references are included for those three studies. The last section of Figure 3.8 gives information about a set of questions developed by Fran Norris that, at the time of the Loma Prieta study, had not actually been used in a questionnaire. The specifications document the source of the questions and note that the set was adapted (i.e., we changed the set by dropping some of the questions) because of time constraints. When surveyors are ready to analyze their data, they can refer back to such specifications both to refresh their memories about the decisions they made earlier and (why they made them) and to find complete references for the sources of their questions and other information.

Checklist for Writing Instructions

✓ Decide whether general instructions for the respondent will be given in a cover letter, as part of an introduction to the interview, or both.

✓ Tell respondents what they are being asked to do and what the study is about.

✓ Identify places where transitions are needed (e.g., change of topic, context for questions that follow).

✓ Determine whether detailed instructions need to be provided for a subset of questions.

✓ Determine which general instructions need to be provided for interviewers (e.g., instructions on probing, editing, how to handle questions).

✓ Decide whether instructions for interviewers are going to be given in briefings, specifications, the questionnaire, or all three.

Checklist for Writing Specifications

✓ Briefly describe the objective of the study.

✓ Describe the study sample.

✓ Describe any tracking done of the sample.

✓ Describe the timing of data collection and tracking.

✓ Provide instructions for conducting interviews.

✓ Provide answers for interviewers to use in response to anticipated questions.

✓ Describe why each question is asked.

✓ If questions are adopted or adapted from other studies, explain the reasons for such decisions and provide complete citations to the other studies.

✓ Index the specifications for easy reference.

Projecting the Surveyor's Ideas
Onto Respondents

Surveyors in all substantive areas are concerned with being as objective as possible in how they develop research questions and collect data to test those questions. Because all researchers are human beings, it is probably impossible to eliminate all aspects of **subjectivity** from a research project, but the aim should be to minimize **bias** and subjectivity as much as possible. The various suggestions that we have made regarding how to decide on a research question, write the questions, and create the response categories are all intended to help the surveyor achieve the ultimate goal of maximizing the **objectivity** of the data collected. In collecting data from and about people, one of the most difficult things that surveyors must do is to minimize the extent to which they project their own ideas about how people behave or what they think onto the survey respondents.

The *ways* in which questions are asked, the *number* of questions and the *order* in which they are asked, the ranges and types of *response categories* provided, and the *instructions* given all provide surveyors with opportunities for making the data come out the way *they think* the world is organized. If, for example, we are convinced that a lot of people leave their homes after an earthquake, that they leave because of structural damage to their homes, and that they stay out of their homes for a long time, we can construct a questionnaire that will tend to confirm our perceptions by ignoring many of the recommendations we have made in this chapter.

One of the simplest ways we could have biased the estimates of evacuations that we got in the earthquake studies would have been to ask respondents about the number of evacuations they had heard about rather than restricting our questions to what the respondents themselves experienced. Asking respondents to report on evacuations they had heard about undoubtedly would have raised the number of evacuations reported, but the increase would have been an artificial one, because it is likely that multiple respondents would have heard about the *same* evacuation. If both Respondent A and Respondent B had told us they knew someone who left his or her home after the earthquake and we failed to find out who that person was, when he or she evacuated and why, and how long the person stayed away from home, we would have been likely to conclude that *two* evacuations occurred when, in fact, both respondents might have been reporting the same evacuation.

Similarly, if we were biased toward thinking that evacuations occur only because of structural damage to buildings, we might create just two answer categories for a question about evacuation, "building or structural damage" and "other," and have the interviewer read both of those answer possibilities to the respondent. The fact that we make available no other reason for evacuating may well result in respondents' overreporting that they left their homes because of structural damage.

Figure 3.9 shows the question about evacuation that we actually used in the Northridge study. If we had had the biases suggested above (and were not vigilant in striving for objectivity in spite of our biases), there are many things we could have done in designing this question to maximize the chances that the data collected would support our biases. First, as noted above, we could have restricted the answer categories to "building or structural damage" and "other." Because people leave their homes for many reasons, most of which do not involve structural damage to their homes, if we had done this, we would not have found out about respondents' wide range of reasons for evacuation. Second, we could have constructed the question so that the respondent could give only one answer; this would have resulted in our concluding that evacuation is motivated by a single factor when, in fact, it is often motivated by a combination of factors. And third, we could have instructed the interviewer to read all of the answers to the respondent, which might have increased the possibility that primacy or recency effects influenced the answers given—that is, respondents might have overreported the first or last reason read by the interviewer from the list of answers.

Figure 3.9.   Assessing Reasons for Evacuating After an Earthquake

9. As a result of the earthquake, did you evacuate your home, or leave it for any period of time because of damage, possible damage, or how you were feeling?

    YES, LEFT HOME . .ASK A 1

    NO . . . . .SKIP TO Q10 . . . .2 V173

A. Why did you leave your home?

CIRCLE ALL THAT APPLY

    1. OWN DECISION BECAUSE OF
       STRUCTURAL DAMAGE 1 V174
    2. SUGGESTED BY OFFICIAL 1 V175
    3. NO DRINKING WATER 1 V176
    4. GAS LEAKS 1 V177
    5. NO ELECTRICAL POWER 1 V178
    6. INVITATION FROM FRIEND/
       RELATIVE 1 V179
    7. TOO UPSET TO STAY 1 V180
    8. AFRAID OF FURTHER
       DAMAGE 1 V181

---

9. TO MAKE CONTACT
   WITH OTHERS 1 V182
10. BECAUSE OF A PREDICTION
    OF NEXT EARTHQUAKE/
    AFTERSHOCK 1 V183
11. OTHER 1 V184

SPECIFY:_____ V185

In this section we have demonstrated just a few of the ways in which surveyors can restrict or bias the information they collect about people through the construction of questionnaires. Improperly designed and poorly tested questionnaires always present a risk. Consequently, surveyors who use questionnaires to collect data must always remain aware of what their own biases are and be vigilant about developing techniques that will keep those biases from creeping into their questionnaires. In general, it is easier to control for bias in interview surveys than it is in mail surveys or other studies using self-administered questionnaires because in interview studies the surveyor can control both the order in which questions are asked and whether or not categories are read to respondents.

Checklist for Minimizing Bias

✓ Be aware of your own biases.

✓ Develop neutral questions.

✓ Ask enough questions to cover the topic adequately.

✓ Pay attention to the order of questions.

✓ Provide an exhaustive range of response categories.

✓ Write clear and unbiased instructions.

✓ Take sufficient time to develop questionnaire.

Pretesting, Pilot Testing, and Revising Questionnaires

The first draft of a questionnaire is never perfect and ready to administer. All questionnaires should be pretested or pilot tested. Surveyors use **pretests** to test sections of questionnaires. In some cases, surveyors employ experienced interviewers or focus groups in pretesting. In a **pilot study**, the complete questionnaire is tested using the administrative procedures that will be used in the study. The numbers and types of pretests and pilot tests that surveyors need to conduct vary with the "histories" of their questionnaires and the questions in them.

QUESTIONNAIRES BASED ON EARLIER RESEARCH

The questionnaire that we used in the Northridge study was modified from questionnaires used in two prior studies of community populations following California earthquakes. When a surveyor has used the bulk of a questionnaire before, in a previous study, the time he or she will need to devote to pretesting or pilot testing is substantially reduced, because the surveyor already has information about how long it takes to conduct interviews and about problem questions or sets of questions that need to be modified. The major objective of pretesting in such cases is to test new or modified sections of the questionnaire.

Sometimes novice surveyors mistakenly assume that they do not need to pretest any questions they have adopted or adapted from question batteries developed by other researchers. In fact, they definitely need to pretest such items or sets of items within the context of the questionnaire being developed. Often, the questions that surveyors adopt or adapt from other researchers have been used only in stand-alone studies, in which they were the only questions asked in an interview. Alternatively, the questions may have been asked originally in contexts that are very different from the one the adapting or adopting surveyor intends to study.

QUESTIONNAIRES DEVELOPED FROM SCRATCH

If surveyors are developing questionnaires from scratch, they must allow ample time for multiple pretests and pilot studies. The questionnaire we used in the Trinet Study is an example of one that was developed from scratch. To begin the construction of the questionnaire, we conducted two focus groups with participants who were selected because of their high level of experience and expertise in the area of emergency response. The focus groups had a number of suggestions for the research team, and we combined these with input from the various groups represented on the research team in developing the questionnaire's various content areas. The biggest problem we faced came from the restrictions on the content of the interview caused by our limited research budget, which required that we keep the average length of the telephone interview to no more than 30 minutes. Thus, one important aspect of all the pretesting activities was making sure that the interview met the necessary time constraints.

Over the development period, the research team designed eight different versions of the questionnaire. All members of the research team reviewed the early drafts, and the revisions generally involved the simplification of instructions, the reformatting and rewording of questions for clarification, and the addition or deletion of questions based on the study's objectives and priorities. We pilot-tested several versions of the questionnaire, but the major pilot testing was done with the fifth draft. That particular pilot test clearly indicated (a) that the interview (and hence the questionnaire) was too long, given the available budget; (b) that the questions were too burdensome, both in the time it took to answer them and in the types of information requested; and (c) that respondents thought the surveyors were trying to sell them something. All of these problems demanded that the questionnaire undergo substantial further modification, with the result that we conducted two more pilot tests before the questionnaire was finalized.

It sometimes happens that even after a questionnaire is finalized and the interviews have started, the surveyor finds out that he or she must once again make changes to the questionnaire. This happened in the Trinet Study. Two weeks after the interviews started, we found out that the CBS television network had aired a news segment about earthquake early warning systems and had made information about such systems available through the network's Web site. We hypothesized that exposure to such information might influence how a person would respond to the interview. Consequently, we added the question shown in Figure 3.10. To obtain the same data from all the respondents in the study, interviewers had to call back those persons who had already been interviewed and ask them this set of questions. This turned out to be a very important modification. We found that the 40 respondents (21.5%) who said they had heard or read something in the media about earthquake early warning were much more likely to say that they would be very or extremely likely to implement an early warning system.

Figure 3.10.   Questions Added to the Trinet Study After Interviews
                  Had Started

35A. Earthquakes are a frequent topic of conversation
      in California. Articles about earthquakes appear
      in newspapers and magazines. Discussions are
      held on radio and television, and information
      appears on the internet. Thinking about things

that you have read and heard, have you gotten any recent information about earthquake early warning or alert systems from television, radio, etc.

> NO . . . . . .SKIP TO Q36 . .1
>
> YES . . . . .ASK A 2

A. What was the most recent thing you heard or read about earthquake early warnings or alerts?

RECORD AS GIVEN

B. Where did you hear or read that information?

> TELEVISION 1
> RADIO 2
> NEWSPAPER 3
> MAGAZINE 4
> INTERNET 5
> OTHER .6
> SPECIFY:_____

C. Approximately when did you hear or read that information?

RECORD AS GIVEN

VALUE OF PRETESTS AND PILOT TESTS

In the Trinet Study, we conducted both pretests within the research group and pilot interviews with persons similar to those in the intended sample. Both provided us with valuable information, and both convinced us to modify sections of the questionnaire substantially. One of the very important things we learned was that some respondents thought we were trying to sell them an early warning system, when, in fact, we were trying to find out how much respondents thought a hypothetical system would cost and what they thought their agencies or institutions would be willing to pay for an early warning system. The irony was that, in fact, no system existed at the time that the survey was conducted, and even members of the research team had no idea what such a system might look like or what it would cost.

Surveyors can evaluate many things by conducting pretests and pilot tests. They can learn how well their questions and instructions are understood and how comprehensive their response categories are. They may learn that they need to change the sequence of questions or modify their planned administrative procedures. Sometimes a surveyor needs to ascertain how well a translated version of a questionnaire works. Pilot tests can also help surveyors estimate how much the data collection will cost in time and money.

Surveyors should always conduct pretests and pilot tests prior to the actual data collection, evaluate the results carefully, and apply what they learn in making changes to the questionnaire and the study design. When a surveyor identifies serious or multiple problems during a pretest or pilot test, he or she should make revisions as needed and continue with pretesting until he or she is confident that the data collection instrument is effectively and efficiently obtaining the data needed to test the research question validly and reliably. Respondents for pretests and pilot tests should always be representative members of the survey's target population.

Surveyors should always try to budget enough time into their study plans for sufficient testing of the questionnaire. In the Trinet Study, we began the development of the questionnaire in September 1999 and completed it at the end of March 2000—the research team devoted 7 months to developing, pretesting, pilot-testing, and finalizing the questionnaire. Surveyors often fail to incorporate sufficient development time into their overall research plans. When this happens, the result is often a hastily constructed questionnaire that is inadequate for obtaining the necessary information.

Checklist for Conducting Pretests and Pilot Tests

✓ Decide whether pretests, pilot tests, or both are needed.

✓ Decide whether multiple pretests or pilot tests will be needed.

✓ Decide how much time needs to be allocated to the development and testing of the questionnaire.

✓ Decide how pretests will be conducted—in focus groups, with interviewers, in group administrations, or through telephone interviews?

✓ Decide what the sample is for the pilot test—should it be representative of the final population or only of selected segments of the final population?

✓ Pay careful attention to the results of pretests and pilot tests:

- Do the respondents understand the questions?

- Are instructions clear?

- Is the order of questions appropriate?

- Do surveyors, interviewers, and respondents clearly understand the objectives of the study?

- Have costs been projected accurately?

4 Format of the Questionnaire

Neophyte surveyors make two common errors in developing questionnaires to use in telephone surveys: They indicate in instructions or advance letters that the interview will "only take 5 minutes," and they format the questionnaire to make it look as short as possible. Often, an unsophisticated surveyor will attempt to make an entire questionnaire fit on two sides of one page. The surveyors' stated objective in both cases is "to increase response rates." Both are errors, however; in fact, they may *reduce* response rates for a number of reasons. If a research question is worth studying, collecting the necessary data from an individual to shed light on that question can rarely be accomplished in less than 5 minutes, regardless of how the data are collected. In a telephone survey, it takes the interviewer 5 minutes just to introduce him- or herself, determine that he or she has contacted the designated respondent or household, and explain the purpose of the interview.

The emphasis that some surveyors place on making the questionnaire "look short" is particularly perplexing when they are designing telephone surveys, given that their respondents will never see the questionnaire. In computer-assisted telephone interviewing, even the interviewer sees the entire questionnaire only during training.

When you have gone to all the trouble to develop a questionnaire and conduct telephone interviews, you want to be certain that all that work results in the collection of sufficient information to answer your research question. We know people who have eliminated demographic questions from telephone interviews because they wanted "to save time," only to discover during data analysis that without demographic information on their respondents, they were unable to answer certain important questions about their sample populations.

In our discussion in this chapter, we focus on the formatting of questionnaires for paper-and-pencil administration of telephone surveys, but many of our recommendations are equally applicable to the formatting of questionnaires used in computer-assisted telephone interviewing.

Length

In the context of a telephone survey, *length* refers to the amount of time it takes to conduct the interview. Because the questionnaires used in telephone surveys are usually more complex and tailored to respondents than those used in mailed or other self-administered surveys, the length of telephone interviews can vary substantially across respondents. Look back at Figures 3.1, 3.4, 3.6, and 3.9 in Chapter 3. All of these questionnaire excerpts include screening questions—that is, questions designed to find out whether a respondent has or has not done something, does or does not know something, does or does not have particular attitudes or opinions, or has or has not experienced something. Depending on what the objectives of the telephone survey are and what the respondent answers in response to a screening question, the interviewer either asks or skips a subsequent set of questions. For example, if a person answers yes to the first question in Figure 3.1, indicating that he or she had some form of injury, the interviewer then asks a series of questions about the injury. If, in contrast, the respondent answers no, the interviewer skips Questions 17A-F and goes on to Question 18. This is called **branching.**

In the Loma Prieta and Northridge studies, the length of the interviews varied with the number of earthquake-related experiences the respondents reported. Interviews with respondents who experienced injuries, damage to their homes, and evacuation from their homes were substantially longer than those with respondents who did not have these experiences because the interviewers had to ask the follow-up questions about injuries, property damage, and evacuation.

As we noted in Chapter 3, one of the surveyor's major objectives in pretesting and pilot-testing the questionnaire for a telephone survey is to find out how long it takes to conduct the interviews. Because telephone interviews are tailored for different respondents, the surveyor must take care during pretesting to interview people with a range of experiences. The objective is to find out the average time of the interview.

The rule of thumb that many surveyors follow is that an average telephone interview should take no more than 30 minutes, but we have conducted telephone surveys in which the average interview was 60 minutes or more. Whether a survey can be successful with interviews longer than 30 minutes depends on the respondents' motivation and interest in the topic under study, the funds available for the study, and the skill of the interviewing staff.

Readability

Surveyors sometimes think that how a questionnaire looks, or its readability, is important only for self-administered questionnaires. They assume that readability does not matter in a questionnaire used for interviews because, after all, the interviewer is the only one who sees the questionnaire. This is a bad assumption. It is important for surveyors to provide interviewers with questionnaires that are user-friendly and easily understood. Whereas the surveyor's goal in formatting a self-administered questionnaire is to help the respondent move through it, in formatting a questionnaire for a telephone survey, the surveyor's aim should be to help the interviewer move through the questionnaire.

One of the most valuable things the surveyor can do for the interviewer in **formatting** the questionnaire is to leave generous amounts of space between questions, between each question and its set of response categories, and between the response categories. Space is as important as content in the presentation of a questionnaire. A questionnaire with generous spacing and good-sized margins, printed in a clear, easily readable **font**, will help the interviewer collect complete, valid, and reliable data.

Vertical Format

Notice that in the earthquake studies (see Figures 3.1, 3.6, and 3.9 in Chapter 3), we used a **vertical format** for our questions and answer categories. There are other methods for maximizing the clarity and order of a questionnaire as well, such as the use of shading, boxes, and arrows; a questionnaire may also be set up in a newspaper column format. The 2000 U.S. Census form provides an example of a questionnaire that uses boxes, arrows, and a newspaper column format to clarify how the respondent should proceed through the questions (see Figure 2.6 in Chapter 2).

We like the vertical format for two reasons. First, it simultaneously differentiates the question from the possible response categories and differentiates the response categories from each other. If, for example, we had used a horizontal format for Question 17A in Figure 3.1, we might have ended up with something like this:

When exactly were you injured?
Were you injured:

During the earthquake itself 1
Immediately after the earthquake 2
Within the first 48 hours
    after the earthquake 3
During an aftershock 4
Some other time 5

or even this:

When exactly were you injured?
Were you injured:

____ During the earthquake itself
____ Immediately after the earthquake
____ Within the first 48 hours after the earthquake
____ During an aftershock
____ Some other time

Many surveyors think that interviewers are unable to work with precoded questions such as those used in our examples. Instead, they have the interviewers put check marks next to appropriate answer categories. Then, for reasons we have never been able to explain, they put the spaces for the check marks *in front of* the answer categories, *and* to save space, they use a horizontal format! What is wrong with this strategy?

First of all, most people in the United States, and especially professional interviewers, are used to filling out precoded questionnaires. Interviewers have no difficulty circling numbers or working with other precoded formats, such as on a CATI system. Second, we read from left to right in English. Putting answer spaces to the *left* of the words or phrases to which they correspond is counterintuitive. Third, horizontal formatting of answer categories increases the likelihood that interviewers will make errors. In the second example above, an interviewer might easily confuse the alternatives and put a check mark in the blank before "Some other time," which corresponds to an answer of "Some other time," when what the respondent *really* said was that the injury occurred "During an aftershock." Similarly, in the first example, even with the precoding and the dots linking each verbal response with its numeric code, the interviewer may mistakenly select the number physically *closest* to the answer the respondent gives rather than the code linked to it by dots.

Finally, a vertical format in which codes are already assigned and placed to the right of the response categories makes data entry from paper-and-pencil-administered telephone surveys much easier and leads to fewer errors. With most answers lined up on the right of each page, the person doing data entry can simply follow the codes down the side of the page when entering the data.

The one exception to vertical format in our examples is shown in Questions 16A-C in Figure 3.2 (Chapter 3). For these stem questions, instead of simply asking the interviewer to circle the numbers that correspond to the parts of existing warning systems the respondent says he or she might use in an earthquake early warning system, we ask the interviewer to record either "yes" or "no." Also in this example, we break our general rule of not including "don't know" alternatives in the list of answers. We made this decision because this was particularly important information in the Trinet Study, and the inclusion of a yes/no column tends to emphasize the importance of obtaining a thoughtful answer from the respondent on each item. Here, also, we expected that many respondents honestly would not know whether they would use certain components, and furthermore, in many environments (such as schools) such things as "automatic shutdown or activation procedures" may not exist. A horizontal format is also useful when the same answer categories will be used for a set of questions—as, for example, in the adapted versions of the Brief Symptom Inventory (Figure 2.7) and the Mississippi Civilian Scale (Figure 2.8), in the household roster shown in Figure 3.4, and in the set of questions on preparedness behaviors shown in Figure 2.5.

Figures 2.5, 2.7, 2.8, and 3.4 all provide examples of **grids.** Using a grid format can enable a surveyor to save space on a paper-and-pencil questionnaire when a series of questions to be asked will use the same selection of answer categories. Complex grids such as the household roster in Figure 3.4 and the questions on preparedness in Figure 2.5 are not easily used in CATI systems, as they involve substantial programming. Grids are particularly popular with surveyors who are writing series of questions to be used in developing scales or indexes such as those seen in Figures 2.7 and 2.8.

Surveyors can also use grids to format multiple sets of question sequences such as those in the household roster in Figure 3.4 and the questions on preparedness behaviors in Figure 2.5. Complex grids have two advantages. First, they save space. Look at Figure 2.5, for example. This series of questions could have been set up as follows.

47. Did you store water:

       Before the earthquake, . . .ASK A 1

       After the earthquake, ...ASK A 2

       Both before and after, or . .ASK A 3

       Not at all? . . . . .GO TO Q25 4

    A. Did you store water:

       For a future earthquake, . .1

       For some other reason, or .2

       For both reasons? 3

48. Did you store canned or dehydrated food:

       Before the earthquake, . . .ASK A 1

       After the earthquake, ...ASK A 2

Both before and after, or　. .ASK A 3

Not at all?　. . . . . .GO TO Q25　. . . .4

A.　Did you store food:

For a future earthquake,　. .1

For some other reason, or　.2

For both reasons? 3

There is nothing wrong with formatting these questions this way; indeed, on a CATI system they would essentially be set up this way. But, given that the questionnaire includes items on some 20 different preparedness behaviors, in this format the sequence of questions will take up a lot of space.

The second advantage to the surveyor of using complex grids containing multiple questions is that they maximize the surveyor's ability to "match" information across questions. Neophyte surveyors often ask questions about family members as follows:

How many people live in your household?

_____

RECORD AS GIVEN

How old are the people who live in your household?

_____

RECORD AS GIVEN

How many males live in your household?

_____

RECORD #

How many females live in your household?

_____

RECORD #

The problem with this strategy is that after the data are collected, the surveyor has no way of "matching" the age and the gender of each person in the household. In contrast, the grid setup used in the household roster in Figure 3.4 not only facilitates the collection of complete data on the household and each household member, it allows us to describe the basic characteristics of each member of the household.

Obviously, in order to use complex grids successfully in telephone surveys, surveyors must (a) develop formats for the grids that are clear and that include sufficient instructions for interviewers and (b) train and monitor interviewers carefully.

Spacing

Notice that in our examples, we have left substantial space between questions and response categories and have used dots to indicate clearly which numeric code is associated with which answer. In these examples, we have used at least double spacing between questions and between each question and its response categories. Within each set of answer categories, we have used 1.5 spacing. Notice also that we have indented the sets of answers under the questions to help clarify where one question stops and the next begins. Where we have dependent questions—for example, 17A-F in Figure 3.1 and 6A-E in Figure 3.6—these questions are similarly indented. This helps the interviewer follow the skip instructions that correspond to the answers given to Questions 17 and 6, respectively. Respondents who say yes to Question 17 are asked Questions 17A-F, whereas those who say no are next asked Question 18. The combination of indentation, spacing, and instructions that are set off from the rest of the text—in this case, by capital letters—helps the interviewer move expeditiously through the interview.

Printing the questionnaire as a booklet (that is, folding the pages in the middle lengthwise and stapling them at the fold, known as *saddle stapling,* to form a "book") is a format we particularly like to use when funds are available to do it. Questionnaires that are printed this way look more professional than other kinds of questionnaires. When using the booklet format, we generally use 8 1/2-by-17-inch paper, because this allows us to use larger print. Aside from looking professional, questionnaires printed in booklet form are ideal for complex grids. The household roster in Figure 3.4 is designed for use in a booklet, with the first page printed on a left-hand, even-numbered page and the second printed on the facing right-hand page. With this setup, the interviewer can see the questions and instructions on the left-hand page while he or she records answers in the grid on the right-hand page.

Often, surveyors produce the pages of questionnaires on word processors, and the page size is then reduced during printing and production of the booklets. In the process, however, the print is also reduced. Small print or ornate print can be difficult for interviewers to read, especially those over age 50 who need to wear reading glasses or who have difficulty seeing in poor light. We recommend using at least a 10-point pitch size (12-point is even better) and an easily read font with equal character spacing, such as Courier. Surveyors should avoid using italics, which are difficult to read, and fonts that use proportional spacing (i.e., the letter *m* takes up more space than the letter *i*), as they can cause alignment problems (and extreme headaches) in the setup of a questionnaire.

Print and Paper

There should be good contrast between the printed words and the paper on which the questionnaire is printed. We recommend that, when in doubt, surveyors use black print on a white background. Some colors of paper, such as the currently fashionable neon colors, are difficult for interviewers to look at for long periods of time. Also, surveyors should avoid using colors that lower the contrast for color-blind persons. There is one situation in which printing questionnaires on different colors of paper can be very helpful, however. If there are different forms of the questionnaire for different respondents (say, a version in English and one in Spanish), the surveyor may want to print them on different colors of paper (the Spanish version on light blue paper and the English version on white paper, for example). Then the surveyor will be able to separate the two versions easily when the questionnaires are piled up for distribution, editing, and data entry.

As our examples show, we use combinations of **boldface type**, <u>underlining</u>, and CAPITALS when we want to emphasize something in the text of a question or give instructions to the interviewer. We consistently use all capital letters in providing instructions—for example, the instructions "CIRCLE ALL THAT APPLY," "GO TO Q2," and "ASK A." We use boldface and sometimes underlining to emphasize key words or phrases for the interviewer—for example, "<u>other</u> personal property" in Question 8 in Figure 2.4.

Surveyors also use other techniques, such as shading or boxing information. As we noted earlier, we do not recommend the use of italics because we have found that italicized text is difficult for interviewers to read, but other surveyors do use italics for emphasis or in instructions. We also do not recommend putting too much information in bold type. Some surveyors print all of their instructions in bold, but we have found that if a page contains a lot of instructions in bold, the text of the questions themselves and the response categories can get lost, with the result that the interviewer sees the instructions very well but misses key phrases in the questions or key answer alternatives.

Consistency

Whatever the size and format of print you select for the questionnaire, the key is to be consistent. If you decide that instructions contained within the body of the questionnaire are going to be underlined, then you should make sure that *all* the instructions in the body of the questionnaire are underlined and that underlining is *not* used to indicate emphasis in the text of questions. Instead, use boldface type for emphasis.

You should also be consistent in the spacing you insert between questions and in the use of indentations. If you decide to use single spacing within the text of individual questions and double spacing between questions, then be sure that you do so throughout the questionnaire. Notice that our examples are consistent in the way the answer categories are lined up. In Figure 2.4 (Chapter 2), the text of all the questions is aligned on the same indent, and the answer categories for all questions are similarly aligned on a further indent, with the beginnings of all the answers lined up and the respective codes lined up.

Splitting Questions Between Pages

A common error that new surveyors often make is to split a question between pages, either separating the instructions for a section from the questions they are describing or separating related and dependent questions across pages. Sometimes this occurs because the surveyor is trying to save space, but often it happens simply because the surveyor doesn't think. Take a moment to look at Figure 3.2 in Chapter 3. Imagine that there was sufficient space on a prior page for the introduction to Question 16 but insufficient space for the question itself. Some surveyors would go ahead and put the introduction on the prior page and then wonder why interviewers subsequently have difficulty with the flow of the questions that follow.

Another common error is to break up related questions. For example, a surveyor might place the introduction and the text of Question 16 on one page because there is sufficient room, but then place Questions 16A-C on a subsequent page. Because Questions 16A-C are logically dependent on

Question 16, this practice increases the probability that the interviewer will misread or never see Questions 16A-C or administer those questions incorrectly.

Finally, look at Question 8A in Figure 2.4 and Question 9A in Figure 3.9. Both questions are followed by long lists of possible responses. Yet another common error is to split such a list of possible responses between two pages (again, surveyors most commonly do this to save space). When such a list is split up, interviewers often fail to see the complete list and, as a result, never read to respondents any of the responses found on the second page. This may result in interviewers' "forcing" responses into answer categories. For example, imagine that the last four answers to Question 8A in Figure 2.4 (from FENCES/FENCE WALL DAMAGED through OTHER) appear on a separate page from all the other answers. Now, imagine that a respondent tells the interviewer that the roof of his or her garage was damaged. Not seeing any reference to garages on the first page, the interviewer might decide to code the answer under "CEILING/ROOF DAMAGED" or may simply fail to record it. Splitting up a list of response choices is particularly problematic if the respondent is asked to select a single answer from a list the interviewer reads, because the interviewer simply may not read the last answers in the list when they are on a different page.

Occasionally, a list of response choices is too long to be printed on a single page even if the question starts at the top of a page. If a list must continue onto a second page, the questionnaire should be printed in booklet form, so that the question and the first part of the list of responses (or the first part of the sequence of questions) can appear on a left-hand (i.e., even-numbered) page and the continuation of the list (or sequence of questions) can appear next to it on the facing right-hand page. A significantly less attractive option is to include a note at the bottom of the first page that clearly indicates that the question continues on the next page.

When surveyors discover that they have one or more response lists that are too long to fit on a single page, they may want to consider the possibility that they have not pretested their questionnaires adequately, or that they are seeking to obtain responses that are too detailed. Another pitfall of extremely long response lists is that they can lead to so few responses in each answer category that it is difficult to draw conclusions about the answers with any confidence. If a surveyor cannot reduce the response categories for a question sufficiently that they fit within a reasonable space on the questionnaire, it may mean that he or she should use multiple questions instead. Alternatively, the surveyor might consider asking the question in an open-ended format and then using content analysis to decide on answer categories after the data collection is complete.

The general rule is that if a question has a large number of response categories, the surveyor should start the question on a new page. Similarly, the first question in a long sequence of related questions should begin on a new page. It is all right to leave part of a questionnaire page blank; sometimes, it is even desirable to leave a whole page blank if that is what the surveyor needs to do to place questions on facing pages and thus maximize their clarity for the interviewer.

Checklist for Formatting Questionnaires

✓ Do not give unrealistic time estimates.

✓ Ask enough questions to obtain the information needed.

✓ Use space between questions.

✓ Use vertical format, space, boxes, arrows, shading, or other devices consistently to maximize the clarity and order of questions.

✓ Do not avoid precoded response categories, but clearly indicate the code that corresponds to each response.

✓ Consider the use of grids.

✓ Use a booklet format when possible.

✓ Make sure there is good contrast between the print and the paper.

✓ Use at least 10-point pitch; better yet, use 12-point pitch.

✓ Use an easily read, equally spaced font, such as Courier.

✓ Avoid the use of italics.

✓ Use bold, underlining, and CAPITALS judiciously and consistently for emphasis and instructions.

✓ Do not split instructions, questions, and associated responses between pages.

Coordinating With Data Entry Personnel and Data Processors

As the paper-and-pencil questionnaire is being developed, the surveyor needs to consider the needs of persons who will be doing the data entry and data processing. We have already recommended the **precoding** of closed-ended questions with clear indications of where and how answers are to be recorded. We also recommend that the surveyor set up the protocol by which the data will be entered into the computer before the questionnaire is actually finalized and then provide variable names on the questionnaire itself at the time it is printed.

Figures 2.4, 3.4, 3.6, and 3.9 provide examples of sets of questions for which the data entry program was preset and the variable names that corresponded to each question in the data set were included on the questionnaire when it was printed. Notice in Figure 2.4 that one variable is assigned to Question 8 because only one answer to the question will be coded. In contrast, in Question 8A, 20 variables are set up, one for each of the listed alternative responses and one for the blank associated with the "OTHER, SPECIFY" category. For the 19 variables that correspond to one of the alternative answers, including "OTHER," we already know that a 1 will be entered into the data set for every answer that is listed, meaning in V134, for example, "Yes, the respondent's chimney collapsed." To convert the questionnaire into a complete codebook, data entry personnel must know what to code if a 1 is not circled. Usually the surveyor will establish a standard code such as 2 for the answers that are not circled.

Depending on the data entry program, the data entry person will enter either text or numeric data for V147, the "OTHER, SPECIFY." If the interviewer circled the 1 that corresponds to "OTHER," the data entry person will first record a 1 for V146. If the data entry program allows for strings of text or alphanumeric data to be entered into the master data set, V147 will be prespecified to accept text data and the data entry person will type the response verbatim into the data set. Some data entry programs do not allow string text variables to be combined with numeric files. In such cases, the surveyor specifies a code, possibly 1, that indicates that "yes, a text answer was recorded by the interviewer, but it is stored in a different data set."

Some survey researchers object to having coding information on the questionnaires because they believe that interviewers do not understand the information and are likely to be confused by it. In our own research, we have not noticed that such information confuses interviewers. Furthermore, we like the efficiency of including the variable names on the questionnaire because the questionnaire, as administered, can then become the basic codebook for the data set.

Ending the Questionnaire

The surveyor should end the questionnaire by inviting the respondent to comment on its content, to make suggestions about what the surveyor might have missed, and even to complain about the questionnaire itself. Such questions are often referred to as "ventilation" questions, because they allow respondents to ventilate their feelings about the topic or the questionnaire.

Finally, the questionnaire should end with a message thanking the respondent for his or her time and cooperation. This is a courtesy due any study participant.

Camera-Ready Copy

If the surveyor has considered all of the points discussed above and resolved any problems with the questionnaire design, and if the content of the questionnaire has been carefully proofread and all errors found have been corrected, the questionnaire is "camera ready," or ready for duplication and production. Usually, questionnaires are either photocopied or set up for offset printing. We discuss these procedures and what they cost in detail in Chapter 6.

Checklist for Finalizing the Questionnaire

✓ Format the questionnaire to facilitate data entry.

✓ Afford the respondent the opportunity to comment on the interview and the questionnaire.

✓ End the questionnaire with a message thanking the respondent.

✓ Carefully proofread the questionnaire one final time and make any necessary corrections.

✓ Duplicate or print the questionnaire.

Correspondence and the Motivation of Respondents

We noted in Chapter 2 that telephone interviews may or may not be preceded by mail or telephone contacts. In the case of the Trinet Study, we made three prior contacts with the potential respondent before the actual interviews were conducted. Because the respondents were selected to represent institutions such as schools, hospitals, and utility companies, we first contacted each institution by phone to find out who among the institution's staff was most knowledgeable about and concerned with emergency preparedness and response. In some cases the relevant person was easily identified, whereas in other cases we had to make multiple phone calls to get a name, title, address, and phone number for the designated respondent. We then sent each designated respondent two letters, one on the letterhead of the California Institute of Technology (see Figure 2.1) and one on the letterhead of the University of California, Los Angeles (Figure 2.3).

If the surveyor has access to potential respondents' addresses, compliance with the survey can be increased by a well-written advance letter that explains the purpose of the study, tells how and why the individual was selected to be a respondent, and cites meaningful reasons the individual should participate. The advance letter should stress how important it is for the individual to participate in the interview and how important that person is to the research. It is also beneficial for the advance letter to be signed or endorsed by someone with positive name recognition for the respondents. For example, if the sample is composed of individuals who belong to a particular professional organization, it may be helpful for the president of the organization to endorse the study, unless, of course, members of the organization are likely to distrust the leadership.

Surveyors should include or at least consider including the following 12 elements in any correspondence intended to motivate respondents.

1. Use of letterhead

2. Information about sponsorship

3. Dates

4. Salutation

5. Information on the purpose of the study

6. Reasons an individual's participation is important

7. Motivating information (in the absence of advance letters)

8. Information on incentives being offered to encourage respondent participation

9. Realistic estimate of the time required to complete the interview

10. Information on how and why the respondent was chosen

11. Explanation of confidentiality and how the data will be handled

12. Provision of a name and phone number to call for information

Figures 2.1 through 2.3 (Chapter 2) provide examples of two advance letters and an information sheet that we used in the Trinet Study.

USE OF LETTERHEAD

The quality of the presentation of all survey materials plays an important part in stimulating respondent interest. All surveyors advocate the use of professional letterhead for advance letters because it helps establish the importance of the study, gives information about study **sponsorship,** and serves indirectly as a means of personalizing contact with the potential respondent. Being contacted by a recognized, reputable organization serves to legitimate the importance of the study in the respondent's mind, and also emphasizes for the respondent the uniqueness of his or her position as a source of information.

INFORMATION ABOUT SPONSORSHIP

Survey materials sent to respondents should state specifically who is conducting and/or sponsoring the study, as the examples in Figures 2.1 and 2.3 illustrate. Because the Trinet Study was a joint activity of the three Trinet partners (the U.S. Geological Survey, the California Division of Mines and Geology, and Caltech), EQE International, and the UCLA Center for Public Health and Disasters, *all* groups were noted as sponsors in the first advance letter. Because UCLA's Survey Research Center was conducting the interviews, the second letter stated, "In the next week or two, an interviewer from the UCLA Survey Research Center (SRC) will be calling to schedule an interview with you."

DATES

It is impossible to overstate the importance of including accurate dates on advance letters and other materials sent to respondents. Many surveyors simply neglect to put dates on letters, but others do not fully think out the sequence of administrative procedures, and as a consequence, the dates that appear on their advance letters differ substantially from the actual dates of the **mailings.** If the advance letter states that an interviewer will be calling "in the next week or two," it is important, first, that the date on the letter be identical to or within a day or so of the postmarked date on the envelope and, second, that the mailing be timed so that each potential respondent receives the letter 1 to 2 weeks before the interviewer calls.

SALUTATION

The salutation used on an advance letter can make a difference in how fully the respondent is engaged. When it is possible, surveyors should personalize each salutation rather than use global salutations such as "Dear Respondent," "Dear Resident," or "Dear _____ Member"; a personalized greeting increases the respondent's sense that the surveyor is sincere and that the respondent's participation is important to the study. Surveyors cannot always send advance letters for telephone surveys, but when they can, they should also make the effort to personalize the salutations they use (as we were able to do in the Trinet Study).

PURPOSE OF THE STUDY

All materials aimed at motivating respondents should clearly explain the purpose of the study. Notice that both of the advance letters for the Trinet Study (Figures 2.1 and 2.3) explained the purpose of the study. Most of the first advance letter was devoted to explaining the study's purpose, and the second letter restated the purpose in the first paragraph and then gave more detailed information about the content of the interview.

REASONS AN INDIVIDUAL'S PARTICIPATION IS IMPORTANT

Materials intended to motivate respondents should explain why each individual's participation is important. In the first advance letter in the Trinet Study (Figure 2.1), we made such appeals to the respondent in the first sentence and in the last sentence. In addition, in the fourth paragraph we encouraged potential respondents to discuss with colleagues whether and how an earthquake early warning system might be used. In the second advance letter (Figure 2.3), the last sentence of the first paragraph focused on the importance of that particular respondent's participation: "We feel that in your position as . . . , you could provide us with very valuable information." We repeated the appeal in the next to the last paragraph, which reads: "Your participation in this study would be very much appreciated and very helpful. We hope you will schedule an interview when you receive the call from SRC."

MOTIVATION IN THE ABSENCE OF ADVANCE LETTERS

When surveyors use random-digit dialing to develop samples for telephone surveys, they do not know who the respondents will be in advance and do not have names or addresses that they can use to send advance letters. Consequently, interviewers must do all the work of motivating potential respondents to participate when they make first contact with these individuals. An interviewer must present information about the study verbally to the potential respondent as part of the initial interaction: information about the objectives of the survey, the sponsoring agencies, why the respondent was selected, and why his or her participation is important. The interviewer communicates this information by using a prepared text developed by the surveyor, but he or she must also establish rapport with the potential respondent and be comfortable handling any questions the individual may have.

Although it is important for surveyors to provide potential respondents with thorough information, there is a fine balance to be struck between providing enough information and providing too much. Look for a moment at the two advance letters in Figures 2.1 and 2.3. Now imagine calling someone you don't know, and after saying, "Hello, I am Dottie Gray from the Xylophone College Research Center," starting to read the text of one of the letters verbatim. Obviously, what works to introduce a study in the context of an advance letter is not the same as what works with a potential respondent over the telephone. The average person will not want to listen on the phone to a long introduction, formally phrased, such as can be presented in a letter. The trick is for the interviewer to deliver essential information in a conversational manner. Figure 4.1 displays an example of a verbal introduction to a survey.

Figure 4.1.   Introducing a Study Verbally

Good morning/afternoon/evening. I'm (. . .) calling from the Survey Research Center at UCLA. We are conducting a study to find out about Los Angeles area residents' experiences with both the recent Northridge earthquake and other earthquakes they may have experienced. The experiences and actions of people like yourself regarding earthquakes will help state and local legislators, policy makers, and planners develop earthquake preparedness programs for the future.

Your household is one of many that have been scientifically selected to represent all households in Los Angeles County. The usefulness of this survey depends upon the participation of every household we select. I want to assure you that this interview is confidential and completely voluntary. Your name will not be connected with the findings of our study. You have the right to refuse any or all questions in the survey. If you have questions about the confidentiality of this survey, you may contact UCLA's Vice Chancellor for Research, 1247 Murphy Hall, Los Angeles, California, 90095-1405, (310) 825-7934.

The interview will take approximately 40 minutes depending on how much you have to say. If you want more information about the survey, you may call the Survey Research Center's Field Director, Tonya Hays, at (800) xxx-xxxx.

QUESTION FOR SPANISH ONLY: Would you prefer to do the interview in English or Spanish?

Because less information can be provided verbally and the information provided is harder for the respondent to retain, the surveyor must anticipate the kinds of questions that potential respondents might ask (see Chapter 6) and provide interviewers with ways to answer those questions. Interviewers should receive training on answering such questions, and they should be provided with relevant information in the interviewer specifications (discussed in Chapter 3). For example, the excerpt from a set of interviewer specifications shown in Figure 3.7 includes headings in the left-hand column that anticipate four kinds of questions a potential respondent might raise: questions about the purpose of the interview, why his or her household was selected, how long the interview will take, and the confidentiality of the data collected. Although the surveyor cannot possibly cover every question a respondent might ask in the interviewer specifications, the suggested responses can provide an interviewer with a good starting point.

Even when surveyors are conducting RDD telephone studies, they may find it useful to prepare advance letters. Such letters can be helpful in convincing wary individuals to become respondents. We often encounter situations in which potential RDD respondents ask interviewers to send advance letters so that they can see the letterhead, have concrete information about who we are and why we are calling, and have contact information they can use to check out the legitimacy of the study before giving their consent to be interviewed. In such situations, they provide us with their names and addresses so that we can send them letters.

INCENTIVES TO ENCOURAGE RESPONDENT PARTICIPATION

Incentives used to encourage respondent participation often overlap with information about the purpose of the study and how the respondent was selected for the study. That was clearly the case in the Trinet Study, where respondents were selected because of their positions in particular institutional settings and because they were assumed to be knowledgeable about the topic under study. In the case of the earthquake study samples, we still appealed to each respondent as a person, but we emphasized, first, that each respondent was selected to represent not only him- or herself but also others like him or her, and, second, that policy makers and others need information from people who had experienced earthquakes in order to develop better procedures for protecting and assisting others in the future.

Surveyors can motivate potential respondents to participate in surveys in many ways. Response rates are always highest when the subject matter of the study has some personal relevance for the respondents, or when respondents believe that by participating they are contributing to some other, greater good. Both techniques were relevant in our earthquake studies and in the Trinet Study.

Monetary or Material Incentives

Sometimes surveyors provide monetary or other material incentives (small gifts such as pencils or pens, notepads, calendars, or raffle tickets) to encourage individuals to participate in surveys and thus increase response rates. Some surveyors prefer to enclose a gift with an advance letter if one is being used; others use the promise of a gift as an inducement to complete the interview, telling the potential respondent that a gift will be sent after the interviewer has returned the completed interview to the researcher. When surveyors use raffle chances or lottery tickets as incentives, the winners are chosen from among those who responded.

One problem with providing material incentives in community samples is that the surveyor needs the names and addresses of the respondents. When a sample is generated through random-digit dialing, the surveyor has the cooperating respondents' telephone numbers, but not their names or addresses. To receive any promised incentive, a respondent must be willing to give the interviewer his or her name and address at the end of the interview. Obviously, this means that the data are not anonymous and that the confidentiality of the data has been reduced. The surveyor must take steps to guarantee that all of the data, including the newly collected names and addresses of respondents, are protected, so that complete confidentiality is maintained and the information respondents have provided cannot be linked to individual respondents.

There is some controversy among survey researchers over the use of material incentives to increase response rates. Some believe that the data collected from individuals who receive such incentives are unreliable. These surveyors reason that the use of incentives "buys" responses from individuals who normally would not respond and who will pay little or no attention to the import of the study when responding to the interview. Other surveyors feel that the use of incentives is entirely appropriate; indeed, in some circumstances, it is the only way to obtain a satisfactory response rate. These surveyors argue that material incentives serve merely to assure respondents that the surveyors believe their time is valuable and worth compensation.

Whether or not to use material incentives is up to the individual surveyor. If you decide to use an incentive and you want to give respondents something other than cash, you must give some consideration to the appropriateness of the gift you provide.

Other Forms of Motivation

We are sure that surveyors have utilized an infinite variety of other methods in their efforts to motivate respondents and increase response rates. Sometimes surveyors try to motivate respondents by offering to supply them with abbreviated reports of the survey results. Many respondents enjoy being able to compare their answers to the results and like knowing that they are part of a research project. Offering this form of incentive is a relatively inexpensive means of increasing response rates. However, surveyors should not offer such rewards if there is any chance that they might not be able to provide them, or if the results will not be known until so far in the future that respondents won't remember participating in the study. (And, of course, in order to send respondents summarized results, the surveyor must have at least their addresses.)

We used a summary of the results of the Northridge earthquake study in a somewhat different way—to motivate respondents to participate in a second interview related to the El Niño storms of 1997-1998. When we conducted the original survey, we did not promise our respondents anything, but we did ask those who were willing to give us their addresses in case we decided to do a follow-up study; we did not get their names. When the El Niño storms occurred, we decided to try to reinterview the Northridge participants to see how they had fared in a second natural disaster. To reestablish contact with our respondents, we mailed them a letter and enclosed a four-page summary of the results from the Northridge study (see Figures 4.2 and 4.3).

REALISTIC ESTIMATE OF THE TIME REQUIRED TO COMPLETE THE INTERVIEW

The surveyor should instruct interviewers to provide potential respondents with a direct or indirect **estimate of the time** required to complete the interview. If the surveyor has determined how long the interview will take with the *average respondent,* the interview is relatively short, and the questionnaire does not involve much custom tailoring—in other words, most questions are asked of most respondents, without large sections being skipped for certain respondents—the interviewer can provide a direct estimate of the time needed. We stress *average respondent* here because people differ, both in the amount of time they take to think about and answer questions and in what they have to say. If the interviewer gives a direct time estimate, he or she should clearly indicate that it represents only an average, and that some respondents will take less time and some will take more time. The interviewer should not attempt to give a direct estimate of time needed until the questionnaire has been thoroughly pretested and pilot work has been completed.

UNIVERSITY OF CALIFORNIA, LOS ANGELES   UCLA

BERKELEY · DAVIS · IRVINE · LOS ANGELES · RIVERSIDE · SAN DIEGO · SAN FRANCISCO   SANTA BARBARA · SANTA CRUZ

UCLA CENTER FOR PUBLIC HEALTH AND DISASTER RELIEF
SCHOOL OF PUBLIC HEALTH
P.O. BOX 951772
LOS ANGELES, CALIFORNIA 90095-1772
TELEPHONE: (310) 794-6646
FAX: (310) 794-1805

February, 99

Dear Northridge Earthquake Study Participant:

Since the fifth anniversary of the Northridge earthquake just passed, we wanted to thank you for participating in UCLA's study of the Northridge earthquake. Your description of your experiences in the Northridge earthquake was very helpful. We learned a lot of about how earthquakes affect people and their neighborhoods. This information will help to improve the responses to future disasters. We appreciate your taking the time and effort to be interviewed.

Results from this study have been published in numerous scientific articles. We have enclosed a brief report of the study. We hope that you find it interesting.

Our next step in this study is to find out how people in Los Angeles County have recovered from the earthquake. We are asking people who were interviewed in the original study to participate in another telephone interview. In the near future, someone from the Survey Research Center at UCLA will be calling you to ask you about your experiences since the Northridge earthquake.

We hope that you will want to take part in the continuation of the Northridge study. Since we can only interview those that we interviewed in the first part of the study, your participation is necessary for the study to be successful. As in the earlier interview, your participation in this interview is completely voluntary and all information will be confidential. If you have any questions about the study, or would like more information, please call Dr. Kimberley Shoaf at (310) 825-4053. Thank you in advance for your support in this study.

Sincerely,

Linda B. Bourque, Ph.D.
Principal Investigator

Kimberley I. Shoaf, Dr.P.H.
Co-Investigator

Figure 4.2a.   Letter Used to Invite Northridge Study Respondents to Participate in a Second Study

UNIVERSITY OF CALIFORNIA, LOS ANGELES   UCLA

BERKELEY · DAVIS · IRVINE · LOS ANGELES · RIVERSIDE · SAN DIEGO · SAN FRANCISCO   SANTA BARBARA · SANTA CRUZ

UCLA CENTER FOR PUBLIC HEALTH AND DISASTER RELIEF
SCHOOL OF PUBLIC HEALTH
P.O. BOX 951772
LOS ANGELES, CALIFORNIA 90095-1772
TELEPHONE: (310) 794-6646
FAX: (310) 794-1805

February, 99

Estimado Participante del Estudio del Temblor de Northridge:

Al pasar el aniversario del Temblor de Northridge, nosotros queríamos expresarle nuestro agradecimiento por su participación en el estudio de ese temblor por UCLA. Sus respuestas a nuestras preguntas de sus experiencias han sido muy beneficiosas. Hemos aprendido mucho en cuanto al como los terremotos afectan a la población. Esta información nos ayudará a mejorar la manera de responder a desastres en el futuro. Reconocemos el tiempo y el empeño apreciable que tomó para ser entrevistado

Los resultados de este estudio han sido publicados en varias revistas científicas. Hemos incluido con esta carta un breve resumen del estudio. Esperamos que lo encuentre interesante.

El proximo paso en este estudio es averigüar como han recuperado del temblor la gente en el Condado de Los Angeles. Estamos pidiendo que los que fueron entrevistados en el estudio original hagan otra entrevista por telefono. En los proximos meses, alguien del Centro de Estudios y Encuestas de UCLA estará llamandole para preguntarle en cuanto a sus experiencias desde el Temblor de Northridge.

Esperamos que usted quiere ser una parte de la continuación del estudio de Northridge. Sólo podemos entrevistar a los que fueron entrevistados en la primera parte del estudio, asi que su participación es esencial para el exito del estudio. Como siempre, su participación en esta entrevista será completamente voluntaria y toda información que nos de será confidencial. Si tiene alguna pregunta en cuanto al estudio o si quiere más información, favor de llamar a la Dra. Kimberley Shoaf al (310) 825-4053. Le queremos agradecer de ante mano por su participación en esta parte de nuestro estudio.

Sinceramente,

Linda B. Bourque, Ph.D.
Investigadora Principal

Kimberley I. Shoaf, Dr.P.H.
Co-Investigadora

Figure 4.2b.   Letter Used to Invite Northridge Study Respondents to Participate in a Second Study

Northridge Earthquake
Survey Report

UCLA
Center for Public Health and Disaster Relief
and
UCLA Survey Research Center

Photo thanks to FEMA library at www.fema.gov

Figure 4.3a.   Study Report Enclosed With Invitation to Participate in a
Second Study

Northridge Earthquake Survey

On the morning of January 17, 1994 a magnitude 6.7 earthquake awoke Los Angeles County residents. Between August 1994 and May 1996, 1,830 residents of Los Angeles County were interviewed about what happened to them in the 1994 Northridge earthquake. These people were randomly selected to represent the experiences of the 3 million households in Los Angeles County. Each person thus represents thousands of other people who are similar in age, sex, education, income and lifestyle. Here is some of what these participants told us about the earthquake.

Damage to Home and Property

About one-third of the people reported that their home or personal property was damaged by the earthquake. Most damage was minor, but cost families about $18,000. The small number of people who had major damage to their home had the highest costs to deal with. This major damage included such things as collapsed roofs or walls, the house coming off of the foundation or the total destruction of the house.

Percent Reporting Damage

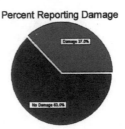

Type of Damage	% Reporting	Average Dollar Amount of Damage Reported
Personal Property	24.2%	$1,775
Contents of House	5.0%	$3,859
Exterior Structures	2.5%	$3,389
Exterior Structures and Contents	1.2%	$8,185
Minor Structural Damage	35.8%	$13,599
Minor Structural + Exterior and/or Contents	22.8%	$30,012
Major Structural Damage	8.5%	$59,804

Figure 4.3b. Study Report Enclosed With Invitation to Participate in a Second Study

Injuries

About 8% of survey participants said that they were injured in the earthquake.
Most of the injuries were mild cuts and bruises. However, about 10% of those who
were injured needed some type of medical care for their injuries.

Types of Injuries

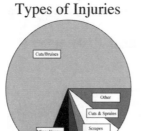

Medical Care for Injuries

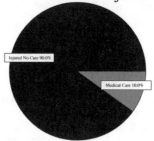

Transportation

A number of local freeways were damaged by the earthquake and this affected the
people in our study. About 2/3 of our participants commuted to either a job or
school on a regular basis. For a small number of them, their commute times
actually decreased during the time
that the freeways were out. For
another 65%, the freeway problems
did not change the amount of time it
took to get to their job or school.
For the remaining 30%, the freeway
problems from the earthquake
increased their commute times
anywhere from 1 minute to more
than 1 hour.

Change in Commute Time

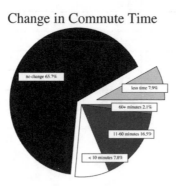

Figure 4.3c.   Study Report Enclosed With Invitation to Participate in a
Second Study

Use of the Survey Results and Future Studies

The information we received from the people interviewed has been very helpful. We have learned more about the causes and effects of damage to homes. This can help engineers make homes safer in future earthquakes. It has also helped us to prepare programs to reduce injuries and avoid traffic problems. We have shared these findings with other researchers and disaster planners in Los Angeles County and across the country.

Researchers at UCLA will be following up on this study. We will be calling participants from the Northridge study soon. We want to find out more about how they have recovered from the Northridge earthquake and their experiences in other more recent events. Please be expecting our call sometime after the first of the year. The information you share with us is very important and will help us to continue improving the safety of our communities in future disasters.

For more information about the study, you can contact:
Dr. Kimberley Shoaf or Dr. Linda Bourque at (310) 825-4053.

> Si quiere recibir una copia de este reporte en Español,
> por favor llame a la Dra. Kimberley Shoaf al (310) 825-4053

UCLA Center for Public Health and Disaster Relief
UCLA School of Public Health
Box 951772
Los Angeles, CA 90095-1772
(310) 825-4053
email: kshoaf@ucla.edu

Figure 4.3d. Study Report Enclosed With Invitation to Participate in a Second Study

When the surveyor anticipates that the interviews may take a relatively long time or may require respondents to invest considerable thought, they may want to instruct the interviewers to indicate the probable time needed in an indirect way. For example, if the surveyor and the interviewer know that interviews with people who experienced a lot of things as a result of an earthquake take 45 minutes to complete but interviews with people who had few things happen take 20 minutes, the interviewer may be better off setting up a future interview appointment than trying to race through an interview with a respondent who tells the interviewer up front that he or she has to pick up a child at school in 20 minutes.

HOW AND WHY THE RESPONDENT WAS CHOSEN

Any materials intended to motivate respondents should tell them how and why they were chosen to participate in the survey. Respondents are chosen in many different ways. In the earthquake studies, respondents were selected through **simple random sampling.** It is not necessary for surveyors to explain the intricacies of sample selection to respondents, but they should provide a lay explanation that lets the respondents know that only certain people are being interviewed and those persons are being selected in a way that ensures that all the types of people who live in the community are represented in the study. Respondents often think that if they refuse to be interviewed the surveyors will simply go on and interview someone else instead. In a rigorously conducted RDD sampling survey, respondent replacement is never done. Therefore, it is important for interviewers to tell potential respondents that their interviews cannot simply be replaced with other interviews, and that, in fact, the representativeness of the sample will be lessened by their refusal to participate.

In the Trinet Study, respondents were selected because they worked in certain institutions (e.g., education, health, emergency response, transportation, and utilities) in jobs that meant they had certain levels of expertise. In that study, we mentioned the selectivity of the sample in the advance letters (Figures 2.1 and 2.3), and the interviewers mentioned it again when they made the calls to schedule the interviews.

EXPLANATION OF CONFIDENTIALITY AND HOW THE DATA WILL BE HANDLED

Both federal law and research ethics require that subjects of all research studies be provided with information about how the collected data will be used and how their privacy or the confidentiality of their data will be ensured. In studies that use them, advance letters offer the perfect opportunity for informing respondents about how data will be used. In the Trinet Study, we explained how the data from the study would be handled in the fourth paragraph of the second advance letter (see Figure 2.3).

Some studies collect truly anonymous data, in that the surveyors make no effort to log the identities of respondents or to contact nonrespondents. When the data are anonymous, once the interviews are completed, the surveyor has no information about who was interviewed, including their names, addresses, telephone numbers, or any other information that would allow them to be "picked out" of the data set and identified. The example studies used here were not anonymous; they were confidential. In the Trinet Study, we knew the identities of the respondents before we interviewed them. At the same time, it was important that we provide as much confidentiality to respondents as was possible within the requirements of the study. It was in our interest and in the interest of the respondents to maximize the probability that respondents' answers were honest and complete. One of the major issues we had to address was that of assuring respondents that the information collected would not be available to personnel at Caltech or other institutions sponsoring the study. In the advance letter, we stated that "only persons from SRC and CPHDR will have access to the interview data," and that was, indeed, what happened. Although we were, respectively, the principal investigator of the Trinet Study and the director of the Survey Research Center, neither of us ever saw or handled completed interviews. We examined information only after it was available in machine-readable aggregate data files.

In the earthquake studies, we had no prior contact with the respondents, so the introduction used by the interviewers emphasized the confidentiality of the interviews. Specifically, the interviewers told potential respondents that identifiers (e.g., phone numbers) would be stripped from the data files and filed separately, and that the information collected would be reported only in aggregate summary form.

PROVISION OF A NAME AND PHONE NUMBER TO CALL FOR INFORMATION

The surveyor must always provide respondents with a name and phone number of someone who will be available to answer questions about the telephone survey. This person should be accessible and should be able to answer questions or respond to other requests the respondents may have. Often, this will be the person (or persons) who signs the advance letters when they are used. In the Trinet Study, we provided the names and titles of the principal and coprincipal investigators on the UCLA study. The letterhead provided the full address and phone numbers. When no advance letters are sent out, the surveyor must provide the interviewers with complete information about the people respondents can contact for further information. Often the interviewers are able to provide potential respondents with any information they need, but there are always some who will call to verify the purpose or sponsorship of a study, to assure themselves that the organization is legitimate or that confidentiality will be maintained. Other respondents will have questions about the content of the interview or how their names were selected for the sample. If an interviewer is unable to give a respondent a name and number when the respondent requests them, the respondent is unlikely to complete the interview.

We recommend that, whenever possible, the surveyor offer respondents the option of calling the project collect. Unfortunately, this was not possible in our example studies because telephones within the University of California system cannot be set up to accept collect calls, and we were unable to provide an off-campus number for respondents to contact. Surveyors should never give out the home phone numbers of project staff for such purposes.

Checklist for Motivating Respondents and Writing Advance Letters

✓ Explain the purpose of the study.

✓ Describe who is sponsoring the study.

✓ Consider sending advance letters, if it is possible.

✓ Consider using other methods, such as newsletters or flyers, to publicize a study conducted within a restricted population (e.g., a university faculty, a professional organization).

✓ Explain how the respondent was chosen and why his or her participation is important.

✓ Describe incentives, if used, and how they will be distributed.

✓ Directly or indirectly provide a realistic estimate of the time required by the average respondent to complete the interview.

✓ Explain how the confidentiality of the respondent's data will be protected.

---

5 Populations and Samples

$$\mathbf{I}$$n a telephone survey, information is collected by phone from a group of people. These people can represent themselves as individuals or they can represent households, institutions, or other entities. The methods by which they are selected for study also vary. In this chapter, we address the following topics concerning the populations and samples used in telephone surveys:

- Populations and methods of sampling from populations
- The creation of random-digit dialing samples
- How list-assisted selection modifies RDD samples
- How interviewers select designated respondents within households
- How surveyors report sample response rates
- How surveyors compare samples to populations

Because random-digit dialing and modifications of RDD are unique to telephone surveys, we focus in this chapter on the creation, use, and evaluation of RDD samples.

A Population or a Sample?

Surveyors can collect data either from populations or from samples of individuals, households, institutions, or organizations. A population consists of all the individuals or groups that meet certain criteria. For example, we can talk about the population of California residents, the population of households in Los Angeles County, the population of the United States, the population of immigrants, the population of hospitals, the population of financial institutions, the population of members of the American Public Health Association, or the population of countries that belong to the United Nations. The 2000 U.S. Census is a practical example of a data set collected from a population of households.

Sometimes researchers use the term *population* interchangeably with the term *universe*. At other times, these two terms reference different constructs, with a universe being defined as all the people or entities that meet the designated criteria and a population being defined as all the people or entities that can be located, identified, or listed as being in the universe. For example, it is well-known that the U.S. Census never gathers data on certain groups of people even though they technically reside in the United States. Census researchers have been particularly concerned with attempting to gather complete data on the homeless in the last three decennial censuses. In some cases, population and universe are essentially equivalent; in other cases, they may be quite different.

In designing a telephone survey, a surveyor may want to collect information from everyone in a certain population. This is feasible if the total number in the population is reasonable and a complete list of the population exists, but it is both impractical and unnecessary when the population is extremely large. (For a discussion of why surveyors can use samples instead of populations, see **How to Sample in Surveys**, Volume 7 in this series.) For example, it is unreasonable to conduct telephone interviews with the 24,621,819 persons age 18 and over who live in California, but it is reasonable to conduct interviews with the population of 110 general acute care hospitals in Los Angeles County.

The term *sample frame* is also sometimes used interchangeably with *population,* but there is a subtle difference: The **sample frame** is the actual list of households, phone numbers, institutions, or individuals from which the participants in a survey come. Often the sample frame is equivalent to the population, but sometimes it includes only a subset of the population. For example, in creating a sample of students at a particular university, the surveyor obtains a list of all the students enrolled at the university and then selects students from the list. The exact composition of such a list changes over the school year, however: Generally, more students are enrolled in the fall than later in the academic year; some students graduate, others drop out, and others go on leave status. *When* the surveyor gets the list determines exactly how many students and which students are available to be selected. Similarly, when a surveyor creates a sample frame using random-digit dialing, he or she is creating a sample frame that is a selection of all telephone numbers in a geographic area.

Types of Samples

A **sample** is part of a population. Instead of collecting data from every person, household, institution, "unit," or "element" in a population, the surveyor selects a sample—a subset of persons or units in the population—from whom to collect data. The types and sizes of samples, or the numbers of units selected, vary with the resources available, the extent to which the surveyor wants to be able to "generalize to" or "infer" back to the population, the research questions under study, and the "prevalence" or frequency with which characteristics important to the study are known or thought to be represented in the population.

Samples are of two general types: probability and non-probability. We discuss these two types, as well as systematic samples (a third, unique type of sample) below.

PROBABILITY SAMPLES

The creation of **probability samples** is based on statistical laws of probability. When a surveyor draws a probability sample, he or she knows that it is possible to determine the probability, or likelihood, of being in the sample for each person, household, or unit in the population. In order to create a probability sample, the surveyor must have a physical list of the population of interest or be able to generate a list, at least in the abstract. We briefly describe below three types of probability samples: simple random samples, stratified samples, and cluster samples.

Simple Random Samples

To create a **simple random sample**, the surveyor starts with a list of all the people or units in the population. For example, imagine that we have a list of all of the undergraduates enrolled at the University of California, Los Angeles, at the end of the second week of classes in the fall quarter of 2001. Suppose there are 25,000 names on the list, and we want to select a sample of 500. We decide to use a table of random numbers to select our sample (Figure 5.1 shows a single page from a random numbers table).

Once we have selected a name off of the list, we delete that name from the list. This is sampling *without replacement.* If we were instead sampling *with replacement,* we would not delete the name from the list, and the person would have a chance to be selected a second (or even third or fourth) time for the sample. Sampling with replacement creates an unbiased

(text continues on page 184)

TABLE 8 Random Numbers

Line/Col.	(1)	(2)	(3)	(4)	(5)	(6)	(7)	(8)	(9)	(10)	(11)	(12)	(13)	(14)
1	10480	15011	01536	02011	81647	91646	69179	14194	62590	36207	20969	99570	91291	90700
2	22368	46573	25595	85393	30995	89198	27982	53402	93965	34095	52666	19174	39615	99505
3	24130	48360	22527	97265	76393	64809	15179	24830	49340	32081	30680	19655	63348	58629
4	42167	93093	06243	61680	07856	16376	39440	53537	71341	57004	00849	74917	97758	16379
5	37570	39975	81837	16656	06121	91782	60468	81305	49684	60672	14110	06927	01263	54613
6	77921	06907	11008	42751	27756	53498	18602	70659	90655	15053	21916	81825	44394	42880
7	99562	72905	56420	69994	98872	31016	71194	18738	44013	48840	63213	21069	10634	12952
8	96301	91977	05463	07972	18876	20922	94595	56869	69014	60045	18425	84903	42508	32307
9	89579	14342	63661	10281	17453	18103	57740	84378	25331	12566	58678	44947	05585	56941
10	85475	36857	53342	53988	53060	59533	38867	62300	08158	17983	16439	11458	18593	64952
11	28918	69578	88231	33276	70997	79936	56865	05859	90106	31595	01547	85590	91610	78188
12	63553	40961	48235	03427	49626	69445	18663	72695	52180	20847	12234	90511	33703	90322
13	09429	93969	52636	92737	88974	33488	36320	17617	30015	08272	84115	27156	30613	74952
14	10365	61129	87529	85689	48237	52267	67689	93394	01511	26358	85104	20285	29975	89868
15	07119	97336	71048	08178	77233	13916	47564	81056	97735	85977	29372	74461	28551	90707
16	51085	12765	51821	51259	77452	16308	60756	92144	49442	53900	70960	63990	75601	40719
17	02368	21382	52404	60268	89368	19885	55322	44819	01188	65255	64835	44919	05944	55157
18	01011	54092	33362	94904	31273	04146	18594	29852	71585	85030	51132	01915	92747	64951
19	52162	53916	46369	58586	23216	14513	83149	98736	23495	64350	94738	17752	35156	35749
20	07056	97628	33787	09998	42698	06691	76988	13602	51851	46104	88916	19509	25625	58104
21	48663	91245	85828	14346	09172	30168	90229	04734	59193	22178	30421	61666	99904	32812
22	54164	58492	22421	74103	47070	25306	76468	26384	58151	06646	21524	15227	96909	44592
23	32639	32363	05597	24200	13363	38005	94342	28728	35806	06912	17012	64161	18296	22851
24	29334	27001	87637	87308	58731	00256	45834	15398	46557	41135	10367	07684	36188	18510
25	02488	33062	28834	07351	19731	92420	60952	61280	50001	67658	32586	86679	50720	94953

Abridged from William H. Beyer, ed., *Handbook of Tables for Probability and Statistics*, 2nd ed. © The Chemical Rubber Co., 1968. Used by permission of CRC Press, Inc.

Figure 5.1a. Excerpt From a Random Numbers Table

SOURCE: Abridged from William H. Beyer, ed., *Handbook of Tables for Probability and Statistics*, 2nd ed. © The Chemical Rubber Co., 1968. Reprinted from R. Lyman Ott, *An Introduction to Statistical Methods and Data Analysis*, 4th ed. © Wadsworth, 1993.

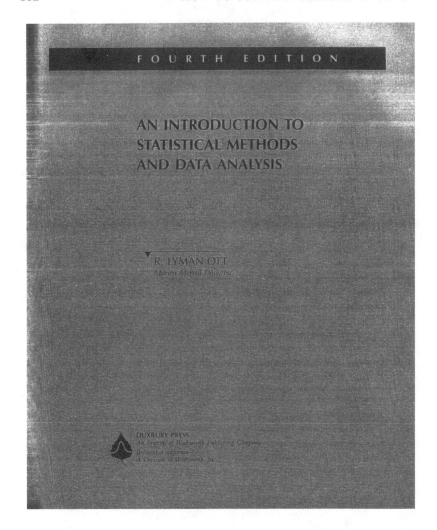

Figure 5.1b. Excerpt From a Random Numbers Table

SOURCE: Abridged from William H. Beyer, ed., *Handbook of Tables for Probability and Statistics*, 2nd ed. © The Chemical Rubber Co., 1968. Reprinted from R. Lyman Ott, *An Introduction to Statistical Methods and Data Analysis*, 4th ed. © Wadsworth, 1993.

Production Editors: Kirby Lozyniak/Susan Krikorian
Designer: Susan Krikorian
Print Buyer: Ellen Glisker
Copy Editor: Linda Thompson
Cover Design: Marshall Henrichs
Compositor: Techset Composition Limited
Printer: R.R. Donnelley & Sons

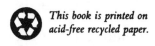

This book is printed on acid-free recycled paper.

Printed in the United States of America

2 3 4 5 6 7 8 9 10—97 96 95 94 93

Library of Congress Cataloging-in-Publication Data

Ott, Lyman.
   An introduction to statistical methods and data analysis /
R. Lyman Ott.—4th ed.
   p. cm.
   Includes bibliographical references and index.
   ISBN 0-534-93150-2
   1. Mathematical statistics. I. Title.
QA276.O77 1992   92-31934
519.5—dc20   CIP

Figure 5.1c. Excerpt From a Random Numbers Table

SOURCE: Abridged from William H. Beyer, ed., *Handbook of Tables for Probability and Statistics,* 2nd ed. © The Chemical Rubber Co., 1968. Reprinted from R. Lyman Ott, *An Introduction to Statistical Methods and Data Analysis,* 4th ed. © Wadsworth, 1993.

sample, but when a study is focused on people (or house-holds or institutions), it does not make economic sense to let a person (or household or institution) be selected multiple times for the sample, because then, technically, the surveyor should collect data from that person (or household or insti-tution) twice.

The practice of probability sampling rests on a number of assumptions, one of which is that the selection of one per-son (or other unit) does not in any way influence the selec-tion of the next person—that is, the selection of every person in the sample is "independent." For telephone sur-veys, surveyors sample without replacement because it would not make much sense to collect data from any person twice.

Surveyors use random numbers tables such as the one illustrated in Figure 5.1 or, increasingly, random numbers generators available in various software programs to make sure that each person in the sample is an independent selec-tion. To select our sample of 500 UCLA undergraduates, we need to take 500 5-digit numbers from the random numbers table.[1] To do this, we must start by "randomly" selecting a "first number" in the table. Let's say that our "random" first number is the first 1 in the fourth row of the table excerpt displayed in Figure 5.1. We next go across the rows in sequence and pull off 500 numbers, each made up of 5 digits. The first number will be 16793, the second number will be 09306, the third number will be 24361, the fourth number will be 68007, and, if we continue across the row, we get, in sequence, 85616, 37639, 44053, 53771, 34157, 00400, 84974, 91797, 75816, and so on. Looking at this array of numbers, we can quickly see that all but four numbers (16793, 09306, 24361, and 00400) are larger than 25,000 (the total number of undergraduates). If we assign a number to each student name on the list of undergraduates, from 00001 to 25000, we can use only those numbers from the random numbers table that fall between 00001 and 25000 in selecting our sample (or, alternatively, we could number the list from 00000 to 24999).

Clearly, when the number of units in the population represents a relatively small proportion of all numbers with the same number of digits, using a random numbers table or a printed list of random numbers will generate many non-usable numbers. Take the present example: There are 100,000 numbers that have five digits, 00000-99999. If there are only 25,000 persons in the population, we can expect that only 25,000/100,000, or 25%, of the numbers will be usable.

Assume that we go ahead with this method and finally obtain 500 usable numbers. We must now apply our numbers to our list of undergraduates. Based on the first four usable numbers noted above—16793, 09306, 24361, and 00400—we find the 16,793rd, 9,306th, 24,361st, and 400th students on the list of 25,000. These four students are in our sample. The fact that the 16,793rd student is the first one selected in no way influences or "predicts" that the 9,306th student will be the second one selected.

When surveyors draw simple random samples, they assume that the distribution of characteristics of persons in the sample will be similar to the distribution of characteristics in the population. For example, if 52% of the population is female, they expect that 52% of the sample will be female. There is always a chance, however, that the proportion of females in the sample will be substantially different from the proportion of females in the population. Earlier, we noted that probability sampling is based on the concept of statistical probability. Recall the normal or bell-shaped curve in statistics. A normal distribution is symmetrical, and the mean, median, and mode all occur at an identical place in the distribution. The normal curve is based on an infinite number of probability samples from a population. Above, we said that 52% of the population is female. This is the true proportion of females in the population, or a *population parameter*. There is no variance in a population parameter. In contrast, the proportion of a sample that is female *can* vary.

Imagine drawing a sample of 100 people from the population; call each one up on the telephone and ask each person's gender. Now "throw the sample away." Draw another sample; call each one on the phone and ask each one's gender. Keep doing this an infinite number of times. For each of these samples, you can calculate the proportion of females in the sample. Now graph the proportion of females from each of your infinite samples. This is the sampling distribution, a normal curve on which the mean, median, and mode all equal 52%, the "true" population parameter.

Obviously, in real life, it is too costly and time-consuming for surveyors to draw multiple samples. But the surveyor uses characteristics of the normal curve to "gamble" that the sample he or she draws "represents" the true distribution of gender in the population. In other words, the surveyor assumes that 68% of the time the proportion of females in the sample will be within plus or minus one standard deviation of the population parameter of 52%. There is, however, a 32% chance that the sample will be outside that area of the normal curve, and at least a small chance that the proportion of females in the sample is either 0% or 100%. Surveyors sometimes use stratified samples and other techniques to reduce their chances of selecting samples that are wildly unrepresentative of their populations of interest.

Stratified Samples

Simple random sampling is not always the most efficient or best way to select a sample of respondents. Surveyors assume when they draw probability samples that the samples appropriately represent larger populations, but this does not always happen. **Stratified sampling** can increase the accuracy of the selected sample and decrease the likelihood that population subgroups are misrepresented in the sample. Surveyors use stratified sampling in two ways: first, to ensure that important characteristics of the population are accurately represented in the sample, and second, to ensure that small groups in the population are adequately represented in the sample.

Proportionate stratification. Surveyors want to be certain that important subgroups are appropriately represented in their samples. Take, for example, our sample of UCLA undergraduates. Of the 25,000 undergraduates, 4,319 are freshmen, 4,358 are sophomores, 8,014 are juniors, and 8,309 are seniors. We want our sample to have the same proportions of freshmen, sophomores, juniors, and seniors that are found in the population. Thus, we want our sample of 500 undergraduates to have 86 or 87 freshmen (17.3%), 87 sophomores (17.4%), 160 or 161 juniors (32.1%), and 166 seniors (33.2%). To obtain this distribution, we first stratify, or divide, our list of undergraduates by class standing, so that the 4,319 freshmen are on one list, the 4,358 sophomores are on a second list, the 8,014 juniors are on a third list, and the 8,309 seniors are on a fourth list. Then we use a random numbers table or a random numbers generator on a computer to select the correct number of students from each list: 86 or 87 of the 4,319 freshmen, 87 of the 4,358 sophomores, and so on.

The sample will then have the same proportions of freshmen, sophomores, juniors, and seniors as there are in the population. The probability that a particular student is selected for the sample is approximately equal for all strata. Because this probability is approximately equal, we do not have to make any special adjustments in the data during analysis.

Disproportionate stratification. Now, assume that we want to evaluate services for disabled students at UCLA, and, as part of that evaluation, we want to select a sample of disabled students and a comparison sample of students who are not disabled. In the 2000-2001 school year, 1,324 students received one or more services from UCLA's Office for Students With Disabilities. If we select a simple random sample of 500 students, on average only 5.3% of our sample, or 26 students, would be listed with the Office for Students With Disabilities, and we run the risk that an even smaller number of disabled students are selected. A comparison of 26 disabled students with 474 nondisabled students does not provide enough statistical power for the data analysis (for more on statistical power, see **How to Sample in Surveys,** Volume 7 in this series). We would be better able to compare the two groups if we had a larger number of disabled students in our sample. To obtain a sample with a larger number of disabled students, we stratify on disability status, but in this case we overrepresent disabled students in our sample to ensure that we can accurately describe them.

Again, we want a sample of 500, but we want it to be evenly divided between those listed with the Office for Students With Disabilities and those not listed with that office, so we select 250 students from the list of 1,324 who received services from the Office for Students With Disabilities and 250 from the other 23,676 (25,000 – 1,324) undergraduates. Again, we stratify the list of undergraduates into two groups: those listed with the Office for Students With Disabilities and those who are not. We then use a random numbers table or computer-generated list of random numbers to select our sample from the two lists, but this time the probability that a student will be selected is much higher for disabled students than it is for nondisabled students. The approximate probability that a disabled student is selected is 250/1,324, or 18.9%, whereas the approximate probability that a nondisabled student is selected is 250/23,676, or 1.06%.

Disproportionate stratified sampling has ramifications for the analysis of the data collected from the sample. As long as the two groups are kept separate in the analysis and compared only with each other, the fact that they were disproportionately sampled presents no problems. But if, instead, we want to combine the disabled and nondisabled groups, or *strata,* in our sample so that we can compare undergraduates at UCLA with undergraduates at UC Berkeley, then we must weight the sample so that the proportion that each group represents in the sample is the same as the proportion it represents in the population. We can think of this in two ways: (a) In our sample, disabled students are *overrepresented* relative to nondisabled students; or

(b) in our sample, nondisabled students are *underrepresented* relative to disabled students.

As we noted above, the probability that a disabled student is in the sample is 18.9%, whereas the probability that a nondisabled student is in the sample is 1.06%. Thus, disabled students are 17.83 times (18.9/1.06) more likely than nondisabled students to be in the sample. In weighting the data, we can either multiply the data of the nondisabled students by 17.83, so that the weighted sample now contains 4,457.5 nondisabled students and 250 (5.31%) disabled students, or multiply the data of disabled students by .056, so that the weighted sample now contains 13.99 (5.3%) disabled students and 250 nondisabled students.[2]

Disproportionate stratified sampling is useful when a surveyor must obtain adequate numbers of particular kinds of persons (or other sampling units) in the sample when their proportion in the population is very small. As long as the strata are kept separate during the analysis, analysis is straightforward. But, as the above discussion probably makes obvious, when the surveyor must reweight the strata back to the proportions they represent in the population from which they were drawn, analyses often become difficult to conceptualize and to explain to others, because some of the elements in the sample become either fractions or multiples of themselves.

Cluster Samples

Cluster sampling is another form of probability sampling in which the researcher divides the sample frame or population into subgroups prior to drawing the sample. But whereas surveyors use stratified sampling to increase the homogeneity within each subgroup (or stratum) on some characteristic (e.g., class standing, disability status), they use cluster sampling to construct subgroups (clusters) that are internally heterogeneous on important characteristics.

Surveyors use cluster samples primarily in studies that employ in-person interviewing for data collection. When respondents selected for a sample live within a "cluster," the costs associated with traveling between interview sites are reduced. Cluster samples are not usually used in telephone surveys.

In a study of residents of California, for example, a surveyor might try to find one geographic area within which it can be demonstrated that the households or individuals (or whatever unit is being studied) capture the heterogeneity of important characteristics of households or individuals in the state—that is, the proportion of males and females, the age distribution, the distribution of ethnicities, and so on, are "like" those of California as a whole. Usually the surveyor cannot find a single cluster that represents the larger population and must, instead, select multiple clusters. So, for example, if the surveyor is studying the behavior of elementary school children, he or she would select multiple schools to represent the population of all schools to which he or she wishes to generalize. For a general population of households, the surveyor might select census tracts or blocks within census tracts.

The appropriate selection of clusters depends on the surveyor's having recent data about the population he or she wishes to sample. We strongly recommend that surveyors consult with sampling statisticians if they want to select cluster samples. The probability of a person, household, or institution getting into a cluster sample differs with the number of clusters selected, the size of the clusters, and the relative homogeneity or heterogeneity within each cluster.

SYSTEMATIC SAMPLES

Surveyors often use systematic samples because it is tedious to select names (or other units) manually from a sample frame or list of the population when both the sample and the population are large. Although many researchers assume that systematic samples are simple random samples, they are in fact a form of complex random sample. To create a systematic sample, the surveyor needs a list of all of the elements or sampling units in the population, a random start point, and an interval by which the sample is going to be selected from the population. In the example of undergraduates at UCLA, the interval for a systematic sample of 500 would be 50 (25,000/500)—that is, every 50th student on the list would be selected for the sample. We begin by selecting a random start point between zero and the interval value on the list, which in this case is 50. Assume that we randomly select 32. Until we select the random start point, every student on the list has an equal chance of being in the sample, and that probability is 500/25,000, or 2%. But once we select the start point, each student's probability of being in the sample goes to either 100% or 0%. Student 32 is in the sample, and then the next student selected is student 82, and then student 132, and so on. Every 50th student has a 100% chance of being in the sample; all students between these students have no chance, or a 0% probability, of being selected.

NONPROBABILITY SAMPLES

There are many different kinds of **nonprobability samples**, and researchers have used varying terms for the different kinds in discussing them in the literature. When a surveyor uses a nonprobability sample, he or she has no way of evaluating how good or bad the sample is or the extent to which the sample represents some larger population. It is always better for surveyors to use probability or systematic samples rather than nonprobability samples, but sometimes surveyors cannot "list" or describe the populations in which they are interested, and, as a result, they must use nonprobability samples. Surveyors also use nonprobability samples when they pretest questionnaires and data collection procedures.

There are three general types of nonprobability samples: convenience or accidental samples, snowball or network samples, and quota or purposive samples. A **convenience sample**, as the name implies, is a sample made up of people or groups that are "convenient" to the surveyor. "Man-on-the-street" interviews conducted by the news media are examples of convenience sampling. The interviewer goes to a public place, such as a busy street corner, and selects people to interview from those who walk by.

Researchers often use **snowball** or **network samples** when the groups in which they are interested are difficult to identify or locate; often this is because the groups are somehow involved in illegal behaviors, and thus no lists are available. To begin snowball sampling, the surveyor obtains the names of one or more people or groups with the characteristic of interest and conducts interviews with those contacts. At the end of each interview, by which time the surveyor hopes that he or she has gained the trust and confidence of the respondent, the surveyor asks the respondent to provide names and contact information for other people like the respondent. The surveyor then interviews those persons and, again, asks them for names of people with similar characteristics. In this way, the sample consists of a network of connected individuals.

Surveyors who use snowball sampling have different ways of deciding when it is time to stop seeking additional subjects. Sometimes they decide to stop when they believe they have interviewed enough people or groups, and sometimes they stop when they reach a point where new respondents are suggesting the names of persons the surveyors have already interviewed.

Quota or **purposive samples** are also nonprobability samples, but they involve more controls than snowball samples or convenience samples. Instead of having interviewers go to a street corner (or other location) and simply pick respondents from among the people who pass by, the surveyor gives the interviewers some rules to follow. For instance, the surveyor tells interviewers to interview equal numbers of men and women, or to pick people of different ages, or to select every 10th person who walks by. Or the surveyor may have interviewers work in a location at different times of the day and on different days of the week, on the assumption that different people are in the area at different times of the day and week.

The problem with all of these examples, however, is that the interviewers have the final control over who gets interviewed. An interviewer may count off 10 people but decide that he or she does not want to approach and attempt to do an interview with the 10th person because that person is walking a Doberman pinscher and is clearly armed with pepper spray. If an interviewer "pretends" that an actual 10th person is not a 10th person, the surveyor will usually never find out about it. Such interviewer selection of respondents can also happen in probability samples if surveyors are not vigilant in training and supervising the interviewers.

TRINET STUDY SAMPLE

The Trinet Study provides an example of a nonprobability sample that was purposive and in which designated respondents were identified by the surveyors, not left to interviewers to select. We first decided that the goal was to interview 200 representatives of institutions in Los Angeles County, with 50 interviews being conducted in each of four institutional sectors: education, emergency services, health care, and utilities and transportation. No single list existed that represented the population of all such organizations, so we identified institutions through a variety of sources, including public-use lists such as the Office of Emergency Services Mutual Aid Region Directory, the Los Angeles County Department of Health Services lists of health care sites by service planning areas, and the Los Angeles Unified School District's list of schools; Internet searches for individual organizations' Web sites as well as lists of specific types of organizations; telephone directories; and personal contacts and recommendations from experts in the field.

We purposively selected potential respondents to represent a range of organizational types within each sector and geographic distribution across the county. We also attempted to include both public and private entities. We monitored the sample throughout the data collection period to maximize the likelihood that we would have a range of respondent types in the final sample. For example, as each wave of data collection was completed, we analyzed nonresponders by type and location so that we could replace them with similar organizations in the following wave. Once we had identified a site as a potential respondent, a member of the office staff called the site to find out who in the organization was most knowledgeable about emergency response procedures. That person then turned the name of that person and his or her identifying information over to the Survey Research Center for actual data collection.

TABLE 1 Types of Responses by Institutional Sector									
	Education (n = 62)		Emerg Svcs (n = 53)		Health Care (n = 59)		Util & Trans (n = 49)		Total (n = 223)[a]
	%	(n)	%	(n)	%	(n)	%	(n)	%	(n)
Completed interviews	80.6	(50)	92.5	(49)	88.1	(52)	81.5	(40)	85.7	(191)
Refused	12.9	(8)	1.9	(1)	5.1	(3)	12.2	(6)	8.1	(18)
Unable to contact	4.8	(3)	0	(0)	5.1	(3)	2.0	(1)	3.1	(7)
No eligible respondent	1.6	(1)	5.7	(3)	1.7	(1)	4.1	(2)	3.1	(7)

[a]Note: This does not include one case in Utilities & Transportation that we included in the final data set even though the interview was conducted as part of the pilot testing.

Figure 5.2.   Example Report on the Disposition of Potential Respondents in a Purposive Nonprobability Sample, Trinet Study

SOURCE: Riopelle, Bourque, and Shoaf (2001, p. vii).

Figure 5.2 shows a table from the Trinet Study that displays the response rates and distributions of the final sample. Notice that interviews were successfully conducted with 85.7% of those contacted, 8.1% refused to be interviewed, 3.1% were never contacted, and at 3.1% of the sites we were unable to identify anyone as knowledgeable about emergency procedures. The high response rate in this study was in large part the result of the amount of prescreening conducted before any telephone interviews were attempted. In all but one sector, we reached or came close to our quota of 50 interviews. We were able to conduct only 40 interviews in the utilities and transportation sector because our original list contained essentially the complete list of such organizations in Los Angeles County that met the study criteria. In the other sectors, substantially more groups exist in the county than we were able either to list or to contact.

Checklist for Selecting Respondents

✓ Do you want to generalize to a larger population?

✓ Is the "element" or "unit" in your study a person, a household, an institution, or something else?

✓ Will you interview everyone in the population or a sample of the population?

✓ Is there a list of the population, or can you create one that meets your needs?

✓ How large will your sample be?

✓ Will it be a probability sample or a nonprobability sample?

✓ If it will be a probability sample, will it be a simple random sample, a stratified sample, or a cluster sample?

✓ If it will be a stratified sample, will selection be proportionate or disproportionate?

✓ If it will be a nonprobability sample, why have you made that choice, and what kind of nonprobability sample will it be?

A high response rate in a purposive or quota sample does *not* make a nonprobability sample into a probability sample. The fact that the surveyor takes great care in selecting the participants and monitoring data collection should increase the resulting sample's representativeness, but it does not enable the surveyor to know how representative of the population the sample is. In the Trinet Study we did not have a list of the population of all institutions in Los Angeles that could have qualified for the study. Without such a list, we cannot estimate the probability that any particular institution or group of institutions was represented in the sample.

Random-Digit Dialing

Random-digit dialing is a method of selecting the sample frame for a probability sample that is unique to telephone surveys. We used RDD procedures to select the samples for both the Loma Prieta study and the Northridge study. Two kinds of RDD can be conceptualized: one in which the researcher uses no lists or other techniques in drawing the telephone numbers, and one in which the researcher uses existing lists of numbers and other techniques to create more efficient sample frames. We describe an example below in which no lists or other techniques are used in developing the sample frame of phone numbers. In fact, most RDD samples used in research are created with the assistance of lists and other techniques, the researchers' objective being to develop more efficient sample frames. Researchers use multiple sources and techniques in developing these list-assisted RDD sample frames.

SELECTING AN RDD SAMPLE

To select a random-digit dialing sample representing a particular geographic area, a surveyor must know the telephone area codes and trunk or prefix numbers that are contained within and roughly coterminous with the geographic area under study. Unfortunately, area codes generally do not follow county or city boundaries. Figure 5.3 shows a map of the area codes in Los Angeles County; notice that area codes 213, 323, and 310 are completely inside the boundaries of Los Angeles County, but area code 909 straddles Los Angeles County, San Bernardino County, and Riverside County. Because we wanted a sample of households in Los Angeles County for the Northridge study, we had to include all of the area codes in the county. However, we knew before we drew the sample that some numbers associated with some of those area codes—for example, 909, 818, and 562—would not be associated with households in L.A. County, so we also used information about the trunk numbers that are associated with area codes.

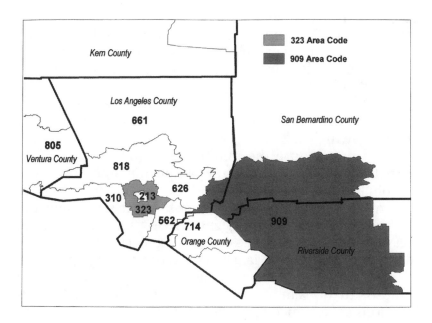

Figure 5.3.   Map of Los Angeles County Showing Area Codes

Figure 5.4 shows a partial list of the trunk numbers associated with the 310 area code as well as the towns or areas of the city in which the trunk numbers are in use. Unfortunately, this information is less than perfect. For example, we both live in Venice, a community that is part of the city of Los Angeles; Venice is located south of the city of Santa Monica. We both live within the 310 area code, and our trunk numbers are 821 and 915. Note that the list says that both these trunk numbers are in an area called Mar Vista, which is east of Venice. We have friends and neighbors in Venice who have trunk numbers of 396 and 399, which, according to the list, are trunk numbers in Santa Monica.

Some people request particular trunk numbers when they arrange for their telephone service, often because certain trunk numbers are associated with areas of the city that they believe are desirable. For example, the trunk numbers associated with Beverly Hills are particularly popular because they are thought to indicate higher socioeconomic status. The point here is that anyone selecting an RDD sample should be aware that trunk numbers, like area codes, do not necessarily follow county, city, or neighborhood boundaries and may not even be located in the geographic areas where they are expected to be.

Thus, the surveyor has to take two important steps, one before and one after he or she draws an RDD sample. First, before drawing the sample, whenever possible, the surveyor should try to reduce the number of "wrong numbers" by restricting the generation of the sample frame to only those combinations of area codes and trunk numbers that are within the geographic area of interest. At the same time, the surveyor must not get overly enthusiastic about eliminating area codes and prefixes, because in the process he or she may inadvertently eliminate large sections of the geographic area of interest from the sample frame. The exception to this rule is those situations in which entire area code and prefix combinations are assigned to single large, nonresidential entities or used for specific telephone services, such as cell phones, public telephone booths, or faxes and modems. For example,

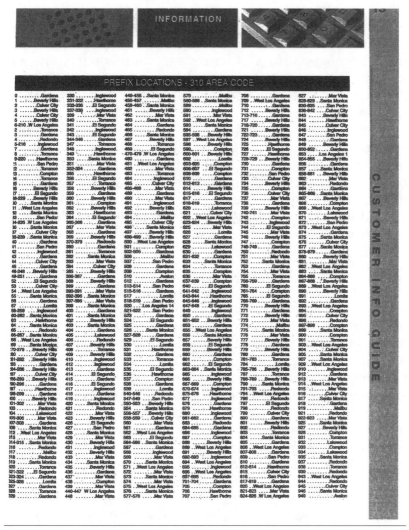

Figure 5.4. Example of Prefixes in the 310 Area Code

the combination of area code 310 and the prefix 825 is entirely assigned to the University of California, Los Angeles. UCLA is located in the western portion (known as the Westside) of the city of Los Angeles. If we want to draw an RDD sample of Los Angeles households on the Westside, it would be acceptable for us to remove (310) 825 from the trunk numbers from which we generate our sample. (There is no consistent rule for such assignment of area code and trunk number pairings; practices vary among telephone service providers, and some telephone service providers are more cooperative than others in providing this information to researchers.)

Second, once the surveyor has drawn the sample frame and telephone numbers successfully yield qualified households, businesses, or respondents, the surveyor must remember to find out where each household or business is located. In the case of the Northridge study, households that were located outside Los Angeles County were not eligible to participate.

Creating the Sample Frame

Figure 5.5 shows all of the area codes that have at least some phone numbers located in Los Angeles County and the prefix or trunk lines associated with the numbers in Los Angeles County. It appears that all of the prefixes associated with area codes 213, 818, 310, and 323 represent phones in Los Angeles County, but only a few prefixes associated with area codes 805, 562, and 661 represent phones in the county. Notice that the lowest prefix number assigned is 200 and the highest prefix number assigned is 999. Not all prefix numbers may be active within an area code; in this example, only two prefixes, 853 and 561, in the 805 area code represent phone numbers located in Los Angeles County.

Within a given prefix, a total of 10,000 phone numbers can be generated, ranging from 0000 to 9999. At any given time, the full bank of numbers usually is not active, meaning that some phone numbers have not been assigned. The third column in Figure 5.5 provides examples of what banks of numbers might be active for each prefix.[3] In our example, numbers 0000 through 5000 for prefix 200 in area code 213 are indicated as active. These would be the phone numbers starting with (213) 200-0000 and ending with (213) 200-5000.

Area Codes in Order Established	Trunk/Prefix Number Associated With L.A. County	Example of Active Bank of Numbers	Population of Phones	
			N	%
213	200	0000-5000	5,001	
	201	0073-9093	9,021	
	202	0000-9999	10,000	
	203	0100-0900	801	
	204	0000-5999	6,000	
	.			
	999	1000-7000	6,001	
			36,824	28.0
805	853	0000-6033	6,034	
	561	0000-4044	4,045	
			10,079	7.7
818	200	1000-8000	7,001	
	201	0000-7213	7,214	
	.			
	997	0000-3029	3,030	
			17,245	13.1
310	200	5000-8999	5,000	
	201	0000-9999	10,000	
	.			
	999	4500-9999	5,500	
			20,500	15.6
562	520	0000-7500	7,501	

Figure 5.5. Creating a Random-Digit Dialing Sample Frame for Los Angeles County

Area Codes in Order Established	Trunk/Prefix Number Associated With L.A. County	Example of Active Bank of Numbers	Population of Phones	
			N	%
	561	0000-2549	2,550	
	836	0000-8200	8,201	
	853	0011-3000	2,990	
			21,242	16.1
323	200	5000-9000	4,001	
	202	0000-4500	4,501	
	203	0000-3900	3,901	
	.			
	998	0000-3200	3,201	
			15,604	11.8
661	561	0200-5432	5,233	
	784	0000-2000	2,001	
	853	7000-9999	3,000	
			10,234	7.8
TOTAL POPULATION OF PHONE NUMBERS			131,728	100.0

Figure 5.5.   Continued

Pretend for purposes of our example that only the prefixes that are actually listed in Figure 5.5 are both active and located in Los Angeles County. That would be prefixes 200, 201, 202, 203, 204, and 999 for area code 213; prefixes 853 and 561 in area code 805; prefixes 200, 201, and 997 in area code 818; and so on. To create a sample frame, we must enter all of the active phone numbers associated with each of these area codes and prefixes into the computer. For this example, 131,728 phone numbers have to be generated within a computer: 36,824 for area code 213; 10,079 for area code 805; 17,245 for area code 818; 20,500 for 310; 21,242 for area code 562; 15,604 for area code 323; and 10,234 for area code 661. This is the population of telephone numbers. This list is self-weighting—that is, the proportion of telephone numbers on the list from the 213 area code represents the proportion, 27.95% (36,824/131,728), of all telephone numbers on the list that are active that are in the 213 area code.[4]

Now that the surveyor has generated the population of telephone numbers, he or she must create a sample frame from which the actual respondents will be selected. The size of the sample frame is determined by the desired sample size, the kinds of persons or groups that will be interviewed for the study, and the proportion of phone numbers that the surveyor estimates will not yield qualified respondents. For example, if a surveyor wants a probability sample of households, it is usually the case that about one in six phone numbers will represent a household. The other five phone numbers may be assigned to businesses, modems, fax machines, or cell phones; may be temporarily out of order or temporarily not in service or assigned; or the surveyor may be unable to identify how they are assigned because no one ever answers them or they always reach answering machines. If, for our example, we want to interview at least 600 people, we need to draw 3,600 phone numbers randomly from the population of phone numbers. We might draw the 3,600 numbers all at one time, or we might draw them in successive draws of smaller subsamples, for example, 300. These 3,600 phone numbers are the sample frame for the study.

Once the numbers are drawn, the surveyor assigns them to interviewers, who attempt to contact each number and determine whether or not it is an eligible household. If it is an eligible household, the interviewer proceeds to conduct the interview with the designated respondent. The interviewers continue to "work" the numbers until the desired number of people are interviewed, the full list of numbers is exhausted, or the surveyor runs out of money for data collection. Occasionally the full set of numbers is exhausted before the sample size is obtained. This has happened to us in the past, and it almost happened in the Loma Prieta study.

Conversely, the interviewers may complete the desired number of interviews before they have exhausted all of the telephone numbers that were generated and released. If the surveyor is to report a valid outcome analysis and response rate, however, he or she must have the interviewers dial every number sampled and released to achieve an outcome for each. Although it is best to interview the additional households, that is not always fiscally possible. The surveyor must, however, identify the outcome for all the telephone numbers and report the sample outcome accordingly.

One way the surveyor can avoid this problem is by dividing the original sample into subsamples, or replicates. If the telephone numbers in the replicates are selected randomly, each replicate is a representative version of the original sample. Replicates can be released on an "as needed" basis, so if the surveyor finds that he or she has reached the goal number of completed interviews, the interviewers need to complete the dialings only in the replicates that are currently open; they do not need to dial any numbers in the "untouched" replicates. The principle is that if the replicates are pulled randomly, each one represents a miniature version of the sample, so the sampling frame will function as intended regardless of the number of replicates used to achieve the goal.

In our example, the selection of phone numbers out of the population was made using simple random sampling. We drew a simple random sample in replicates for the Northridge study, but for the Loma Prieta study we prestratified the phone numbers to create a disproportionately stratified sample in which households located in areas of high earthquake shaking, such as Santa Cruz and San Francisco/Alameda/Oakland, were oversampled relative to their proportion in the population.

LIST-ASSISTED RDD SAMPLES

Surveyors can increase the efficiency of RDD samples by using available lists to reduce the number of nonworking business and nonresidential numbers. Sources of such lists include published telephone directories and computerized databases of business numbers and working numbers. One source of lists is Donnelley Marketing Information Services (located in Stamford, Connecticut), which publishes U.S. telephone directories. Surveyors can also purchase RDD-generated lists from Survey Sampling, Inc. (SSI; in Fairfield, Connecticut) and GENESYS Sampling Systems (in Fort Washington, Pennsylvania); these firms are equipped to create list-assisted RDD samples to meet surveyors' needs.

According to SSI, there are approximately 96.7 million telephone households in the United States, but approximately 30% of those households have unlisted numbers, either by choice or because of mobility. SSI uses a variety of procedures to select and screen household samples, including maintaining a database of 11 million business telephone numbers against which the numbers selected for a sample can be compared. Those identified as business numbers can then be either replaced or flagged, depending on what the surveyor requests. Similarly, surveyors can request that SSI remove or flag disconnected numbers.

We purchased a list-assisted RDD sample from SSI for the Northridge study. The sample was list-assisted in the sense that we set a lower boundary on the proportion of listed telephone numbers in a selected prefix that were residential. For example, if less than 30% of the listed telephone numbers in a prefix were residences, that prefix was excluded when the sample was generated. We obtained the sample for the Loma Prieta study from GENESYS. That sample frame was list-assisted in that once the sample was generated, it was compared against a listed directory for the area in order to eliminate known commercial listings. As a result, fewer numbers needed to be generated in order for us to obtain the required number of completed interviews. When a sample is not list-assisted, as many as 20 numbers may have to be drawn for each completed interview; in contrast, a list-assisted sample can sometimes reduce that number to 2-3 for each completed interview.

The **Waksberg-Mitofsky procedure** is another form of list-assisted sampling that was designed to increase the number of working residential numbers in the sample. A Waksberg-Mitofsky sample is somewhat analogous to a two-stage cluster sample. First, primary sampling units are drawn that are clusters or blocks of 100 numbers identified by the first eight digits of the phone number: (xxx) xxx-xx00 through (xxx) xxx-xx99. A number out of this cluster or block is randomly selected and called. If it is a working residential number, the block of numbers is kept in the sample frame; if it is not, the block of numbers is dropped. Once all of the clusters or blocks of numbers have been selected, all the numbers in each block are called until the desired sample size is reached. There is a substantial literature on the Waksberg-Mitofsky procedure that has resulted in both a number of criticisms and modifications in its usage.

Checklist for Developing an RDD Sample

✓ How large a sample do you need?

✓ Will you develop the sample frame, or will you purchase a sample?

✓ Will the creation of the sample frame be list-assisted, and, if so, in what way?

✓ Does the sample need to be stratified or targeted in some way?

✓ How many callbacks will you incorporate in your study?

✓ How many phone numbers will you need to obtain the desired sample size?

Selecting the Designated Respondent

Often surveyors do not think about specifying who will be interviewed in a household—that is, who will be the **designated respondent**—once the household is successfully contacted. This failure can result in an unrepresentative final sample, both because some groups of people (e.g., retirees) are more likely than others to be at home and because some people (e.g., teenagers) are more likely than others to answer the phone. Generally, researchers conducting telephone surveys have as their objective either obtaining a representative sample of all households in a given area or obtaining a representative sample of all adults 18 and over in an area. If the objective is households rather than individuals and the surveyor feels comfortable assuming that any adult in the household can "represent" the household in responding to the survey, then he or she need not give the interviewer any instructions on how to select a respondent within a household. Alternatively, if the surveyor wants the sample to represent all adults in the population, he or she must provide the interviewer with a method by which to select a respondent from among all the adults in the household. The surveyor must also clearly instruct the interviewer that, once the interviewer has selected a respondent within a household, he or she is to interview that person and only that person in that household.

The literature on the selection of designated respondents discusses four different procedures: the use of Kish tables, the use of Troldahl-Carter-Bryant (TCB) tables, the Hagan and Collier method, and the last/next birthday method. We feel that using Kish tables is the best way to select respondents, and that is the method we usually use, but many surveyors think that using Kish tables reduces response rates, because the selection process in this method takes more time than other methods. We have not found that to be true. In the Northridge study, we randomized households to either the Kish table method or the last/next birthday method for selection of the designated respondent, and we found no readily discernible differences between the two procedures in refusal rates.

KISH TABLES

To use **Kish tables,** the surveyor preassigns to each interview, in sequential order, the number of one of the 12 Kish tables.[5] When an interviewer successfully contacts an eligible household, he or she asks the person who answered the phone for the names, ages, and genders of all persons 18 and older who are permanent residents of the household. The interviewer lists the household members in the same order for all interviews, generally from oldest to youngest. Once the interviewer has listed all the members of the household, he or she consults the particular Kish table that has been preassigned to that interview. Kish developed these tables to ensure that all members of a household have an equal chance of being selected for a survey. Figure 5.6 shows the set of 8 Kish tables. Each table is to be used with a certain proportion of households in the sample.

Look at Table B1 in Figure 5.6. Imagine that the interviewer has listed six adults in the household, from oldest to youngest, and Table B1 is the Kish table that was preassigned to the interview. The first row of Table B1 represents the number of adults in the household; the second row of Table B1 represents the person on the list who should be interviewed in the household. According to Table B1, if six adults live in the household (the top row), the second person is the designated respondent for the study (the second row). If, instead, Table E2 had been assigned to the interview, the fifth person would have been the designated respondent.

Now imagine another household for which the interviewer has listed two adults. If Table A was preassigned to that interview, the first person is the designated respondent. But if, instead, Table D had been assigned to that household with two adults, the second person would be the designated respondent.

| TABLE A: | If the number of adults is: | 1 2 3 4 5 6+ |
| | Then select adult number: | 1 1 1 1 1 1 |

| TABLE B1: | If the number of adults is: | 1 2 3 4 5 6+ |
| | Then select adult number: | 1 1 1 1 2 2 |

| TABLE B2: | If the number of adults is: | 1 2 3 4 5 6+ |
| | Then select adult number: | 1 1 1 2 2 2 |

| TABLE C: | If the number of adults is: | 1 2 3 4 5 6+ |
| | Then select adult number: | 1 1 2 2 3 3 |

| TABLE D: | If the number of adults is: | 1 2 3 4 5 6+ |
| | Then select adult number: | 1 2 2 3 4 4 |

| TABLE E1: | If the number of adults is: | 1 2 3 4 5 6+ |
| | Then select adult number: | 1 2 3 3 3 5 |

| TABLE E2: | If the number of adults is: | 1 2 3 4 5 6+ |
| | Then select adult number: | 1 2 3 4 5 5 |

| TABLE F: | If the number of adults is: | 1 2 3 4 5 6+ |
| | Then select adult number: | 1 2 3 4 5 6 |

Figure 5.6. Kish Tables Used in Selecting a Designated Respondent in a Household

NOTE: There are 8 unique tables. Tables B1, B2, E1, and E2 are each assigned to 1/12, or 8.3%, of the households in the sample. Tables A, C, D, and F are each assigned to 1/6, or 16.6%, of the households in the sample. For practical reasons, then, sets of 12 tables are created for assignment to households in sequence, where Tables A, C, D, and F are duplicated and interspersed into the original set of 8 tables. See Kish (1965, pp. 396-401).

TROLDAHL-CARTER-BRYANT TABLES

When an interviewer uses the **Troldahl-Carter-Bryant tables,** he or she does not necessarily make a complete list of all adult residents. Instead, the interviewer asks how many persons there are in the household of a certain age (for example, 18 and over) and how many of these persons are of a certain gender (usually male). The interviewer then consults the preassigned TCB table to determine who is the designated respondent. Figure 5.7 summarizes the Troldahl-Carter-Bryant selection process. Research suggests that the TCB procedure underrepresents males in telephone surveys because they are less likely to be at home when interviewers call, and that in households with three or more adults of the same sex, the oldest and youngest persons may be overrepresented, and persons in between may be underrepresented, in the final sample.

Troldahl-Carter-Bryant (TCB) Tables	Questions:	(1) How many persons *xx* years or older live in your household, including yourself? (2) How many of these are women?		
(Ask how many persons live in the household, how many of them are women, and then use TCB selection charts.)	Row B	Col. A		
	Number of Women in Household	Number of Adults in Household		
		1	2	3	4 or more
	0	man	youngest man	youngest man	oldest man
	1	woman	woman	oldest man	woman
	2		oldest woman	man	oldest man
	3			youngest woman	man or oldest man
	4 or more				oldest woman

Note: The intersection of Col. A and Row B determines the sex and relative age of the respondent to be interviewed.

Figure 5.7. Troldahl-Carter-Bryant Tables

SOURCE: Adapted from Aday (1996, p. 131, Fig. 6.3, "Procedures for selecting the respondent—selection tables").

HAGAN AND COLLIER METHOD

The **Hagan and Collier method** simplifies selection of the designated respondent further. When using this method, the interviewer simply asks to speak with the youngest or oldest adult male in the household. If no male is there, the interviewer asks to speak to the corresponding female (that is, if the selection rule was "youngest male," then the interviewer asks to speak to the youngest female). As Aday (1997) has observed, "There are . . . some ambiguities in directly implementing the Hagan and Collier approach, and no extensive methodological research is yet available that compares this to other methods of respondent selection" (p. 129).

LAST/NEXT BIRTHDAY METHOD

The method of using the last or next birthday within a household to select a respondent has become increasingly popular over the past decade. Here the interviewer asks the person who answers the phone, "In order to determine whom to interview, could you please tell me, of adults [xx] years of age or older currently living in your household, who had the most recent [has the next] birthday? I don't mean who is the youngest, just who had a birthday last [who has a birthday next]."

Research has generally shown that the **last/next birthday method** is valid, but its validity is dependent on whether the person answering the phone accurately knows the birth dates of all the adults in the household.

COMPARISON OF THE FOUR METHODS

Of the four methods discussed above, only the Kish table procedure requires the surveyor to create a roster of all adults in the household. To use Troldahl-Carter-Bryant tables, the interviewer must find out the total number of adults in the household and their gender distribution, but he or she does not have to match the age and gender for each adult. The

Hagan and Collier and last/next birthday methods do not even find out how many adults live in the household or what the gender distribution is. Unless the surveyor includes questions to gather additional information about the household composition later in the interview, neither of the last two methods provides information the surveyor can use to estimate the probability that a given household resident will be selected. As a result, the surveyor cannot estimate whether the resultant sample accurately represents the population of adults in the area of study.

Checklist for Selecting the Respondent

✓ Do you need to interview a particular person or type of person?

✓ Is the unit of analysis a household or an individual?

✓ Do you need to create a roster of all of the adult residents of a household?

✓ Will you get the data you need if you interview the person who answers the phone, or do you need to get information from other people in a household or other setting?

✓ Which procedure will you use to select designated respondents?

Reporting Response Rates

Many surveyors do not know how to give complete sample reports and calculate response rates. In 2000, the American Association for Public Opinion Research published guidelines for reporting response rates for in-person surveys, telephone surveys, and mail surveys; we strongly recommend that all surveyors familiarize themselves with and follow these guidelines. (For publication information on these guidelines, see the "References and Suggested Readings" section at the end of this book.)

Two of the biggest problems in reports on telephone surveys is that surveyors often do not provide information about the number of callbacks they used in their studies or about the phone numbers they never successfully contacted. Figure 5.8, which comes from our report on the Loma Prieta study, demonstrates some of the things that surveyors should report about their samples. Remember that the Loma Prieta study was conducted using paper-and-pencil methods. We purchased a list-assisted RDD sample from GENESYS. Because we wanted to make sure that we had enough respondents in the areas where the heaviest shaking occurred, the sample of phone numbers was prestratified, and households within the San Francisco/Oakland area and the Santa Cruz area were oversampled.

As Figure 5.8 shows, the sample frame consisted of 270 numbers drawn for the San Francisco/Oakland strata, 270 numbers drawn for the Santa Cruz area, and 1,100 numbers drawn for the rest of the five-county area (San Francisco, Alameda, Santa Cruz, Santa Clara, and San Mateo Counties). The top section of the figure shows how phone numbers were distributed that were screened and found to be ineligible for the study. Notice that 218, or 19.8%, of the numbers in the five-county area were disconnected. A similar proportion were disconnected in the Santa Cruz area, but a substantially higher proportion were disconnected in the San Francisco/Oakland area. Going down the first column for the five-county area, we see that 159 numbers were not residences, the numbers had changed for 25 numbers, there was no qualified respondent at 17 numbers, 20 numbers reached fax machines, and 6 numbers reached computer modems. So, of the 1,100 numbers we started with, 445 numbers, or 40.5%, were contacted and found to be ineligible for the study. Note that about the same proportion of numbers were found ineligible in the Santa Cruz area, but that substantially

Outcome	Strata					
	Five County		San Francisco/Oakland		Santa Cruz	
	N	%	N	%	N	%
Telephone numbers generated	1,100	100.0	270	100.0	270	100.0
Disconnected	218	19.8	76	28.1	47	17.4
Nonresidential	159	14.5	60	22.2	46	17.0
Number changed	25	2.3	3	1.1	7	2.6
No qualified respondent	17	1.5	6	2.2	4	1.5
Fax machine	20	1.8	3	1.1	—	—
Modem	6	0.5	4	1.5	2	0.7
Total screened as eligible	445	40.5	152	56.3	106	39.3
Total usable	655	59.5	118	43.7	164	60.7
Refusal	116	17.7	14	11.9	25	15.2
Language barrier	27	4.1	5	4.2	3	1.8
Resident incapable	11	1.7	1	0.8	3	1.8
No answer (9+ attempts)	24	3.7	8	6.8	6	3.7
Answering machine (7+ attempts)	26	4.0	7	5.9	5	3.0
Completed interviews	451	68.9	83	70.3	122	74.4
Response rate (%)	68.9-74.5		70.3-80.6		74.4-79.7	
Probability household selected	5/10,000		5/10,000		31/10,000	
Weights	1.00		0.96		0.16	

Figure 5.8. Example Report on the Disposition of Numbers in a Disproportionately Stratified RDD Sample Frame, Loma Prieta Study

more numbers (56.3%) in the San Francisco/Oakland area were screened as ineligible.

These ineligible numbers do not "count" for purposes of calculating response rates. The loss of these numbers represents the loss that is associated with any sample frame that is created through random-digit dialing. Because this frame was selected with list-assistance, note that approximately half of the original numbers are now gone. Left are 655 numbers in the five-county area, 118 numbers in the San Francisco/Oakland area, and 164 numbers in the Santa Cruz area from which we hoped to obtain, respectively, 400, 100, and 100 interviews. These numbers (655, 118, 164) represent the basis for determining the denominator for later calculating response rates.

If we continue going down the first column, we find that 116 numbers, or 17.7% of the 655, refuse to be interviewed even after attempts at refusal conversion. A total of 27 households cannot be interviewed because we are interviewing in only English and Spanish, and 11 respondents are unable to be or incapable of being interviewed. It is the next two numbers that are of particular importance; these represent figures that surveyors frequently fail to consider in describing their samples. Within the five-county area, 24 phone numbers were never answered after more than nine callbacks spread out over a range of days and times, and 26 phone numbers were always answered by answering machines. When we finished our interviews, we did not know whether these numbers were or were not assigned to residences. Thus, we calculated the response rates twice, once assuming that these were eligible households that we failed to contact, and a second time assuming that none of these numbers represented eligible households. The first response rate calculation is 451/655, or 68.9%. The second is 451/(655 − 24 − 26), or 451/605, or 74.5%.

Notice that the response rates for the two oversampled strata are higher. This reflects the fact that we believed it was particularly important to try to get at least 100 interviews in each of these strata, and with the San Francisco/Oakland stratum, after screening for ineligibles, we started with only 118 numbers from which to obtain a sample of 100. As a result, we conducted more callbacks on these numbers in an attempt to get the desired 100 interviews. Because we ended up with only 83 interviews in the San Francisco/Oakland stratum, we could have elected to select another sample or replicate of phone numbers from that area, but we decided that 83 interviews were sufficient.

The response rates reported here are substantially higher than those often obtained by commercial companies. The difference is largely determined by the number of callbacks incorporated into the field procedures. The higher the number of callbacks, the higher the response rate, but also the higher the cost of the survey.

Comparing Surveys to Other Data Sets

It is always wise for surveyors to compare their telephone surveys to other available data sets that are thought to represent the same geographic area or population. The availability of U.S. Census data on the World Wide Web makes this relatively easy to do. The biggest problem surveyors have in making such comparisons is that the available census tables do not always report population characteristics in ways that are directly analogous to the surveyors' samples. Figure 5.9 displays a table from a report on the Loma Prieta study that compares the Loma Prieta sample to the 1990 U.S. Census. Remember that our sample was persons 18 and older who resided in households with telephones in five Bay Area counties. As the notes to the table indicate, data from the 1990 Census about gender and the percentage of persons over 44 years were reported for people 18 and older, but data on the percentage married were reported for persons 15 years and older, data on the percentage residing in California since 1985 or before were reported for persons 5 years and older, and data on the percentage employed were reported for persons 16 years and older. So the denominators for the 1990 Census data are not always directly comparable to the denominators in the Loma Prieta study.

Nonetheless, the 1990 Census data allow us to make some judgments about the validity and representativeness of our sample. Note first that 100% of our sample lived in households with telephones, whereas between 94% and

Characteristic	Loma Prieta Earthquake Study Sample Geographic Area of Subsamples			1990 Census Geographic Area of Subsamples		
	Five County	San Francisco/ Alameda	Santa Cruz/ Santa Clara	Five County	San Francisco/ Alameda	Santa Cruz/ Santa Clara
% Households with phones	100	100	100	98.5[1]	94.9[1]	98.0[1]
Group quarters: % Living in institutional group quarters[2]	0[3]	0[3]	0[3]	1.00[4]	0.21[4]	0.57[4]
% Living in non-institutional group quarters[5]	0[3]	0[3]	0[3]	1.40[4]	0.93[4]	1.13[4]
% Living in military quarters	0[3]	0[3]	0[3]	0.27[4]	0.44[4]	0[4]
% Female	56.1[3]	59.0[3]	52.5[3]	50.2[3]	49.3[3]	49.7[3]
% < 44 years old	46.0[3]	56.1[3]	56.6[3]	62.1[3]	58.9[3]	65.2[3]
% Non-Hispanic Caucasian	69.4[3]	57.3[3]	88.5[3]	65.6[6]	58.2[6]	85.9[6]
% Married	51.0[3]	20.5[3]	45.9[3]	47.4[7]	29.4[7]	49.8[7]
% Residing in CA since 1985 or before	94.7[3]	95.2[3]	95.9[3]	87.4[8]	78.7[8]	90.4[8]
% With H.S. diploma or	90.9[3]	90.4[3]	90.2[3]	81.4[3]	73.3[3]	84.2[3]

Figure 5.9. Example Comparing Respondents in the Loma Prieta Survey to the 1990 U.S. Census

SOURCE: Bourque and Russell (1994, p. 35).

	Loma Prieta Earthquake Study Sample Geographic Area of Subsamples			1990 Census Geographic Area of Subsamples		
Characteristic	Five County	San Francisco/ Alameda	Santa Cruz/ Santa Clara	Five County	San Francisco/ Alameda	Santa Cruz/ Santa Clara
equivalent						
% Employed	68.1[3]	69.9[3]	71.3[3]	65.9[9]	59.6[9]	68.5[9]
Per capita income	$15,000[4]	$16,208[4]	$15,625[4]	$16,492[4]	$22,108[4]	$14,997[4]
% Own residence	61.2[3]	27.7[3]	59.0[3]	55.6[1]	16.7[1]	58.3[1]
Total n: All people	451	83	122	4,050,592	230,733	98,750
Total n: Occupied households	451	83	122	1,482,234	111,050	37,478

Notes:
[1]Occupied housing units
[2]Includes people living in correctional facilities, nursing homes, psychiatric hospitals, juvenile facilities, schools/hospital for chronically ill or disabled
[3]People 18 years old
[4]All people
[5]Includes people living in rooming/boarding houses, group houses, halfway houses, communes, maternity homes, off-campus college quarters, college dorms, emergency shelters, religious quarters, and individuals encountered on the street
[6]Householders
[7]People 15 years old
[8]People 5 years old
[9]People 16 years old

Figure 5.9.   Continued
SOURCE: Bourque and Russell (1994, p. 35).

98.5% of the population lived in households with telephones. Immediately, we see that between 1% and 3% of the population, depending on the stratum, could not be in our study because they lived in institutional or noninstitutional group quarters or in military quarters. The population 18 and over was almost equally divided between males and females in 1990, but our sample was disproportionately female. This is typical in all surveys. To assess whether we have differentially more females in our survey than others do, we might want to compare our gender distribution with that obtained in other studies conducted in the Bay Area or California during the same period.

Our sample tended to be older than the population in general, which is also typical for surveys, but the ethnic distribution, when we look only at the proportion of non-Hispanic Caucasian, was quite similar to the overall population. More of our respondents lived in California before 1985, more had high school diplomas, and more owned their own residences, but the proportions of married and employed and the per capita income in the sample were quite similar to the population as a whole.

Respondents in telephone surveys, like those in all surveys, tend to be older, more affluent, and less transient than the general population. Those who participated in the Loma Prieta and Northridge studies are no exception. But by comparing the characteristics of our sample with those of the population, we can estimate the extent to which our sample under- and overrepresents certain kinds of people and qualify our findings accordingly.

Notes

1. Most software programs used for generating random numbers will allow the researcher to specify the size of the population from which the sample is being drawn. This increases the efficiency of the sample selection process because the program selects only random numbers that can actually be used. In our example using UCLA undergraduates, we would specify the size of the population to be 25,000, and the program would select 500 random numbers between 1 and 25,000.

2. Disabled students represented 5.3% (1,324/25,000) of the total undergraduate student population, and nondisabled students represented 94.7% (23,676/25,000). So, $.947X = 250$, where X = the total sample. To solve for X, $250/.947 = 263.99$, which is the adjusted size of the sample with the proportions of disabled and nondisabled reweighted to their appropriate proportions in the sample. Then, 13.99 students, or 5.3% of the adjusted sample, are dis-

abled, and the data collected from 250 disabled students are weighted by 13.99/250, or .056.

3. The active area codes and prefixes for Los Angeles County are correct in this example, but we created the hypothetical list of active banks of numbers.

4. In this example, we assume that the surveyor knows all the active banks of numbers before he or she starts. In fact, surveyors often do not know either the number of active banks or the number of active numbers within a bank. In such cases, they must estimate the number of numbers they will have to call before reaching a household. When surveyors identify large numbers of inactive numbers within banks, they should call the appropriate telephone companies to try to find out the assignment status of numbers. Unfortunately, telephone companies in Los Angeles frequently do not provide such information.

5. There are 8 unique selection tables and 4 of them are repeated, to yield a total of 12 selection tables (see Engelhart, n.d.; Kish, 1965, pp. 398-401).

6 Data Collection and Data Reduction

In this chapter, we explain how surveyors should go about recruiting the people who will conduct the interviews and training them for the task of interviewing. We discuss the skills and personality traits of good interviewers and some techniques of interviewing, and we address how survey researchers should monitor and supervise interviewers. We also discuss how surveyors can maintain quality control over the data collection while keeping an eye on their budgets and time schedules. We then address the topic of how interviews are transformed into data through the processes of editing, coding, data cleaning, and data entry. We conclude the chapter with a discussion of how surveyors can estimate the costs of telephone surveys.

Interviewers

RECRUITING INTERVIEWERS

Interviewers play one of the most important roles in survey research. No matter how much attention you have paid to the planning and design of your survey, the value of the final product is dependent on the attention you pay to the selection and proper training of interviewers. Furthermore, the overall length of the data collection period and the efficiency and economy of the interview process are, in large part, dependent on interviewer quality.

You can recruit interviewers in many ways, including through newspaper advertisements; through postings at local colleges and universities, community-based organizations, churches, and temporary employment agencies; through word of mouth among current employees and colleagues; and through listings with human resources development agencies. When recruiting bilingual interviewers, you should utilize the resources found within the appropriate linguistic communities; for example, you might place job ads in newspapers published in the languages sought, contact community agencies that serve the linguistic populations in which you are interested, and distribute notices among the language departments and foreign student organizations of local schools.

If you do not plan to conduct surveys on an ongoing, routine basis, you do not need to establish sources that will provide you with potential candidates over a long period. One-time-only or very occasional surveys are often conducted with the personnel at hand, such as in-house office staff. In some such cases, if the budget allocated to the project can afford it, a few temporary workers will be hired to conduct the interviews. Regardless of the source, you should always screen the potential pool of interviewers for individuals who have the characteristics most highly associated with good interviewing.

CHARACTERISTICS OF GOOD INTERVIEWERS

A successful interviewer is a person who likes people and is genuinely interested in others. He or she is outgoing without being overwhelming or aggressive, engaging rather than intrusive. At first contact, this individual reveals a warm and friendly personality and, especially important for a telephone interviewer, a welcoming, pleasant speaking voice. The successful interviewer has a speaking voice that is clear and modulated, neither too quiet nor too loud. He or she is able to enunciate clearly and to talk at a comfortable pace, neither sounding like an auctioneer nor taking overly long to complete a sentence. The successful interviewer's speaking style is free of "uhs," "ers," and "ums." In addition, the successful interviewer understands that a respondent's first impression of the interviewer sets the tone for all subsequent interactions, and so he or she is skilled at establishing rapport with potential respondents.

The interview process is a dynamic one, and the successful interviewer is able to think quickly and to make appropriate judgments based on excellent "people skills." A skilled interviewer can generally tell if a respondent is becoming annoyed, is losing interest, has misunderstood a question, is hesitant to respond to a question, or is otherwise not performing as desired. He or she can sense how the respondent is reacting and take appropriate steps to remedy the situation in a satisfactory way—that is, in a way that prevents the respondent from terminating the interview and also guarantees that the information collected is not biased or untrue.

Interviewers must also be able to read well, to read aloud well, to spell correctly, and to write legibly in any languages in which they will be interviewing. If you plan to hire bilingual interviewers, you must have as part of your project team an individual who if fully bilingual in English and the desired other language who can test the applicants for their reading, writing, and speaking abilities in both languages. You should not operate on the assumption that bilingual individuals are fully capable of interviewing in their first or second language.

To be able to read aloud well, an individual needs a broad vocabulary; an interviewer should be able to read aloud smoothly, without having to sound out the words as he or she goes along. Although interviewers will gain experience at reading the questionnaire aloud in training, and increased familiarity with the questions they will be administering will make their reading smoother, some individuals are simply unable to read aloud smoothly even with repeated practice. If your research involves concepts with which your interviewers may not be familiar, or if the questionnaire includes words to which they may not have been exposed previously, you should have trainers rehearse with the interviewers before they begin to interview to be sure they can explain any needed concepts to respondents and that they can pronounce all the words correctly.

It is also extremely important that interviewers be able to write legibly. The data collection process does not end at the completion of an interview. Completed questionnaires must be edited, perhaps coded, and the data entered into a data file. If an interviewer's handwriting is not legible, you may lose data. If you are conducting your survey using computer-assisted telephone interviewing, you would be wise to look for interviewers who, in addition to all the characteristics noted above, are skilled in both typing and the use of a 10-key pad.

RECRUITING TELEPHONE INTERVIEWERS

Before you can plan your approach to recruiting interviewers, you must determine how many you will need. To do that, you must begin by determining the number of completed interviews you require and the desired length of the field period, or the amount of time you have in which to collect the data. Next, you must estimate how much time it will take to identify each respondent; this includes dialing time, time for possible screening and/or random adult selection, and time for obtaining cooperation. To that number, add the time it will take to conduct each interview. You then also need to consider how many hours each day interviewing will take place, and on how many days in a week. With these elements, you can estimate how long it would take one interviewer to complete the entire study. For example, assume it will take 15 minutes to dial the number, screen the household, select the respondent, and gain his or her cooperation. Then assume that the interview itself will take, on average, 30 minutes. The average interview thus takes 45 minutes. To compensate for interviewer time paid that is nonproductive (such as rest breaks, supervisor evaluations, and assignment reviews), add 10 minutes to each interview, bringing the time required for each interview to 55 minutes. If your goal is to complete 500 interviews, you will need 27,500 minutes, or 458 hours, of interviewer time ([500 interviews × 55 minutes]/60 minutes per hour).

Say that your plan is to interview from 3:00 P.M. to 9:00 P.M. on weekdays and from 10:00 A.M. to 8:00 P.M. on weekends, equaling 50 interviewing hours per week. On this schedule, it will take about 9 1/2 weeks to complete the interviews, assuming the 458 interviewing hours required in the above example. You might hire two interviewers who would split the 50 hours a week of interviewing duties. Now, assume that your survey team decides to complete the interviewing in 5 weeks due to the demands of another deadline. To achieve this, both of your interviewers would need to work all the shifts—but this is clearly not possible. Under no circumstances should an interviewer work 7 days a week or put in 12-hour days. For such a shortened schedule, you would need to double the number of interviewers to four, so that all interviewers get days off and there are enough interviewers to cover two shifts on weekends.

You would be wise to recruit and train more than the exact number of interviewers you think you will need, because attrition rates are very high in interviewing. Many individuals find that they do not like this type of work and quit within a few days of starting to interview. Others simply do not perform as well as desired and need to be let go. Other unanticipated events may occur at any time during a study; interviewers may call in sick for one shift or more, or other situations may necessitate interviewers' leaving their positions. Sometimes, interviewers hired on a temporary basis are actively seeking other employment while working on a study, or they may have other competing interests or obligations. We often recruit and train twice as many individuals as we believe we will need (in the above example, we would train eight people). Another precaution: The more difficult the study, the higher the interviewer attrition rate. Difficult studies include those conducted with hard-to-reach populations and those that require an extremely high ratio of screening calls to eligible calls, that deal with particularly sensitive topics, or that require very long interviews.

When recruiting telephone interviewers, you need to be very clear as to the nature of the work. Telephone interviewing is not easy, and when inexperienced interviewers make their first attempts and get their first refusals, many decide that this is not a job they wish to pursue. Further, when the sample population is to be found in households, some of the most productive interviewing hours will be during the late afternoon, in the evening, and on weekends—periods when many people do not wish to work. Interviewers must be available to work evenings and weekends. By being candid about the nature of the work at the outset, you may reduce the attrition with which you ultimately will have to contend.

Among the points you should stress with potential interviewers is that a major portion of the job involves **cold calling** individuals—that is, calling people who are unaware of the study and whom the interviewer does not know and attempting to establish study eligibility by screening them and then interviewing them. Depending on the circumstances of the study, and when samples are developed from known lists, you can ameliorate the difficulty of cold calling somewhat by sending advance letters about the study to the addresses associated with the sampled telephone numbers.

But whether or not potential respondents have received advance notification, telephoning people you do not know and asking them to devote their time to participate in a survey that may or may not be of interest to them is a task few of us would relish.

RDD interviewing is probably the most difficult to accomplish of all telephone interview sampling methods. The task of dialing numbers is, in and of itself, frustrating. An interviewer's job is to complete interviews. If an interviewer is working with an RDD sample that has not been prescreened (that is, in which the random numbers have not been predialed to determine if they are assigned to working telephones and to categorize them as business numbers, households, group quarters, or other types of establishments), the dialing of numbers to find households can be tedious. The ratio of generated or created telephone numbers to eligible households varies considerably across geographic areas, ranging from a low of three randomly generated telephone numbers to find one eligible household to a high of six or more random numbers to find a household. Individuals who thrive on instant gratification, have little patience, and/or get bored easily do not make good telephone interviewers. Persistence is one of the most important attributes in a telephone interviewer.

ELITE TELEPHONE INTERVIEWS

"Elite" telephone interviews—interviews in which the respondents are individuals of high status or who have high levels of responsibility—are among the most difficult to do. Respondents in elite interviews may be the owners of businesses, top executives in corporations, elected officials, medical doctors, or other professionals. Not only do such individuals typically have very busy schedules, with little or no time to spare, they also are generally protected by "gatekeepers" such as secretaries or assistants whose responsibility it is to screen out unsolicited calls to their employers. If you are interested in conducting interviews with high-status individuals, you might send advance letters, but they will probably be intercepted by gatekeepers. If you can obtain e-mail addresses for the elite individuals you desire as respondents, you can send them advance notice electronically; for the present, at least, e-mail has a better chance than conventional mail of going directly to the addressee and, possibly, of being read.

Successful completion of an elite interview depends heavily on the skills of the interviewer, who must convince both the gatekeeper and the designated respondent to cooperate with the interview process. The interviewers hired for this type of study should have strong persuasive skills, should be able to think quickly and cleverly, and must not get discouraged easily. Interviewing elites requires self-confidence and poise; it is not a job for the shy, retiring type.

IN-PERSON VERSUS TELEPHONE INTERVIEWS

It is not uncommon to find that some interviewers prefer in-person interviewing and others prefer telephone contact. Some individuals interact best with others in person, whereas others are able to convey their personalities well vocally. Using strong verbal skills and good vocal tone, these individuals can convey an immediate sense of warmth and security over the telephone and are able to establish rapport with respondents within seconds. When you are recruiting telephone interviewers, you should include in your hiring decision the appeal of each candidate's voice and approach over the telephone.

In summary, then, the ideal telephone interviewer is available to work afternoons, evenings, and weekends. He or she has an engaging personality and pleasant speaking skills, is self-confident, and enjoys challenges. Above all, a good interviewer is persistent in working through his or her assignments and is patient with respondents.

Checklist for Recruiting Interviewers

✓ Choose sources from which to recruit.

✓ Determine the number of interviewers needed.

✓ Keep in mind the qualities of a successful interviewer:

- Likes people and is interested in others

- Is outgoing but not aggressive

- Has a warm, friendly personality

- Has a pleasant speaking voice and modulated speech

- Enunciates clearly and speaks at a moderate pace

- Speaks without hesitation

- Thinks quickly and makes good judgments

- Has good "people skills"

- Has the ability to sense other people's reactions

- Has the ability to read aloud well

- Has the ability to spell correctly and write legibly

- Possesses a broad vocabulary

✓ When interviewing candidates, be specific as to difficulty of the interviewing task.

✓ Select individuals who are available and willing to work during desired interviewing times.

✓ Screen for patience, persistence, self-confidence, and poise.

✓ Conduct evaluations of candidates' reading ability and writing legibility.

Training Interviewers

Many people assume that survey interviewing is easy. Most people participate in conversations daily and are able to ask questions and listen to the answers, so they think, How hard can interviewing be, especially if your half of the conversation is already written for you in the form of a standardized questionnaire? This perception is the downfall of many surveyors, especially those who believe that individuals who apply for jobs as study interviewers will be successful at interviewing because they have conducted interviews as part of their jobs (as social workers, doctors, nurses, employment interviewers, or the like). Surveyors who make this assumption are mistaken. Any individual who has not had prior experience in survey interviewing requires proper training in the skills demanded of a survey interviewer. The quality of interviewer training is reflected in the quality of the data collected.

For practical purposes, we recommend that surveyors train interviewers in groups of no more than 20. If you must train more than one group, you should plan out and document your training program carefully to ensure that all trainees are exposed to the same information and materials. If your different groups of interviewer trainees are not told the same things, or if discussions arise in one training group but not in others, the interviewers trained in the different groups will essentially be working on different studies. You must be certain that all interviewers receive the same information and instructions. If the training is very complex or requires a number of different materials, you may want someone to assist you in training. You may also want to train your interviewers in groups even smaller than 20, so that you can be sure everyone is on the same page, using the same materials, and so on.

During interviewer training, you need to provide your trainees with a variety of study-related materials. First among these is a manual of interviewing practices and procedures, which you must create before training begins. This manual should cover all the basic skills required of interviewers as well as the procedures used in interviewing. Second, you need to provide trainees with a set of interviewer specifications—that is, instructions that are specific to your study and to the questionnaire. You should instruct the interviewers to use these specifications (which give information about the study's intent as well as detailed instructions on how to ask each question in the questionnaire) as a reference tool when they do not have easy access to the help of supervisory personnel. (We discuss the writing of interviewer specifications in some depth in Chapter 3.)

You also need to provide each trainee with a packet of all the basic study materials, including the following: a copy of the screening instrument, if one is used; a copy of the questionnaire; any reference materials the interviewer will need during interviewing; paper and pencil for note taking and recording; a copy of the call record sheet (see Figure 6.1); and contact information. If your project or the study topic has received any recent exposure in the media that may be useful to the interviewers and will not contaminate the results in any way, you should provide information on this as well. Copies of newspaper or magazine articles or summaries of television and radio coverage can help to educate interviewers about the subject of the study and give them a sense of the survey's legitimacy. Such information can also sometimes help interviewers to convince respondents to participate.

The environment in which you conduct interviewer training should be large enough so that everyone is able to sit comfortably at a table or other work area; each trainee should have a sturdy, flat surface to write on. The room should be free of external noise and internal traffic. The lighting should be adequate for all trainees to be able to read comfortably. In addition, climate control is crucial; you do not want your trainees to fall asleep because it is too warm and stuffy or have trouble concentrating because they are trying to keep warm. Many organizations that train interviewers routinely provide trainees with coffee, tea, water,

Figure 6.1. Example of a Call Record Sheet

LOS ANGELES COUNTY SOCIAL SURVEY
CALL RECORD SHEET
Spring 2002

LABEL HERE:
1ST.INT. ID:_____   LOG:_____
2ND.INT. ID:_____   EDIT:_____
ENTRY:_____

CALL #	DAY	DATE	TIME	OUTCOME CODE	COMMENTS/ NOTES
1.					
2.					
3.					
4.					
5.					
6.					
7.					
8.					
9.					
10.					
11.					
12.					
13.					
14.					
15.					

OUTCOME CODES:

NO ANSWER 3.13
BUSINESS/NONRESIDENTIAL PH 4.51
BUSY SIGNAL 3.12
GROUP HOME/SHELTER/ETC.* 4.53
ANSWERING MACH 2.22
LANGUAGE PROBLEM* 2.33
FAX MACH 4.20
CALLBACK NEEDED* 3.21
CELL PHONE. 4.42
REFUSAL INFORMANT* 2.111
PAGER 4.44
REFUSAL RESPONDENT* 2.112
DISC/NONWORKING # 4.30
PARTIAL INTERVIEW (50%+) 1.2
TEMPORARILY OUT OF SRV 4.33
COMPLETED INTERVIEW 1.1
CHANGED OUT OF LA COUNTY 4.41
OTHER 5.0

*SPECIFY IN COMMENTS/NOTES SECTION.

snacks, and lunches; at a minimum, you should supply drinking water.

Depending on your resources, you may want to use slides, videos, or other visual aids during training. One effective method of teaching trainees how to record answers on the questionnaire is to demonstrate correct procedure for them on questionnaire pages projected using an overhead projector. You may also find it useful to show videos of interviewers screening households and conducting interviews. In some cases, you might use such aids to inform the trainees about the nature of the topic under study.

Even if you are using CATI as your data collection medium, you should supply each trainee with a paper version of the instrument. You should encourage trainees to use the paper version to make notes to themselves and to rehearse asking the questions. In addition, it is a good idea to have paper copies of the CATI instrument handy during interviewing, so that if the computer system should crash during a shift, interviewers will still be able to complete interviews. Also, occasionally a respondent will agree to be interviewed only at an unusual hour when the computer system is not up for interviewing.

For individuals who are new to paper-and-pencil interviewing, training ideally should last 3 days or more. It can take close to 2 days just to instruct trainees on basic screening and interviewing skills, such as how to introduce oneself and the study; how to determine if one has reached an eligible household, and, if so, how to select an appropriate respondent; how to build rapport with respondents; how to ask questions; how to answer respondents' questions; how to handle problem situations; how to keep respondents focused on the questions; and how to probe responses.

The use of CATI does not eliminate the need for in-depth interviewing training. In fact, for first-time interviewers, CATI training takes longer and is more extensive than the training needed for paper-and-pencil studies. In addition to interviewing skills and study-specific training, the interviewers must learn how to use the CATI software and how to deal with computer-related problem situations that may arise during the course of interviewing. All of the training materials mentioned above are just as important in training for CATI surveys as they are for training in paper-and-pencil studies. As we have noted, new paper-and-pencil interviewers ideally should receive at least 3 days of training; in contrast, CATI training typically takes a week or more.

CONTACTING ELIGIBLE RESPONDENTS

One of the most important parts of interviewer training involves teaching trainees how to contact eligible respondents. An interviewer's initial contact with a telephone number starts with his or her determining the status of the number called: Is it a working number, a busy signal, an answering machine, a cell phone, a pager or fax number, a business or other institution, a telephone booth, or a nonresponse, or does an individual answer? If an individual answers, the interviewer must first verify the telephone number by asking the person who answered if the number reached is the number assigned. This rules out mistakes in dialing as well as technical problems in telephone line switching. Once the interviewer has confirmed that the telephone number he or she intended to dial is the number reached, the interviewer must identify him- or herself and the organization he or she is representing.

The interviewer should then inform the person who answered the phone that a survey is being conducted and that the call is not for solicitation purposes—that is, the interviewer has no intention of selling anything or of asking for any contributions. The interviewer should then explain the nature and purpose of the survey, describe briefly how this particular household came to be called, and assure the person who answered the phone of the confidential nature of the interview. At this point, the interviewer should determine whether the individual with whom he or she is speaking is 18 years of age or older. If the individual is a minor, the interviewer must ask to speak with an adult household member. If no adult is available, the interviewer should find out when an adult will be available and when would be a good time to call back. When the interviewer subsequently reaches an adult, he or she must reintroduce him- or herself and repeat the study introduction.

If your study involves interviewing individuals under the age of consent (that is, under 18 years of age), you will typically be required to employ an entirely different set of procedures. If any organization involved in your study receives funding from public entities or foundations, you will most likely have to submit a protocol to an institutional review board detailing the procedures that will be employed to obtain the interviews with minors. When respondents are minors, surveyors need to make sure that interviewers obtain parental consent to interview the desired respondents before they attempt to obtain the minors' assent.

If your interviewers will be contacting respondents who may not be American-born or who may have ethnic origins different from those of the interviewers, interviewer training must include some education in aspects of the relevant cultures, especially those that relate to customs of greeting and introductions between strangers. Interviewers need to understand that by using appropriate approaches, they can greatly enhance the possibility of obtaining interviews.

Once the interviewer has determined that the telephone number is correct, that the number belongs to a private household, and that an adult is providing the information, he or she can proceed, either to interview that person or to ask the appropriate screening questions needed to determine the person in the household who is eligible to be interviewed. If the survey is being conducted via CATI, the interviewer should mention that to the respondent to explain the typing sound he or she will hear in the background. An added benefit of this explanation is that respondents are sometimes more tolerant of gaps or hesitations in the interview when they understand that the interviewer is dealing with a computer. If a supervisor may be **monitoring** an interview as it is being conducted, the interviewer must inform the respondent of this possibility prior to commencing the interview. (To monitor an interviewer's work, an interviewing supervisor may listen in on an ongoing interview by means of a mute telephone connection to the interviewer's phone line. This is often referred to as *live monitoring*.)

The most important point to emphasize at this phase of interviewer training is that the interviewer's first cold contact with a potential respondent is critical. You must prepare the interviewers to deal with the wide variety of questions respondents will ask, such as, "Who are you?" "What are you selling?" "What's this for?" "What good will this do me?" "How will you use this information?" "Who is paying for this research?" This is where interviewers must be their most engaging, reassuring, friendly, and knowledgeable. Potential respondents must understand who is calling and for what purpose. Finally, you must be sure your interviewers are trained in the art of assuring respondents either of their anonymity or of the confidentiality of the information they provide. You should have your trainees rehearse the initial contact phase with supervisors until they are relatively unflappable.

ESTABLISHING RAPPORT
AND CONDUCTING THE INTERVIEW

You should teach your interviewer trainees that developing rapport with a respondent means establishing a friendly, comfortable dialogue; it does not mean letting a respondent talk one's ear off. Interviewers should be taught to use non-committal responses (such as "I see," "Uh-huh," or "That's interesting") to volunteered personal information or opinions, so that respondents feel as if they are being heard. If a respondent starts to take the conversation off the subject or to elaborate too much, the interviewer should get the individual back on the subject by saying something like "We have questions later in the interview that address this. Let me continue now. I will get your response then so I don't miss any information," or "We can talk about this more at the end of the interview; right now I need to focus on the questions I must ask so that I don't lose my place or get confused about your answers. I want to make sure I conduct your interview correctly." The interviewer must never offer his or her own definitions, interpretations, opinions, or experiences, as this will bias the respondent's answers.

Good interviewing style includes reading each question from start to finish in an articulate, evenly paced manner. A good interviewer neither rushes through the reading nor drags it out. A good interviewer also reads each question carefully as it is printed on the questionnaire, placing emphasis only where the text calls for it and paying attention to the punctuation. When the interviewer reads the questions properly, the respondent can more easily tell when he or she is expected to respond. Sometimes a respondent will try to give an answer before the interviewer reaches the end of a question (often because the respondent thinks he or she knows what the question is going to be); when this happens, the interviewer should ask the respondent to wait until the interviewer has completed the reading of the question, because he or she has been instructed to read all questions completely.

Often, respondents who try to answer questions before they are fully asked are mistaken about what they are expecting the questions to be. For example, let's take a series of questions about household composition. The interviewer asks the first question, "How many people in total live in your household?" The respondent answers, "Six." The interviewer than asks, "How many of these people are age 65 or older?" and the respondent answers, "One." The next question is, "How many of the people in your household are between the ages of 18 and 64?" The respondent answers, "Two." As the interviewer starts the next question, "How many people in your household . . . ," the respondent says, "Three." The respondent is expecting to be asked how many people are under 18 years of age, but in fact that is not the question, as that piece of information can be ascertained deductively (that is, we know that there are six people in the household and that one is 65 or older and two are between the ages of 18 and 64, so three people must be under 18). The actual question was going to be "How many people in this household are employed for pay at least part-time or more?" If the interviewer were to accept the answer of "three" without completing the question, it would very possibly result in an overestimate of the number of employed people in the household.

If, after listening to an entire question, a respondent provides an answer that does not seem to make sense, the interviewer should read the entire question again, first saying something like, "I think I made a mistake, let me read that question again." This is especially important in CATI surveys, where every item needs a response before the computer will advance to the next question. If a respondent in a CATI survey provides an answer that is not included within the answer menu displayed on the screen or otherwise does not make sense, the interviewer must resolve the discrepancy before entering a response that will take him or her on to the next question.

If a respondent says that he or she does not know what a particular question means, or asks the interviewer to explain the meaning of a word or phrase in the question, the interviewer should read the relevant part of the question aloud to the respondent again and ask the respondent to answer to the best of his or her ability or understanding based on what he or she thinks the question means. The interviewer should never interpret or define anything for respondents. Unless the questionnaire specifically provides definitions for words, concepts, or ideas, the interviewer must tell respondents to provide their own personal meanings for any items about which they are unsure. For example, in answer to being asked, "Have you felt sad or blue most of the time for the past two weeks?" a respondent might ask, "What do you mean by 'sad or blue'?" The surveyor wants to know what the respondent's concept of "sad or blue" is, not the interviewer's definition. Figure 6.2 displays an example of how an interviewer should deal with a respondent's request for clarification of a question.

If a respondent gives an answer that needs further elaboration to make sense or to fit a category, the interviewer needs to probe for more information. Let's say there is a question that asks, "Do you drink bottled water?" with answer categories of yes or no, and the respondent answers "Sometimes." The interviewer should not assume that this answer means yes. Instead, he or she should repeat the question and include the answer categories: "Would you say you drink bottled water, yes or no?"

Respondents often try to give ranges in their answers. For example, to the question "How many times have you gone

---

Figure 6.2. How to Handle a Respondent's Request for
Clarification or Definitions

Q12. INTERVIEWER: The next questions are about your use of prescription drugs on your own. By "on your own," we mean either without a doctor's prescription, or in larger amounts than prescribed, or for a longer period than prescribed. With this definition in mind, did you ever use any drugs, such as sedatives, tranquilizers, painkillers, marijuana, cocaine, or heroin, on your own during the past 12 months?

RESPONDENT: Does that mean Advil? I use Advil all the time. Sometimes I take it a couple of times a day for pain. My doctor told me to take something like Advil if my arthritis was bad.

INTERVIEWER: We are talking here about your use of prescription drugs on your own. That is, taking prescription drugs without a prescription, in larger amounts, or for a longer period than prescribed. In the past 12 months, did you ever use sedatives, tranquilizers, or painkillers on your own, including marijuana, cocaine, or heroin?

RESPONDENT: I just take Advil for pain.

INTERVIEWER: So, would you say yes or no to the question?

RESPONDENT: No.

to the movies in the past month?" a respondent might answer, "Two or three times." Rather than leave it to the researcher to try to decide whether this answer should be coded as "2" or "3," the interviewer must obtain a specific figure by saying, "Would you say that you went closer to two times or closer to three times?" When the interviewer probes in this way, the decision is made on less arbitrary basis, and, more important, it is made by the respondent rather than the interviewer or the surveyor.

Whenever an interviewer uses a probe, he or she should note this fact on the questionnaire (usually by writing a capital P) along with an abbreviated form of the probe used. Figure 6.3 illustrates how an interviewer should mark the questionnaire to show the probes he or she used to obtain more precise answers to questions. (For more on how interviewers should report on the probes they use, see Figure 3.7 in Chapter 3.)

In most surveys conducted using CATI, interviewers do not make note of the probes they use. Although some CATI software allows surveyors to program their instruments to allow interviewers to make text notes in the file at each question, in practice this can be time-consuming and cumbersome.

When interviews will be conducted in any languages other than English, you must be sure that interviewer training includes sufficient education in the customs and cultures of the intended respondents. In many cultures, the very concept of conducting interviews is considered rude and/or intrusive. Similarly, in many cultures the kinds of questions typically asked in interviews touch on topics that are considered taboo to discuss. Such questions include those concerning income, age, and other sociodemographic characteristics. In some cultures, it is thought that if individuals make positive statements about the health and well-being of themselves or their family members, bad luck will ensue. Inexperienced interviewers who were raised in these cultures may complicate the picture further by assuming that individuals in their ethnic groups will not consent to be inter-

---

Figure 6.3. Using Probes to Obtain More Precise Answers

---

5. Do you drink bottled water?

> YES 1
>
> NO 2
>
> Respondent answer: "Sometimes."

> (P) Would you say you drink bottled water, yes or no?
>
> Respondent answer: "Yes, I do."

28. How many times have you gone to the movies in the past month?

> # TIMES IN PAST MONTH:_____
>
> Respondent answer: "Two or three."

> (P) Would you say that you went closer to 2 times or to 3 times?
>
> Respondent answer: "Three."

[Interviewer inserts "3" in answer blank for Question 28.]

---

viewed, or that, if they do, they will not answer many of the questions. This is simply not the case. Interviewers administer questionnaires to individuals of numerous ethnic origins every day, and they get responses to all types of questions. The keys to success in obtaining such data are the interviewer's own ability and confidence.

When you have reached a point during training where everyone is comfortable with the study materials and the instruction you have provided, you should proceed to demonstrate the techniques you have covered. You can do this several ways. For example, you might have one of the trainees attempt to screen and interview another trainee, using dummy forms created for this purpose, while the rest of the group watches. Or you might have a trainer demonstrate interviewing techniques to the group by administering the questionnaire to a trainee or to another individual who has been trained to act like a respondent. If you use someone who is trained to act like a respondent, you should provide him or her with a script for the interview such as the one displayed in Figure 6.4. This script should purposely includes confusing responses, some questions for the "respondent" to ask the interviewer, and other problem situations, so that you can get an idea how the trainee interviewer will handle him- or herself in such a situation.

Trainers differ in how they prefer to handle questions from interviewing trainees that arise during training. Some like to stop and handle questions as they come up, lest they be forgotten later on. This is an acceptable method, provid-

---

Figure 6.4.   Example of a Training Script

---

40. How long ago did you last speak to or communicate with your ex-partner? Was it:

   Within the past week, ...5

   Within the past month, ...4

   Within the past 3 months, ...3

   Between 3 and 6 months ago, or 2

   More than 6 months ago? .SKIP TO Q42 . . .1

RESPONSE: Well, I talked to him on the phone about a month ago, but my daughter got a letter from him last week.

INTERVIEWER SHOULD REPEAT: How long ago did you last speak to or communicate with your ex-partner?

RESPONSE: About a month ago.

INTERVIEWER SHOULD PROBE "ABOUT A MONTH AGO" BY REREADING THE TIME RESPONSE CATE-GORIES.

RESPONSE: Actually, we haven't talked in 3 weeks.

41. How often, if ever, did you and your ex-partner discuss (CHILD) during the last 6 months? Was it:

Never, ...0
Less than once a month, ...1
About once a month, ...2
2 or 3 times a month, ...3
About once a week, ...4
More than once a week, or 5
Daily? 6

RESPONSE: We talk about her every week. About how she is doing in school, what her mood is like, her health, things like that.

INTERVIEWER SHOULD COME BACK: I think I made a mistake on the last question I asked. Let me check with you again. . . . . How long ago did you last speak or communicate with your ex-partner?

RESPONSE: We usually talk on the phone every week, but my ex has been away on vacation so we haven't talked for one month.

ing the trainer is able to get back on focus quickly and does not allow the question-and-answer session to get out of control and take up too much time. Other trainers prefer to ask all trainees to hold their questions until the end of the session. Although this is more orderly than interrupting the flow of the training to take questions, trainees may never ask some important questions because they have forgotten them by the end of the session or are eager to leave when the session is over.

The next step in basic skills training is to have trainees conduct interviews with each other in round-robin fashion. In this exercise, the group of trainees is broken up into pairs and each pair practices interviewing, with one acting as the respondent and the other as the interviewer, while members of the training team observe and offer feedback. The questionnaire is marked off in sections, and at each new section, the trainees reverse roles. At intervals, the existing pairs of trainees are broken up and new pairs are formed; this presents each trainee with new challenges and helps to make the experience more realistic.

In CATI training, the trainees' first exercise should be to practice going through the instrument, entering their own answers or using a preanswered form, so that they can become acquainted with the programming and how the branching and item entry work. They should repeat this exercise numerous times, entering a variety of answers to test all the possibilities, until they feel competent to handle actual interviews. Once they have reached this point, they can conduct mock interviews by calling supervisors on the telephone or by having "respondents" sit at their interviewing stations with them to answer questions.

At the end of the final training session, you should give the new interviewers an assignment: Have each go home and complete a practice interview with a friend or family member. Then have each interviewer return with his or her practice interview at an appointed time when you will be able to sit down individually with him or her and go over the interview, or "debrief" the interviewer. When you review the new interviewers' work, you should keep in mind that interviewing is probably a new skill for them, and it will take some time for them to become expert at it. Indicate their problems or mistakes in a constructive manner, giving suggestions as to how they might have better handled any problems or avoided errors. If any interviewers bring you practice interviews that have many errors or other problems, you will have to decide whether you want to invest more time and resources in their training or let those individuals go.

When you feel that an interviewer is prepared to handle an actual interview, have him or her start by conducting just one. After that first real interview, you (or a supervisor) should review the interviewer's work with him or her and ask about how the interview experience went, paying particular attention to the cold calling, the introduction of the study, the process of obtaining cooperation, and the administration of the questionnaire. Again, this session should be constructive and not accusatory. At this point, you should be able to determine which interviewers are ready to interview, which need a bit more training, and which you do not want to retain.

Checklist for Training Interviewers

✓ Train in groups no larger than 20.

✓ Create and distribute training documents, such as specifications, an interviewing manual, and study-specific references.

- Document the training program if multiple trainings are planned or needed.

- Assemble training materials and final screening and interviewing instruments (include note paper and pencils).

- Provide comfortable seating, sturdy writing surfaces, and refreshments.

- Use questionnaire pages projected by an overhead projector, slides, and/or videos to demonstrate interviewing techniques.

- Demonstrate interviewing procedures and provide group practice time.

- Have each interviewer complete a practice interview after training and provide one-on-one feedback and debriefing before releasing the actual sample for the study assignments.

Supervision, Monitoring, and Verification

When new interviewers start working, you will want to monitor or review all of their work, either personally or with the help of interviewing supervisors. As interviewers develop their skills and confidence and you feel secure in their abilities, the amount of monitoring or reviewing that you need to do will be reduced. Minimally, you should monitor or verify 10% of every interviewer's work throughout data collection. As we noted above, monitoring involves a supervisor's listening to all or part of an interview as it is being conducted. When performing **interview verification**, a field supervisor recalls a respondent to make sure the interviewer called, spoke to the individual he or she claimed to, took the amount of time required for the interview, and asked and recorded the questions properly (the supervisor does this by reconducting part or all of the interview). You should maintain a log for each interviewer in which to keep all information about the monitoring and reviews of his or her work; you should note in this log any mistakes the interviewer makes and any problems the interviewer encounters with the questionnaire, recorded by question number.

Every interviewer should be monitored during every interviewing session—that is, during every work shift. If you do not have the ability to monitor interviewers' telephone calls because all calls are not being made from a central facility, you (or a field supervisor) should review a portion of each interviewer's work as well as have the editors and/or coders keep a log of each interviewer's mistakes and any problems they encounter when working with completed interviews. A supervisor should review each interviewer's log with him or her on a regular basis.

You can also monitor an interviewer's work through interview verification. When the verification process turns up any interviewer errors, you should correct these errors on the interview schedule or questionnaire and review the identified discrepancies with the interviewer. Obviously, if you find that for any given interviewer the verification process reveals a substantial number of problems, you will need to release that individual. Sometimes interviewers pretend to interview people or call friends and interview them instead of the designated respondents. At other times, interviewers may intentionally or unintentionally reduce the number of questions they ask respondents and fill in the skipped questions themselves. Sometimes interviewers falsify dialing outcomes. It is surprising how many ways some interviewers can think of to falsify their work.

You must also monitor interviewers' individual rates of respondent refusals. If some interviewers report more refusals or have more interviews terminated than do others, you must attempt to help them isolate and overcome their problems. The two major contributors to poor response rates and poor sample representativeness are refusals and never-answered telephone numbers. An interviewer's ability to overcome refusal attempts has a strong influence on response rates.

Within a week or two after training is complete and interviewers are in the field, you can identify the better interviewers. They are the ones who achieve the highest response rates, complete the most interviews, and need the least correction, and for whom verification calls result in few or no discrepancies. You should use these interviewers to handle special tasks, such as refusal conversions, attempts to complete partial interviews, or calls to respondents who have not refused but may require special handling. Interviewers who are skilled at these tasks are the individuals who often go on to become trainers or field interviewing supervisors in survey research operations.

EDITING COMPLETED INTERVIEWS

Even when you have made sure that the interviewing has been closely supervised throughout the data collection process, all completed questionnaires should go through one final editing process. In this process, an editor checks to be sure that each question that should have been asked has been answered completely, and that the answer given satisfies the question asked. The editor also checks to be sure that ranges have not been given as answers where they should not have been, and that the interviewer has marked only the answer categories provided for closed-ended questions, unless residual "other" options are provided. The editor also makes sure that answers to open-ended questions are recorded completely and that they fully answer the questions, so that a reader does not have to guess at what the respondent meant. In addition, the editor checks to be sure the interviewer has made appropriate notes on the questionnaire at any point where he or she has used probing to obtain elaboration of any answers. The editor must also check to make sure that the interviewer has followed all skip or branching instructions correctly. After editing is complete, the interview can be forwarded for coding and data entry.

Administration of Data Collection

During the data collection period, you may find that some interviewers require some review or retraining. If you notice that some individuals report high refusal rates, consistently make routine types of errors, do not probe adequately, or have other types of problems, you should conduct a short retraining session to provide in-depth instruction and problem solving for the identified issues.

As we have noted, you must supervise and monitor the interviewing process throughout the data collection period. This includes keeping track of the sample, monitoring the quality of the interviews, monitoring the progress of the sample outcome, establishing schedules, and keeping track of the budget and the time schedule. At the same time, you need to attend to any personnel problems that may arise with the interviewers. One problem to watch for is shift fatigue, or interviewer burnout. On occasion, interviewers will ask to work longer shifts, or to work more days than they are scheduled for. We recommend that you try to avoid having any interviewer spend more than 6 hours a day interviewing.

Interviewing is a very demanding job. Interviewers must do a considerable amount of talking while maintaining an amiable demeanor. Respondents can be difficult to deal with; they may be surly or, conversely, they may want to talk too much about irrelevant issues. Some may require considerable hand-holding in the form of repetition of questions and/or response categories in order to answer questions. When interviewers are tired, they do not respond as well to potential respondents, and this leads to more interview refusals and terminations and a reduced overall quality of work. Tired interviewers may pay less attention to detail and may overlook inconsistencies in answers. Generally speaking, whatever kind of work people do, they are less attentive to it as the work shift progresses; interviewing is no exception.

The number of days an interviewer works in a week is another consideration. We believe that interviewing is too demanding a task for anyone to do for 7 consecutive days. It is best if you can schedule your interviewers so that each works no more than 3 or 4 days in a row before having a day off. If you are conducting a household or population survey, you will no doubt need to have interviewers working every day of the week. You will need to have enough interviewers so that you can stagger their shifts across the 7-day schedule.

CALL SCHEDULING

The most productive calling times for telephone surveys are in the late afternoon and early evening hours and on weekends. The two exceptions are when interviews are being conducted with an elite or institutional sample (such respondents may be available only during traditional work hours— that is, early morning through late afternoon) and at the beginning of a study using an RDD sample, when unusable numbers (such as numbers that are not in service or disconnected or that are assigned to businesses) are being eliminated. Residents in urban households are more likely than residents in rural households to be working away from the home, so interviewers are less likely to find someone at home in urban households during the day. Generally, the best calling times are from 3:00 P.M. to 9:00 P.M., with the last dialing starting about 8:00 P.M., so that an interview started around 8:00 can be completed by 9:00. On Saturdays, dialing can start at 9:00 A.M. and continue until approximately 8:00 P.M. On Sundays it is best to begin dialing no earlier than 10:00 A.M.

You may find that you need to alter calling times and days depending on the type of population you are interviewing. For example, when interviewing households, it may be less productive to call during holiday seasons, on the nights or weekends of major sporting events such as the Super Bowl, or during the Academy Awards broadcast or other heavily viewed television events. When your interviewing involves a national sample that crosses time zones, you need to adapt your start and stop times to the time zones you are calling.

Most CATI software systems provide call-scheduling modules that can be set to the calling times desired. For a national sample, for example, the scheduler can be programmed so that time zone differences are taken into account based on the area codes of the telephone numbers before they are released for calling.

CALLING FACILITY

When your interviewers are placing calls from a centrally located facility (as is almost always the case in CATI studies), it is important that you provide a comfortable and congenial working environment. The interviewing facility should have proper ventilation and good lighting, and the work area should be kept at a comfortable temperature. There should be an adequate amount of work space and proper ergonomic seating for each interviewer.

To keep each shift progressing in an orderly fashion, it is best to stagger interviewers' breaks and mealtimes so that everyone does not leave the facility at once. You should provide an area apart from the interviewing stations where interviewers can go to rest and have something to eat and drink. You should not allow interviewers to bring any food or drink, aside from water, to their interviewing stations. Interviewers who are eating and/or drinking while they are working are likely to spill liquids or food on their work materials. Further, you do not want to risk an interviewer making contact with a respondent when his or her mouth is full of food.

Checklist for Interviewing

✓ Monitor and review interviewers' work.

✓ Maintain an interviewer performance log for each interviewer and review the log with the interviewer regularly.

✓ Be alert for consistent errors, high refusal rates, and inadequate probing.

✓ Establish quality-control procedures.

✓ Monitor the progress of the sample outcome.

✓ Keep an eye on costs and the duration of data collection.

✓ Arrange staggered shifts for individual interviewers to avoid interviewer fatigue.

✓ Schedule calling times to suit the sample area and anticipated respondent availability and to maximize exposure.

✓ Avoid calling during times with competing events such as holidays and major sports events.

✓ Provide a break area where interviewers can have refreshments.

✓ Keep the interviewing area properly ventilated, well lighted, and at a comfortable temperature.

The Data Reduction Process

When your interviews have been collected by paper-and-pencil method (rather than by a computer-assisted method such as CATI) and you have not designed the questionnaire or answer sheet to be optically scanned, your next challenge is to reduce the data collected in the interviews into quantifiable data in a **machine-readable** format. This is accomplished by **data reduction**, or coding and data entry.

Presumably, at the time you developed the questionnaire you had a plan for processing and analyzing the data once they were collected. You may have precoded your questionnaire to the specific software you planned to use for statistical analysis. (There are numerous statistical software packages on the market. If your analysis is relatively straightforward, you may already have a program included in your office software that can provide numeric counts, calculate percentages, and perform simple data sorts.)

Before you can undertake data reduction, you must create a codebook—that is, a set of standardized instructions stating how each piece of information or datum is encoded in the data set. In Chapter 3, we suggested that the question-naire itself can provide the basis for the codebook. Even if the questionnaire you used to collect the data included only closed-ended questions, you must, at minimum, create codes for all questions that will account for missing information, refused answers, and "don't know" responses. You should use the same codes throughout the coding process (for exam-ple, you might use 8, 98, 998, or some other iteration of 8, as appropriate, to code "don't know" for each question in the questionnaire). You must note in the codebook all the codes you use.

You must also include in the codebook the **code frames** you have created after content analyzing any answers to open-ended questions and "other, specify" responses. Today, with the proliferation of personal computers and the ability to store verbatim data in machine-readable form, you do not have to content analyze the responses to open-ended ques-tions and "other, specify" responses and convert them into numeric codes immediately. Some surveyors prefer to wait and code the verbal data when they are getting ready to ana-lyze that particular part of the data set.

For questions requiring numeric answers, the codebook must show the range of acceptable numbers; that is, it must show the codes used for qualified responses as well as those that would be accepted for "refused," "don't know," and no answer. A complete codebook should provide an answer for any question that may arise during coding.

After questionnaires are coded, a coding supervisor should spot-check the coders' work for accuracy. As an added precaution, some surveyors want reliability coding per-formed on open-ended questions. This requires that two coders independently code the same open-ended responses, compare their results, and resolve discrepancies.

Data entry is the final step in the data reduction process. During data entry, the information from the coded question-naire is entered into a software package that will store the data in a file for subsequent analysis. Like all the other steps in the survey process, data entry should be subjected to verification procedures. You can verify the data entry by having some or all of the data from a questionnaire entered a second time and then comparing the two data files for discrepancies. If you find any discrepancies, you must go back to the original questionnaire to determine the correct number or numbers and then correct the data file accordingly. Some surveyors insist on 100% **verification of the data**, whereas others are happy with as little as 10%. At the very least, you should have 100% verification of the identification number assigned to each unique case. If you need to refer back to an interview at any time, you need to be sure that you have the correct questionnaire; the identification number provides the link between the machine-readable data set and the interview.

Estimating Costs

Before you undertake a telephone interview survey, you will undoubtedly need to estimate the costs your proposed project will incur. In this section, we discuss two possible scenarios. In the first, we assume that your survey will be conducted by a professional survey research entity outside your organization and that the survey organization will do the following: provide consulting on the appropriate sampling approach to use, develop the sample, help you develop and design the questionnaire, and handle all aspects of the data collection and data reduction.

The first decision you must make when you set out to estimate costs is what your sample size will be; that is, how big a sample do you need to obtain the information you require? In order to make this determination, you need to have some estimate of the prevalence or proportion of the population you wish to study in comparison to the whole. For example, if you want to interview registered voters in your county from an RDD sample, and you know from your research at the county registrar's office that 50% of all households in the county have at least one registered voter, you know that, minimally, you will have to screen two households to find one eligible household.

The next step is to determine the approximate length, or duration, of the interview. Although you do not have a fully developed questionnaire at this point, you should have a good idea of the types of questions and how many questions you need to ask to meet the study's goals. You can develop an outline based on this information and use it to establish a rough estimate of interview length. If the cost to conduct the study you hope to conduct is more than your budget can meet, you will have to sacrifice sample size, questionnaire length, or both in order to carry out the study within your budget.

GETTING A COST ESTIMATE FROM A SURVEY ORGANIZATION

If you plan to have the survey conducted by a professional survey organization, you need to provide the organization's representative with your sample size and interview length information, along with any other specifications you wish to impose on the survey administration. Such specifications might include, but are not limited to, the number of callbacks you want interviewers to attempt for "no answer" outcomes, how you want refusal conversions to be handled, the extent of monitoring or verification you want performed, and the desired response rate and how you want that rate calculated. Given this information, a potential contractor should be able to provide you with an estimate of cost. You should seek proposals from several survey organizations and, ideally, choose the one that proposes the best design and methods for the most reasonable cost.

Survey organizations vary widely in the amount of detail they provide when costing a survey. Most will simply provide you with a bottom line of costs plus or minus 10%. Some will break the costs down into major subcategories such as sampling, questionnaire development, data collection, data reduction, and report writing. Very few will provide detailed costing for the elements or steps within each subcategory. Depending on the level of detail you wish, you can always ask for a breakdown of the estimate; some organizations will provide such breakdowns when asked.

There is a great disparity in the cost per interview between for-profit and nonprofit organizations and between market research and social science research contractors. Market research companies are nearly exclusively for-profit organizations. For an RDD telephone survey, the cost per completed interview may range from as low as $40 to as high as $400, depending on the organization. Many factors contribute to this disparity. Some commercial companies employ less educated, less experienced personnel, with interviewers, editors, and coders who work for minimum wage, whereas other companies employ more highly skilled and experienced professionals, including interviewers. Higher-level professional staff who work for nonprofit agencies, such as those operating out of public universities and research think tanks, typically have considerable experience and advanced college degrees; the interviewers and clerical-level employees working for these agencies typically have considerable experience and some college education or the equivalent. As is generally true for most occupations, the more skilled and experienced the worker, the better the quality of the product.

Survey companies, and the fees they charge, are also differentiated by the rigor with which they conduct research. Lower-cost companies may simply "burn" through telephone numbers (that is, immediately replace numbers that are not answered or that reach answering machines, instead of redialing those numbers) until they find someone who answers the telephone and interview that person immediately. Such companies do not worry about the representativeness of the sample or its potential lopsidedness in regard to demographics, nor are they concerned about the bias associated with interviewing only those individuals who are immediately ready, willing, and able.

Another cost-cutting technique that undermines the quality of the data is that of restricting sample selection to telephone directories. When only telephone directories are used, the sample is made up exclusively of households with listed telephone numbers. Obviously, in such a sample the household hit rate is higher than that in an RDD sample, but a significant portion of the population has no opportunity to participate in the study.

The differences mentioned above are not the only ones to be found between higher-cost and lower-cost survey contractors, but they are the most critical. Surveyors should always remember that if either the sample or the quality of the interviews is in doubt, the entire study is for naught.

With this in mind, we present below an overview of the costs a researcher might expect to be quoted if he or she were to commission a quality survey organization to conduct a study. For our example, the specification is to complete 1,000 telephone interviews with an RDD sample of randomly selected adult residents of households that will be representative of a highly urbanized county in the United States. Further, because a significant proportion of the population speaks only Spanish, the questionnaire requires translation into Spanish to facilitate bilingual interviewing. A general outline of the questions has been developed, and most of the questions will be closed-ended; however, there are four open-ended questions that will require content analysis and coding.

The survey organization is to conduct 15 pretest interviews in English and 15 in Spanish. The client will write the final report, but the contractor will perform data processing and provide some statistical consultation in data analysis.

The client's specifications further ask for an initial call to each telephone number sampled and released for calling and five callbacks to nonanswered numbers, answering machines, and busy signals. The client requests that refusal conversion attempts be made to refusals that seem to be amenable to recalling. After initial 100% verification of the work of all interviewers, coders, and data entry personnel, the client wants 10% verification of all further work. Finally, the client wants weekly sample reports and work progress reports.

Typically, a survey contractor assigns a project manager to each study. This individual is responsible for all aspects of the project, from beginning to end. The project manager coordinates all sampling, questionnaire design and development, and data collection and reduction, and produces a final report. In a cost estimate, the survey contractor usually shows the charge for this individual as a percentage of time rather than as an hourly pay rate. For example, the contractor plans that this study will take 4 months to complete, during which 50% of the project manager's time will be spent on this project. The project manager's annual billable salary is $75,000, so at 50% time for 4 months, this will cost $12,500. The project manager also most likely has an administrative assistant. Say that the assistant will spend 25% of his or her time on this project over the 4 months, and his or her salary is billable at $3,750 per month. At 25% time for 4 months, the assistant will cost $3,750. The total cost for project management is thus $16,250.

The sampling frame is the first nonmanagement cost to consider. The tasks the contractor will perform include identifying all area codes and prefixes that are within the county under study. Because the client wants a representative RDD sample of the county, the sampling technician can then proceed to design the sampling frame. It would be reasonable for a sampling technician to spend 12 hours on planning, design, documentation, and the estimation of final sample status and response rates, and for a sampling clerk to spend 8 hours obtaining the data on area codes and prefixes. The sampling technician then provides a programmer with the sampling specifications, and the programmer generates the sample in 4 hours of work. Assume that the sampling technician bills at $40 per hour, the clerk at $15 per hour, and the programmer at $30 per hour. Finally, there is a materials cost of $800 for the sample. This figure covers the cost of telephone number replacement, licensing, the production of assignment labels or call sheets that contain the telephone numbers, and miscellaneous supplies. Our example estimate will show a total sampling cost of $1,520.

The next costs to anticipate are those associated with questionnaire development and production. Depending on the nature of the survey organization, a project manager or questionnaire design specialist will work with the client on developing the questions, formatting the questions, and developing the overall pattern of the questionnaire. For the sake of our example, say that over the course of questionnaire development this person will spend 40 hours at $35 per hour, from initial design through final revisions. Typing the developing versions of the questionnaire and the interviewer specifications once they are completed requires the skills of an experienced word processing specialist at a billable hourly rate of $20. The word processing specialist will spend a total of 60 hours to produce drafts and final versions of all materials, for a total cost of $1,200.

Once the English-language materials are drafted and near finalization, the Spanish translations will be done. Typically, translators charge by the word. Although the rate per word varies with the qualifications of the translator, 18¢ per word is a good average cost. The questionnaire contains 5,763 words, so at 18¢ per word this comes to $1,037.34 for translation. The cost for word processing the Spanish version of the instrument will be $528 for a $22 per hour bilingual typist working 24 hours. Because the survey organization will be employing bilingual interviewers, the training manual and interviewer specifications need not be translated.

The last cost associated with questionnaire production is that for duplication of the questionnaires and training materials. If we assume that 20% of the RDD sample will be Spanish-only speakers, at least 100 Spanish-language questionnaires will be needed. In addition, extra copies will be required for training, for the contractor's files, for project files, and so on, so the print quantity is set at 150 copies. Using the same logic for the English-language version, the print quantity will be 450 copies. For the training materials, 20 copies of the training manual and 20 copies of the interviewing specifications will be printed. A call record/screening sheet is also needed for each telephone number to be dialed. The contractor's vendor has quoted $2,400 for all printing charges. The total cost for questionnaire development and production comes to $6,565.34.

Survey organizations do not always separate the costs for pretesting from data collection costs. In this case, however, the client has requested a separate itemization of the cost for the pretest. Because the volume of interviews in a pretest is small, the cost per interview is high, sometimes twice the final per interview cost. The questionnaire is typed as a final draft and copies are made. A few interviewers must be trained to the questionnaire, and a subsample of the RDD telephone sample should be used for obtaining the pretest interviews. The contractor quotes a cost of $175 per pretest interview. If 30 pretests are conducted, 15 in English and 15 in Spanish, the total cost for pretesting will be $5,250.

Next come the data collection costs. The contractor estimates that it will take one senior-level field supervisor and two junior-level field supervisors to handle the interviewers for this study. The billable rate for the senior staff is $25 per hour; for the junior staff, it is $20 per hour. Interviewer time is charged at a rate of $18 per hour. Each of the senior and junior supervisors will spend 40 hours preparing for and conducting the training, for a cost of $2,600, and it will take 10 interviewers 40 hours each to be prepared to begin interviewing, for a total of $7,200. Thus, the labor cost for training is $9,800.

Data collection is the next line item in the contractor's estimate. The charge for one senior and two junior supervisors is $17,500. The senior supervisor will work 25% time for 14 weeks, while one junior supervisor will work 75% time and the other one will work 50% time. Dialing, screening, interviewing, and verification are costed at 1,500 hours at $18 per hour, for a total of $27,000. Telephone expenses are shown to be $5,000. This amount covers phone toll costs plus the base cost of the instruments for the field period. Clerical assistance for record keeping and administrative duties for 14 weeks at 35% time at $18 per hour amounts to $3,528. The final item in this expense line is for materials and supplies at $1,000. The bottom line for data collection is $63,908.

Data reduction is the next line item in the budget. The cost for developing a codebook and programming a data entry instrument is $1,600. Coding is costed at $1,800 and data entry at $1,900. Supervision of the data reduction process is estimated at $1,200 with $500 in expenses. The total cost for setting up the coding and entry process and completing coding and data entry is $7,000.

The final estimate is for data processing and analysis. Programming costs for building a data file and processing the data are charged at $35 per hour for 48 hours, or $1,680. Consultation on statistical analysis is budgeted for 24 hours at $50 per hour, or $1,200. These costs add a final $2,880 to the estimate.

The total estimate for all line items amounts to $103,293.34. This includes all costs from design through data processing and statistical consultation. The contractor will provide the data runs or computer tables for analysis and some analytic assistance to guide the client in writing the report. Additionally, the contractor will provide a clean electronic data file for the client's future use. The average cost per completed interview in this example comes to approximately $167 per case. Figure 6.5 shows what the survey contractor's budget estimate for this study might look like.

COSTING A STUDY FOR IN-HOUSE ADMINISTRATION

Not all surveyors have the luxury of being able to contract out their survey work. To demonstrate how a surveyor might budget for in-house administration of a study, we present a hypothetical example of a small community social service organization (CSO) that is long on enthusiasm and short on funds. The leaders of the organization want to conduct a study to gather data that will help them to plan community programs that are effective and efficient. The CSO has individuals on staff with previous exposure to survey

PROJECT MANAGEMENT		
Manager	4 Months @ 50%	$12,500.00
Assistant	4 Months @ 25%	3,750.00
SAMPLE DEVELOPMENT		
Sampling Technician	12 Hrs. @ $40	480.00
Programmer	4 Hrs. @ $30	120.00
Clerical	8 Hrs. @ $15	120.00
Supplies		800.00
QUESTIONNAIRE PRODUCTION		
Specialist	40 Hrs. @ $35	1400.00
Word Process/English	60 Hrs. @ $20	1200.00
Translation	5,763 @ $18	1037.34
Word Process/Spanish	24 Hrs. @ $22	528.00
Print = 450 English/150 Spanish		
20 Manuals, 20 Specifications		
3,200 Call Record Sheets		2,400.00
PRETEST		
15 English/15 Spanish	30 @ $175.00	5,250.00
DATA COLLECTION		
Training		
Senior Supervisor	40 Hrs. @ $25	1,000.00
2 Junior Supervisors	80 Hrs. @ $20	1,600.00
Interviewers	10 @ 40 Hrs. @ $18	7,200.00
Interviewing		
Senior Supervisor	14 Weeks @ 25%	
Junior Supervisor	14 Weeks @ 75%	
Junior Supervisor	14 Weeks @ 50%	17,500.00
Dial/Screen/Interview/Verify	1,500 Hrs. @ $18	27,000.00
Telephone Expenses		5,000.00
Clerk	14 Weeks @ 35%	3,528.00
Materials and Supplies		1,000.00
DATA REDUCTION		
Codebook/Entry Programming		1,600.00
Code		1,800.00
Data Entry		1,900.00
Supervision		1,200.00
Expenses		500.00
DATA PROCESSING		
Programmer		1,680.00
Statistical Consultation		1,200.00
TOTAL STUDY COST		$103,293.34

Figure 6.5. Survey Organization Estimates of Costs

research from college classes and from their work in larger social service agencies. They have discussed the need for a survey and have found that the organization currently has on staff many of the design-level personnel needed. They decide to estimate what the CSO's out-of-pocket costs would be for the study they want to conduct, to determine whether it is feasible.

Their first step is to establish the number of interviews they need to obtain reliable figures for planning. Then they must determine the approximate length of the interview, both in pages and interviewing time, and estimate the number of telephone numbers that will need to be dialed to obtain this sample. They then must lay out the types of expenses involved in a telephone survey. These include two types of costs: those for expenses (that is, the material goods necessary to conduct the survey) and those for labor that must be expended for the study to be conducted. Expenses for a telephone survey may include the cost of purchasing a telephone sample, telephone charges, printing charges, the cost of incentives (if offered), the costs for any labor required to do tasks that are not covered by in-house staff, supplies, and postage.

A word of caution: The expenditures itemized below reflect approximate costs as of September 2002 and are based on a highly urban workforce center such as Los Angeles. Some of the costs noted may vary considerably across geographic regions; for example, the labor charges that are inherent in certain items will vary from location to location, as will the costs of some other items, owing to variations in the expense of doing business in different areas. In addition, prices on printing and paper generally decrease as the volume purchased increases. The dollar amounts presented here are meant as guidelines only; it is up to individual surveyors to find out the appropriate costs for these items in their own market areas.

Obtaining a Telephone Sample

For a telephone survey, the sample of numbers to dial is the initial requirement. This may or may not represent an out-of-pocket cost, depending on the nature of the study. If the plan is to interview a list sample of clients, the sample will most likely be available with minimal effort. In our example case, however, the objective is to interview households in a geographic area, so the CSO will have to go to an outside vendor to purchase the sample. Of course, the quantity of telephone numbers purchased will have a major bearing on the cost of the sample. The CSO staff members developing the study budget can determine how many numbers are required by first estimating the number of noninterview outcomes they expect. They should get some help with this task from the sampling organization (i.e., the company from which they are purchasing the phone numbers), which can provide them with data on the population sorted according to particular demographic specifications. The sampling organization will charge a setup or data processing fee for processing its data according to the specified criteria; this cost may be minor or may amount to several hundreds of dollars. Additionally, there is a cost for each individual telephone number purchased. Generally, the cost per number is 5¢ or more; pricing depends on the volume of numbers ordered and any services requested, such as prescreening for business or working phones.

Let's say that the CSO staffers' goal is to interview 500 households in the local community. They have identified all of the postal zip codes or all of the area codes and prefixes to be included in the sample, and the sampling company claims that the success rate for its samples is 1 household for every 2.5 numbers provided. This means that the researchers will need 1,250 telephone numbers to complete 500 interviews. However, they must also factor in disconnected telephone numbers, households that will refuse the interview, phones that are never answered, households in which no one speaks any of the languages in which they will be interviewing, and so forth. The CSO staffers determine that, based on their best estimate, they will need six telephone numbers to complete an interview with one household. Consequently, they need 3,000 telephone numbers. Assuming a per number price of 5¢, the total cost for the phone numbers is $150, and the sampling company's setup fee is $100. However, the sampling company requires a minimum order of $500, so, given that the sample will cost at least $500 anyway, the CSO staffers request the largest number of telephone numbers that this dollar amount will cover. They can use the extra numbers for pretesting, and they will have a safety margin in the event that they underestimated how many numbers they would need to complete each interview.

Duplicating the Survey Materials

Next, the CSO staffers must estimate the cost of printing copies of the training manuals, the interviewing specifications, the screening form, and the questionnaire. Their own organization will be unable to provide the volume of photocopying required, so the staffers must project a cost for having all of the study materials duplicated by an outside vendor. As we have noted, their goal is to complete 500 interviews. They will need extra copies of the questionnaire for training purposes and so that interviewers can keep copies of their own on which to make notes for themselves. The staffers will also want extra copies for their study files. Considering all this, they decide to order 600 copies of the questionnaire.

The CSO staffers estimate the length of their questionnaire at 20 pages. The charge for standard photocopying of single-sided pages is 4¢ per page, or 80¢ per copy of the questionnaire. The vendor charges an additional 10¢ per copy for collating the questionnaire pages and stapling them with a single staple in the upper left-hand corner; this brings the total cost of a copy of the questionnaire to 90¢. Thus, the cost for reproducing 600 questionnaires will be $540 plus any applicable sales tax.

Additionally, the study will need call record sheets and copies of the screening form that will be used to identify eligible households. The screening form will be 2 pages long, so each copy will cost 10¢ (the fee for collating and stapling is 2¢ per copy for this run, as the collating and stapling can be done by the machine as part of the copying process, due to the lower page volume). As we noted above, the interviewers will need to call 2,500 telephone numbers to complete 500 interviews. Therefore, the CSO staffers decide to order 2,600 copies of the screener so that they will have an ample supply; the total cost for these copies is $260. Each telephone number will also require a call record sheet, adding a single page of printing of 2,600 copies at 4¢ each, for a total of $104. They also need copies of interviewer training manuals (estimated to be 30 pages each) and interviewer specifications (estimated at 20 pages); they decide to have 40 copies of each of these printed, so this adds another $88 to the printing costs, bringing the total cost for printing all materials to $992.

Supplies and Expenses

Other operating costs that the CSO staffers must anticipate include those for supplies such as pencils, note paper, bottled drinking water and paper cups, tea and coffee, and any other refreshments for survey workers. They estimate these miscellaneous expenses to be $300.

The greatest nonlabor expense of any telephone survey may well be in telephone charges. Depending on the type of telephone service subscribed to and the local calling area (that is, the area one can dial into at no additional cost), these costs can be considerable. In Los Angeles, for example, any call made to a telephone number that is more than 12 miles from the originating number is charged as a toll call. Additionally, Los Angeles County is broken up into nine area codes, and calling from anywhere in the county to all other points in the county entails making long-distance or toll calls. In short, a call that is geographically "local" can cost as much as or more than a call placed to New York City, some 3,000 miles away. Because of the wide variability in rates among the many telephone carriers existing today, it is virtually impossible for us to offer a generalizable model for estimating the telephone costs associated with telephone interviewing.

Assuming that the CSO study we are using as an example—an RDD survey of 500 completed interviews—is conducted in Los Angeles County using standard telephone charges, the cost per completed interview might average $8, including all dialing and screening costs. Therefore, the total telephone costs, not considering the base monthly cost of the phones, would be $4,000.

Labor Costs

Generally, labor costs represent the largest part of any survey budget. Unless the surveyor can recruit volunteers to serve as interviewers or has access to in-house employees who will be made available to the project at no cost, the surveyor's budget estimate must include the cost of the labor required to complete the survey. The first labor cost that must be considered is the interviewers. In Los Angeles, pay rates are higher than they are in many other areas of the country. In our organization, we typically pay interviewers at least $9 per hour to compete with the local labor market for individuals who meet the criteria (discussed above) to be potential interviewers. If we are recruiting individuals who have special skills, such as being bilingual, we of course have to pay more. As a study progresses, we give hourly rate increases every few months to those interviewers who exhibit excellent skills, as shown in their low refusal rates, high rates for completed interviews, and generally high-caliber work. We may go as high as $14 per hour for such individuals. When budgeting, surveyors must remember to include in their estimates the costs associated with training interviewers prior to their becoming productive. In our CSO study example, the staffers estimate that they will need to train 10 interviewers for 2 full days at $9 per hour, which means the training costs for the interviewers alone will be $1,440.

The CSO staffers also must consider supervisory and monitoring costs. A few members of CSO's staff can perform supervisory functions at no out-of-pocket expense to the study, but they cannot cover all the time required, so additional personnel will be needed. Supervisory and monitoring tasks can be performed by the same individuals interchangeably. People who fill such roles typically earn $2 per hour more than beginning interviewers, so in this case the CSO staffers estimate the cost at $11 per hour. The three people hired to work as supervisors and monitors will help set up and conduct the interviewer training, spending 40 hours each on these tasks. This adds $1,320 to the study's training costs.

Ideally, supervisors and monitors should have considerable interviewing experience, and they should conduct some interviews for the study before interviewer training begins. If a surveyor hires individuals for supervisory positions who have no prior survey experience, he or she should make certain that they get some experience interviewing on the study before training begins.

Editors and coders generally are paid at the same rates as interviewers, and key data entry personnel usually earn about as much as interviewing supervisors or more, depending on their experience and local labor market rates. Surveyors do not usually need to hire experienced key entry operators, as individuals with good 10-key skills can adapt easily. The characteristics that surveyors should look for in coders and entry personnel are attention to detail, accuracy in working with numbers, and good deductive logic.

It is usually best to estimate labor costs for data collection by stages: dialing, screening, and interviewing. Once the surveyor has made these estimates, he or she can derive an estimate of supervisory and monitoring time. To estimate the labor costs of data collection, the staffers in our CSO example first estimate how much time it will take an interviewer to dial a telephone number, wait for a response, and record the outcome. They start by allowing 45 seconds for these three actions, which comes to 31.25 hours to dial each of 2,500 numbers once. Because humans are not automatons, however, they decide to pad this figure somewhat to account for paid break time, restroom trips, paid lunch hours, and the like. They settle on the conservative figure of one dialing per minute, or nearly 42 hours for initial dialing.

The CSO staffers assume that after an initial dialing, one-third of the telephone numbers will have been eliminated, either because an interview was conducted or the number was disconnected or was a business or other nonsample number, leaving 833 numbers to try again. On the next round of dialing, they assume that the interviewers will clear another 15%, or 125, of the numbers, this time primarily with interviews. Overall, they still need to allow for 833 dialings, or 14 hours of dialing time. They assume that on the third try, the remaining 708 numbers will take approximately 12 hours to dial, and approximately 600 numbers will then be left to dial. Because by this round of dialing the bad numbers will have been cleaned out and all that remain will be assumed household numbers, the researchers assume that the amount of time it takes to dial each successive round of remaining numbers will stay fairly constant, decreasing only by the number of completions achieved.

Typically, about one-half of the completions desired will be obtained after the third call to the sample numbers, with about 5% to 10% of the completion goal coming from each additional dialing. This, of course, assumes nonreplacement sampling. We have found that in our studies in the Los Angeles area, which is highly urbanized, we must make at least 6 callbacks after the initial call to reach a household, and more often than not, we need 15 or more calls to nonanswered numbers to complete a study. The CSO staffers decide to plan on an initial call and 6 follow-up calls, which means that 102 total hours will be spent in dialing. At $9 per hour, this results in a dialing time cost of $918.

The plan for the CSO study requires that after a household has been identified, it must be screened for eligibility and/or the random selection of a respondent. Screening a household and selecting a respondent may take up to a minute, and this screening does not guarantee that a respondent will be available and ready to interview at that time. The interviewer may need to make a callback appointment or determine an optimal time to call back when the designated respondent will be available. To achieve their goal of completing 500 interviews, the CSO staffers estimate that interviewers may have to talk to 600 households. Because they will not secure an interview with every household they contact, the researchers estimate that screening time will average out to 45 seconds per household, or approximately 8 hours of screening time, for a cost of $72. RDD surveys looking for people with special characteristics (known as *rare events*), such as seniors, members of particular ethnic or racial groups, the very poor, or the very rich, require massive amounts of screening time, and the ratio of households to completed interviews can easily go 20 to 1 or higher. In some cases, screening for rare events can cost more than the total interview time for the study.

The next estimate the CSO staffers must make is that of the cost for interviewing. This is the amount of time required to complete the interview once a number has been dialed, a household has been screened for eligibility, and a respondent is ready to do the interview. Through pretesting, the researchers have learned that it takes 30 minutes to administer the interview. Given that their goal is to complete 500 interviews, they will need to budget for at least 1,000 interviewing hours. They decide to add 10 minutes to the time needed for each interview to allow for interviewer downtime (breaks, lunches, and so on), and so they estimate that, on average, an interview will take 40 minutes to complete. This brings the total time for interviewing to 333.3 hours, which they multiply by $9 per hour to arrive at a total cost for interviewing time of $2,999.

Logically, it appears that the total number of hours required to dial, screen, and interview for this hypothetical study is 444. That means the study could be completed in less than 2 weeks with interviewing being conducted in 6-hour sessions, 7 days a week, and with six interviewers working each session. We do not recommend such a schedule, however. Ideally, this study should be conducted over a span of 3 to 4 weeks. That would allow for adequate calling exposure to all nonanswered telephone numbers and would enable interviewers to make call attempts to nonanswered numbers in the mornings, afternoons, and evenings, both on weekdays and on weekends.

Surveyors should spread out the calling times in telephone surveys to ensure that persons who work odd shifts, who work away from home during the week and return on weekends, or who may be away on vacation during part of the study period have an opportunity to participate. Additionally, some respondents do not have the time or may be too ill to be interviewed when first called but will make an appointment to be interviewed at a later date. When a study is extended over a longer period of time, daily interviewing sessions are staffed with a smaller number of interviewers than were trained. It may turn out that after the first week only three or four interviewers are needed on a shift, and that number will diminish in subsequent weeks.

Regardless of how few interviewers are working a shift, the surveyor should be certain that at least one supervisor works each shift. Generally, one supervisor can manage six interviewers. Depending on the demands of the study, that supervisor may or may not be able to monitor interviewing as well. In our example study, the CSO staffers assume that none of the shifts will employ more than six interviewers at any one time and that the data collection period will be 3 weeks long. Although an interviewing shift may be only 6 hours in duration, the supervisor on that shift will need to work a full 8-hour day to set up the shift assignments, coordinate materials, handle personnel matters, and see to all the administrative details involved with the job.

At a minimum, if the supervisory pay rate is $11 per hour and one supervisor works 8 hours a day, 7 days a week, for at least 3 weeks, the cost for interviewing supervision alone will be $1,848. The CSO staffers decide that in all likelihood they will need at least one other monitor or supervisor working half-time, because there will be too much for one person to do. At the same rate of pay, this adds another $924 to the supervisory costs.

For a one-time-only survey such as the CSO staffers have in mind, it is usually most cost-efficient to retain the supervisors to do the work of coding and entering the data after data collection is complete. Having been through the interviewing process, these individuals know the questionnaire and are best qualified to deal with any questions or problems that arise in the data reduction process. The supervisors will need assistance, however, with keeping sample records, preparing interviewer assignments, and editing the completed questionnaires to pass on to data reduction. These tasks must be done throughout the data collection process, so the person hired to do them in the CSO study will be needed full-time for 4 weeks. At a wage rate of $10 per hour, this adds an additional $1,600 to the estimate.

The cost of collecting 500 interviews in the CSO's proposed study now stands at $16,811. This total does not include any costs associated with paying for the time of the person or persons who will be responsible for designing and developing the study. Design and development tasks include designing the sample; developing the questionnaire, the interviewing specifications, the codebook, and the coding procedures; setting up data entry; performing data processing and analysis; and writing the report. For the CSO example, we have assumed that all these tasks will be performed by existing agency staff. Figure 6.6 summarizes the estimate of out-of-pocket expenses for this hypothetical study.

Setting Up a CATI Facility

In this final section, we offer a brief discussion of the activities and expenses involved in setting up a facility for computer-assisted telephone interviewing. It is unlikely that an organization planning on conducting a one-time telephone survey, a very limited number of telephone surveys over time, or a series of very small telephone surveys will or should consider setting up a CATI laboratory for interviewing. A CATI lab is a facility furnished with banks of telephone calling stations that are generally equipped with personal computers wired to a central server.

The calling stations represent the first expense in a CATI study. These cubicles must be built so that they are as sound-

OUT-OF-POCKET EXPENSES	
Purchase Telephone Sample	$500.00
Print Materials—	
Questionnaires/Screeners/	
Manuals/Specifications	992.00
Miscellaneous Expenses	300.00
Telephone Charges	4,000.00
Training Interviewers	
Supervisors	1,320.00
Interviewers	1,440.00
Interviewing	
Dialing	918.00
Screen	72.00
Interview	2,999.00
Full-Time Supervisor	1,848.00
Half-Time Supervisor	924.00
Clerk	1,600.00
TOTAL EXPENSES TO CONDUCT INTERVIEWS	$16,913.00

Figure 6.6. In-House Cost Estimate for a Hypothetical Study

NOTE: This estimate does not include in-house personnel time required to handle study design and development, questionnaire development, some training and supervision, data reduction, analysis, and report writing.

proof as possible. At the least, each must have side panels to separate the interviewer from other interviewers and a shelf platform big enough to accommodate a personal computer and a telephone. Each telephone in the lab should be equipped with a headset, and, ideally, the walls and floor of each cubicle should be covered in static-reducing, sound-deadening fabric. Each cubicle must also accommodate individual seating that meets the depth and width requirements of local fire codes.

The computers in a CATI lab's interviewing stations may be stand-alone PCs running individual versions of the CATI software or "dummy" terminals linked to a master computer that acts as a server and runs the CATI software, providing the sample, displaying the appropriate questionnaire screen for each PC, and recording the information entered into each PC. The latter setup is preferable in that having one sample location makes sample management more efficient and effective. Regardless of the configuration, the lab must have at least one powerful PC that is capable of storing all the data from all the other PCs, processing sample information, and creating master files of all data collected.

Clearly, the costs of setting up a CATI facility are not inconsequential. Aside from the costs of building and furnishing the lab cubicles, there are the computer costs, starting with a PC for each station, a master PC, and possibly a server. Depending on the computer operating system and the CATI software being used, a primary operating system could cost anywhere from $3,000 to $30,000 (of course, there are cheaper systems in use and far more expensive ones as well; we are speaking in general terms). Individual PCs may cost as little as $900 per unit or as much as $1,500. Even at the relatively low costs of $3,000 for the primary system and $1,000 apiece for 10 PCs, a surveyor setting up a lab will spend $13,000 on computer hardware alone.

The next cost is that for leasing a CATI software program. Again, the prices range widely. A simple system may be available for around $1,000; a more sophisticated system might run $50,000 per year for licensing. Generally, the lower the cost, the less sophisticated the program. And the less the program does, the more human labor is needed to perform the missing functions. Less sophisticated programs have less flexibility in branching, in building complex display screens, in providing question or answer rotations, and in performing background computations or procedures.

Hand in hand with the cost of the CATI software is the cost of a programmer to install and run the program. The caliber of the programmer needed is determined by the sophistication of the system chosen: The more complex the system, the higher the level of expertise needed in a programmer. If the software is simple, the programmer could be a technician who has developed excellent software skills by using and practicing problem solving with other software packages; the cost of hiring such a person could run as little as $35,000 per year. If the software system is very complex, the surveyor may need to find one or possibly more people who have system-level programming skills specific to the operating system in addition to experience with complicated software. For example, the programmer (or programmers) may need to program in PERL, C++, and the like. Individuals with this kind of expertise earn a minimum of $80,000 per year, so if two are needed, that adds at least $160,000 to study costs.

In addition, keeping a computer lab operating requires, at the least, a service contract for the hardware and/or someone on staff who can deal with mechanical problems. When surveyors running CATI labs contract with outside vendors for service calls, they should strongly consider paying extra for agreements that guarantee 1-hour response; the higher cost of this type of service contract is usually more than worth paying when compared with the cost of having interviewing come to a halt for long periods of time.

Finally, setting up a CATI facility requires a large investment in learning and training time. Programmers and/or technicians alike may take up to 3 months to become competent with the software. Many CATI software providers offer valuable training programs for users, but they are not free; taking advantage of these programs will add additional expenses for travel, per diems, and registration fees.

In addition to the costs enumerated above, setting up a CATI facility involves numerous other incidental expenses (for such things as manuals, peripherals, and supplies) that are beyond the purpose of this discussion. And last, but by no means least, computer equipment rapidly becomes outdated. Software companies revise and update their programs on a regular basis. Machines wear out. Memory and storage become filled. A CATI lab is not a one-time investment. To establish a CATI lab, an organization must have the resources and commitment to support it for the long run; the idea of creating such a facility should not be entertained lightly.

There are alternatives to taking that step, however. Organizations that want to conduct surveys but do not plan to conduct numerous surveys with large sample sizes on an ongoing basis have other options. For example, depending on their geographic location, they may be able to rent CATI stations in an already established telephone facility equipped with a CATI system. Or they may be able to use relatively simple CATI software programs run on individual PCs. In this kind of setup, it is even possible to forgo interviewing stations—all each interviewer needs is a telephone, a PC, and a place to sit. In all likelihood, the day is rapidly approaching when user-friendly interviewing software will be available that will enable researchers to develop and conduct nearly any type of study methodology on computers simply by linking on to a Web site to develop, interview, and process the data.

Exercises

1. The president of the United States gives her State of the Union address. A small survey organization wants to find out whether residents of the United States listened to the speech and what they thought of the budget priorities the president outlined. Would a telephone survey be appropriate for this study? If so, which <u>type</u> of telephone survey would you recommend using?

> A paper-and-pencil survey conducted
> by phone over the next 4 weeks 1
>
> A computer-assisted telephone interview
> survey conducted over the next 4 weeks ...2
>
> A telephone survey conducted within
> 4 days with the chief executive officers
> of *Fortune* 500 companies 3
>
> A paper-and-pencil survey conducted
> by phone within 48 hours with a sample
> created by random-digit dialing 4
>
> Do not use a telephone survey 5

2. A researcher is concerned that recent immigrants from Central and South America do not know about and do not use available public health clinics in New York City. What type of study would be appropriate for getting this information?

Observations in public health clinics 1

Telephone interviews with a sample
of New York residents selected by RDD 2

In-person interviews in public health clinics .3

Telephone interviews with the directors of
public health clinics 4

Using the 2000 U.S. Census to find out
where immigrants live and then
conducting in-person interviews
in households 5

Using the 2000 U.S. Census to find out
where immigrants live and then
conducting telephone interviews with
residents of those areas 6

3. The governor of Arizona needs information about
whether small business owners in the state provide
health care for their workers. Would a telephone survey be appropriate for this study? If so, which type of
telephone survey would you recommend using?

Telephone interviews conducted with
the first person who answers the phone
at a sample of businesses selected
from the Yellow Pages of the phone book .. 1

Telephone interviews with the owners
of small businesses that are selected off
of a master list of all businesses
in the state 2

A telephone survey of households
selected using RDD 3

A telephone survey with members
of the Chamber of Commerce in Tucson ... 4

Do not use a telephone survey;
instead, send out a mail survey 5

4. Identify whether or not a telephone survey would be a reasonable way to collect data in each of the following situations:

  A. The school board wants to find out whether the number of high school dropouts has increased, decreased, or stayed the same over the past 10 years.

  B. The police department wants to find out how many people run red lights at a busy intersection.

  C. The Zzyxx Department Store staff wants to find out whether people know that the store sells furniture.

5. Identify whether you would expect high or low response rates in each of the following situations:

  A. A survey conducted on Thanksgiving day

  B. A survey conducted with no callbacks

  C. A survey conducted with inexperienced interviewers

  D. A survey conducted over an 8-week period

  E. Calls made by well-trained interviewers at the end of an 8-hour shift

  F. Interviews conducted in English with a sample of recent Korean immigrants

  G. A survey of physicians conducted on weekends

  H. A survey in which the status of all telephone numbers in the sample had to be determined

  I. A survey conducted on a CATI system

  J. A survey conducted using paper-and-pencil methods

6. You run a health clinic that serves low-income residents in a community. It is your impression that many eligible members of the community do not know that the clinic exists. You decide to conduct a telephone survey to find out whether your impression is correct. You have limited resources, so you look within your own staff for people who can interview, but you also advertise for interviewers. Which of the following kinds of persons would you look for in selecting your interviewers?

   A. Persons with pleasant speaking voices

   B. Persons with strong opinions that they readily state

   C. Persons who are doctors on your staff

   D. Persons who are patient

   E. Persons who are willing to work only in the morning

   F. Persons who talk rapidly

   G. Persons who are easily discouraged

   H. Members of your staff who are bilingual

7. You have now selected 45 interviewers for your health clinic awareness study. What will you need to train them, and how will you go about training them?

   A. Send each of the 45 interviewers 20 copies of the questionnaire and a list of 40 phone numbers of possible respondents. Ask interviewers to call you if they have any questions about the questionnaire and to send you the completed interviews in 2 weeks.

   B. Develop a training manual.

    C. Find a room where you can set up 45 chairs in auditorium style and where the temperature is set at 85 degrees.

    D. Provide coffee and other drinks during training.

    E. Have each interviewer conduct a practice interview with a friend or relative and bring the completed interview to you for review.

    F. Conduct three separate training sessions.

    G. Have trainees participate in role-playing exercises.

    H. Use overheads or other visual aids.

    I. Develop interviewer specifications.

8. Identify why each of the following questions would or would not work well in a telephone survey.

    A. When you take your next vacation, will you take your children with you or go alone, and will you go on a cruise or go backpacking in the Rocky Mountains?

       Go backpacking alone, or 1

       Take a cruise with your children? 2

    B. Some people drink water and some people do not drink water. Would you say that you drink:

       Two cups of water every hour, ...1

       Two pints of water every day, or 2

       Three gallons of water every week? 3

    C. How many times have you been to a doctor's office in the last year? Would you say:

       None, ...GO TO Q53 1

       Once, ...GO TO D 2

Twice, ...GO TO D 3

Three or more times . . . . .GO TO D 4

D. When you went to the doctor the last time was it because you were sick or was it for a "checkup" or other preventive reason?

Because you were sick 1

For a "checkup" or preventive reason? 2

E. When you listen to postmodern music, which of the following characteristics of the musical format do you gravitate to:

CIRCLE ALL THAT APPLY

An allegretto tempo, ...1

Atonal music with hermeneutic overtones, . .2

A scherzo format with a repeated coda, ...3

A sonata form, ...4

A quartet with a descant voice, ...5

Development based on themes of Chopin? . .6

F. Which of the following agents of bioterrorism are the <u>most</u> potent? Would you say:

Tularemia, ...1

Smallpox, ...2

Ebola virus, ...3

Anthrax, ...4

Plague, or 5

Botulism? 6

9. What kinds of instructions will you need for interviewers and respondents for the following set of questions?

A. When I read the word "violence" to you, what do you think of?

_____

_____

_____

B. We hear a lot about crime and violence these days. In your opinion, what causes crime and violence?

Too few guns in houses, ...1

Mothers who work, .2

Too much religion, .3

No respect for other people, ...4

Not enough police, .5

Divorce 6

C. What kinds of weapons are used in robberies?

Guns, ...1

Knives, ...2

Physical violence, .3

Hitting people with furniture 4

D. Which crimes generally are not solved? Would you say:

Murders, ...1

Robberies, ...2

Burglaries, ...3

Kidnappings, ...4

Car theft? 5

E. How much does the public spend on crime?

_____

10. The state superintendent of education wants to find out whether residents of the state think that all schools should go on a year-round schedule. What steps should the superintendent take in developing a telephone survey of residents?

11. In the following list, identify whether each thing increases, decreases, or has no effect on whether or not a representative sample is obtained for a telephone survey.

ITEM	INCREASE?	DECREASE?	NO EFFECT
A. Well-designed questionnaires	1	2	3
B. Answering machines	1	2	3
C. Telemarketing	1	2	3
D. Well-trained interviewers	1	2	3
E. Computer-assisted telephone interviewing	1	2	3
F. Caller ID	1	2	3
G. Random-digit dialing	1	2	3
H. Modems	1	2	3
I. Pretesting questionnaires	1	2	3
J. Starting the interview without explaining the study	1	2	3
K. Sampling from telephone books	1	2	3
L. Paper-and-pencil telephone interviewing	1	2	3
M. Fax machines	1	2	3
N. Adopting questions from others	1	2	3
O. Refusal conversion	1	2	3
P. Callbacks	1	2	3
Q. Completing all interviews within one day	1	2	3
R. 50% of sample has telephones	1	2	3
S. Telling respondents the interview will "only take 5 minutes"	1	2	3
T. Giving a good explanation of how the information collected will be protected	1	2	3
U. Providing information about who to call to find out about the study	1	2	3
V. Translating the questionnaire	1	2	3

12. A corporation is renegotiating its benefits package for all of its employees, both at central headquarters and at all regional offices. Included among the 5,000 employees are executives, managers, skilled workers, and assembly line workers. They need information both on the kinds of benefits employees prefer and the kinds of benefits packages employees would select if different types of packages were made available. The leaders of the corporation have decided that the best way to collect the data is to have a survey house that is unassociated with the corporation conduct telephone interviews, but they ask your advice about whether a population or a sample should be interviewed and, if a sample, the kind of sample to use. What is your advice?

13. What do you need to consider in developing an RDD sample of households in the state of Kansas?

14. A telephone survey is going to be used to find out what a national sample of adults over age 18 know about terrorism, how likely they think it is that terrorist acts will occur within the United States within the next year, and how well prepared national, state, and local governments are to prevent and respond to acts of terrorism. You have been hired to develop the sample. You have decided on a list-assisted random-digit dialing sample of households, but you are debating whether or not the sample design will include selection of a designated respondent within the household. What are the advantages and disadvantages of selecting a designated respondent? If you decide to select a designated respondent, how would you go about making the selection and why would you do it that way?

15. The owners of a local health food store want to find out about the lifestyles of community residents. They design the following questionnaire and hire an interviewer to

conduct telephone interviews with their customers. What suggestions would you make to the owners?

We have designed a questionnaire to find out about your healthy lifestyle. It will only take three minutes for me to interview you, and you will feel much better when you realize how healthy your lifestyle is.

1. Of course you exercise every day, don't you? Yes . . . . .1 No 2

2. When you exercise, do you drink a lot of water? Yes, I drink a lot of water and then I run three miles. . . . 1 Yes, I drink some water and run four miles. . . . 2 Sometimes I drink some water before I run. . . . 3 When I run I drink water, but when I walk I don't. . . . 4

3. How much do you *avoid* red meat? A lot_____ Some_____ Occasionally_____ When I think of it_____

4. How many people live in your household? Is it just you and one other person or are there more people there?

    Only me. 1

    Me plus one person 2

    Something else 3

    Who else is there?_____

5. When you finished school, did you have a high school degree and a college degree or something else?

    High school degree and college degree 1

    Something else 2

6. Rank order the following list of things that make for a healthy lifestyle from 1 to 10.

List	Rank
Eating right	_____
Running at least 10 miles a week	_____
Doing meditation	_____

Getting 8 hours of sleep every night   _____
Eating leafy green vegetables every day   _____
Avoiding situations that make you angry   _____
Avoiding caffeine   _____
Never eating sugar   _____
Thinking good thoughts   _____
Lifting weights   _____

ANSWERS

1. Option 4: This is a situation where you want rapid feedback on the content of the speech. The objective is to find out what residents of the United States think, thus an RDD sample is a good selection. Although a CATI system would make this survey easier to conduct quickly, a small survey firm probably does not have that capability. Paper-and-pencil techniques will be perfectly adequate.

2. Option 5: Conducting in-person interviews in areas known to have a substantial population of immigrants is clearly the best way to get a good sample of immigrants who both know about and attend the clinics as well as those who know about but do not attend the clinics and those who do not know about the clinics. Options 1 and 3 could be used for exploratory, low-budget estimates of the total number of immigrants that actually come into the clinics, but neither option will provide information on those immigrants who do not come to the clinics. Option 6 could also be used, but the problem is that immigrants in New York City are poor and are not likely to have telephones. Thus, a telephone survey would not reach a certain proportion of the immigrants of interest.

3. Option 2: The owner of a small business is the person who decides what benefits will be provided to employ-

ees and is the only person who can be expected to know the range of benefits provided. Employees of the business (Option 1) will not have this information; furthermore, small businesses are not always listed in the Yellow Pages, and the Yellow Pages do not differentiate small businesses from other businesses. Although some members of the Chamber of Commerce (Option 5) may be the owners of small businesses, not all small business owners will be represented; furthermore, that sample is limited to Tucson. A telephone survey of households is unlikely to yield many small business owners. A mail survey could be sent to a master list of small business owners, but response rates would be substantially lower than in a telephone survey.

4. Rather than a telephone survey, a better way to approach Question A is through an examination of trend data of dropouts over time taken from administrative records. For Question B, rather than a telephone survey, structured observations at intersections would be a good approach, perhaps using cameras that are triggered when a driver runs a red light. A telephone survey is the best way to answer Question C—that is, to find out whether people know what the Zzyxx Department Store stocks. A mail questionnaire could be used to address this question, but response rates would be lower. Also, it would be more difficult to disguise the real purpose of the study in a mailed questionnaire, because the respondent can read the entire questionnaire before filling it out.

5. Low response rates would be expected for A, B, C, F, and G. High response rates would be expected for D, E, and H. The *method* by which data are collected (I and J) will have no effect on the response rates. Response rates are determined by characteristics of the questionnaire, the competence of interviewers, and the time and methods devoted to maximizing potential respondents' opportunities to participate.

6. A and D are particularly important characteristics to look for in interviewers. Given that this is a low-income clinic, you may well have patients who do not speak English, so bilingual ability (Option H) may also be important. Persons who readily state their strong opinions (Option B) will not make good interviewers. In general, doctors do not make good interviewers, and few would be willing to devote time to interviewing (Option C). Because telephone interviewing is most productive in the late afternoon and evening, you do not want people who will only work in the morning (Option E). Respondents often find people who talk rapidly difficult to understand (Option F), particularly when interviews are conducted on the phone. Interviewers have to be patient and persistent; you do not want interviewers who are easily discouraged (Option G).

7. Options B, D, E, F, G, H, and I are all important components of good interviewer training. Interviewers need to have space to write on, thorough instruction, and supervised practice. A and C will *not* result in well-trained interviewers.

8. Option C is fine for inclusion in a telephone interview. It requires skips depending on the answer given, but this is easily done by the interviewer. Option D is okay but could be improved by the addition of a residual "other" to the answer categories and probably by other revisions to increase the clarity of the question and the responses. Option A is a bad question for any study, in that it is double-barreled: Where will you go, and who will you go with? Furthermore, the list of alternatives provided in both the question and the response alternatives is incomplete for *both* questions. The question in Option B should restrict the time frame to, for example, a day. The list of alternative responses is not

exhaustive and includes three different time referents: an hour, a day, and a week. Options E and F are filled with jargon and terms specific to particular disciplines (i.e., music and medicine). Even musicians (in the case of Option E) and health professionals (in the case of Option F, particularly before September 11, 2001) would have difficulty with these questions.

9. First, the researcher needs to provide introductory instructions to tell the respondent what the study is about, who is sponsoring it, and how the data will be used and protected. Second, in Question 1, the interviewer needs to know whether he or she is supposed to probe the respondent or simply record only the first thing the respondent says. This part of the questionnaire could also benefit from some kind of transition into Question A, such as "People have different ideas of what violence is . . . ." Third, in Questions B, C, and D, the interviewer needs to know whether he or she is supposed to record a single answer or multiple answers are permitted. Fourth, in Questions B and C, the interviewer needs to know whether or not he or she is supposed to read the responses to the respondent. This is also somewhat of a problem for Question D, but the phrase "Would you say" included in the question provides at least a cue that the interviewer is to read the list of alternatives. Fifth, Questions B, C, D, and E probably should have a residual "other" included in the list of possible alternative answers. Sixth, Question E is pretty vague; it could profit from the specification of a time period (such as a year), comparison to other public expenditures (such as public transportation), and other specifics. Seventh, transitions would be helpful between these questions. This is particularly true between Questions D and E. Eighth, the researcher needs to consider providing definitions for some of the crimes listed; for example, many people do not know

the difference between robbery and burglary. And finally, complete instructions should be prepared for this questionnaire in the form of interviewer specifications and research specifications.

10. The superintendent needs to decide what kind of sample should be used (we would recommend an RDD sample of residences in the state). The superintendent also needs to decide if households will be prescreened for the presence of school-age children and whether or not a procedure for selecting a designated respondent will be used. The superintendent needs to decide how long the interview will be, what its content will be, and who will conduct the interviews, analyze the data, and write the report.

11. A, D, G, I, O, P, T, and U will all tend to increase both the response rate and the representativeness of the sample. B, C, F, H, J, K, M, Q, R, and S will decrease both response rates and representativeness. In addition, if only 50% of the targeted population has phones (R), telephone surveys are clearly not the way to get the data. E, L, N, and V generally will have no impact on the response rates, but well-done and appropriate translations (V) will increase the representativeness of a sample in a multilingual population.

12. We recommend first dividing all employees into strata divided by site of the office (headquarters and all regional offices) and rank of the employee (executive, manager, skilled worker, assembly line worker), and then examining the total number of employees in each stratum. We generally would recommend a stratified probability sample rather than a study of the population, but whether respondents were selected proportionately or disproportionately across the strata would depend on the number of employees in the smallest stratum and the range across the various strata.

Depending on how employees are distributed across strata, in the end it may be just as efficient to interview the entire population rather than a sample.

13. First, you need to consider whether you will develop the sample yourself or purchase one from a corporation. Second, you need to examine how area codes and trunk numbers correspond with the state boundaries. Third, you need to consider whether the RDD sample will be list-assisted and, if so, what method will be used. Fourth, you need to decide whether the sample will or will not be stratified. Fifth, you need to decide how many numbers need to be drawn to obtain the desired sample size. And sixth, you need to decide whether you will interview any adult in the household or whether you will set up a procedure to select a designated respondent.

14. The advantage of not having a designated sample is that it is generally easier to complete interviews and obtain your desired sample size. The disadvantage is that you are making an assumption that whoever completes the interview represents the composite views of the household, and in making inferences from your sample, you can only make inferences to households in the United States, not to all adult residents of the United States. Selecting a designated respondent increases your ability to generalize to all adult residents of the United States. We strongly prefer using Kish tables to select a designated respondent because we think it provides the best method for determining who exactly is represented in your sample, but we are aware that last/next birthday methods are widely used by other researchers.

15. This questionnaire breaks almost every rule of good questionnaire construction. First, the print is too small. Second, italics are used, which are difficult to

read. Third, the owners of the health food store clearly have an "agenda." Their questions do not allow for the possibility that respondents might *not* do the things that the owners consider healthy. Fourth, the responses for Question 3 are all vague qualifiers. Fifth, there is no consistency in spacing or formatting; some response categories are listed vertically, and others are listed horizontally. Et cetera, et cetera.

References
and Suggested Readings

Aday, L. A. (1997). *Designing and conducting health surveys: A comprehensive guide* (2nd ed.). San Francisco: Jossey-Bass.

Basic textbook on the design and administration of all kinds of surveys. Draws on methodological work on surveys in general and health surveys in particular.

American Association for Public Opinion Research. (2000). *Standard definitions: Final dispositions of case codes and outcome rates for surveys: RDD telephone surveys, in-person household surveys, and mail surveys of specifically named persons.* Ann Arbor, MI: Author.

Describes standard codes for researchers to use in cataloging the dispositions of sample cases in surveys, with the objective of improving the quality of surveys and maximizing comparability across public, government, and academic survey research.

Aneshensel, C. S., Frerichs, R. R., Clark, V. A., & Yokopenic, P. A. (1982). Measuring depression in the community: A comparison of telephone and personal interviews. *Public Opinion Quarterly, 46,* 110-121.

Reports on a study that randomized respondents to telephone or in-person interviews. No differences were found in nonresponse to symptom items, preference for specific response categories, reliability, mean level of depression, or proportion classified as depressed.

Aquilino, W. S. (1994). Interview mode effects in surveys of drug and alcohol use. *Public Opinion Quarterly, 58,* 210-240.

Reports the results of a field experiment designed to study respondents' willingness to admit use of illicit drugs and alcohol in three conditions: personal interviews that incorporated the use of a self-administered questionnaire to obtain the sensitive information, personal interviews without a self-administered questionnaire, and telephone interviews. The use of a self-administered questionnaire within a personal interview resulted in somewhat higher estimates of illicit substance use, and telephone interviews resulted in somewhat lower estimates.

Aquilino, W. S., & Wright, D. L. (1996). Substance use estimates from RDD and area probability samples: Impact of differential screening methods and unit nonresponse. *Public Opinion Quarterly, 60,* 563-573.

Compares nonresponse and reports of self-reported tobacco, alcohol, and illicit drug use in two samples of the same population: an RDD sample with telephone screening and a multistage area probability sample with in-person screening but telephone interviewing. Response rates were lower in the telephone screening mode, but the two procedures produced samples that were similar in demographic characteristics and substance-use profiles.

Atrostic, B. K., Bates, N., Burt, G., & Silberstein, A. (2001). Nonresponse in U.S. government household surveys: Consistent measures, recent trends, and new insights. *Journal of Official Statistics, 17,* 209-226.

Compares nonresponse in six continuing household surveys that provide data for key national social and economic statistics in the United States for the years 1990 to 1999.

Barreto, P. (2001, October). Health insurance outreach and enrollment assistance program: Health IDEA, a local intervention. *Clinical Scholars Research Protocol.*

Source of information on the Healthy Families program used as an example in Chapter 1.

Bassili, J. N., & Scott, B. S. (1996). Response latency as a signal to question problems in survey research. *Public Opinion Quarterly, 60,* 390-399.

Examines the effects that questions with superfluous negatives and double-barreled questions have on response quality and the amount of time respondents need to provide answers.

Behling, O., & Law, K. S. (2000). *Translating questionnaires and other research instruments: Problems and solutions.* Thousand Oaks, CA: Sage.

Discusses procedures used to achieve semantic, conceptual, and normative equivalence in the translation of questionnaires.

Biemer, P. P. (2001). Nonresponse bias and measurement bias in a comparison of face to face and telephone interviewing. *Journal of Official Statistics, 17,* 295-320.

Uses data from a special study conducted for the U.S. National Health Interview Survey to illustrate a study design and analytic methodology for evaluating and comparing the quality of survey data in the case of in-person and telephone interviewing.

Biemer, P. P., Groves, R. M., Lyberg, L. E., Mathiowetz, N. A., & Sudman, S. (Eds.). (1991). *Measurement errors in surveys.* New York: John Wiley.

Expanded edition of the papers presented at the International Conference on Measurement Errors in Surveys held on November 11-14, 1990, in Tucson, Arizona. Presents information from diverse perspectives on the most important issues in the field of survey measurement error.

Binson, D., Canchola, J. A., & Catania, J. A. (2000). Random selection in a national telephone survey: A comparison of the Kish, next-birthday, and last-birthday methods. *Journal of Official Statistics, 16,* 53-59.

Compares differential dropout rates at each phase of the screening process for three methods of selecting the designated respondent within a household. The highest proportion of dropout occurred in the screening interview before the informant was asked questions unique to one of the three selection methods, with the highest rates in the Kish condition and second-highest rates in the last-birthday condition. The authors suggest that interviewers rather than respondents are a primary source of the higher rate of refusals when the Kish method is used.

Blasius, J., & Thiessen, V. (2001). The use of neutral responses in survey questions: An application of multiple correspondence analysis. *Journal of Official Statistics, 17,* 351-267.

Examines whether neutral responses are substantive or nonsubstantive— that is, whether the respondent really has a neutral opinion or if the expressed neutral opinion is encouraged by the structure of the question. Also identifies subgroups of respondents who use substantive, nonsubstantive, and neutral categories, respectively, relatively often and relatively seldom.

Bourque, L. B., & Clark, V. A. (1992). *Processing data: The survey example.* Newbury Park, CA: Sage.

Provides a systematic explanation of how to perform data processing using today's technology. The authors adopt a broad definition of data processing that starts with selecting a data collection strategy and ends when data transformations are complete. Much of the material covered has direct applicability to the design, administration, and processing of telephone surveys.

Bourque, L. B., & Russell, L. A. (1994). *Experiences during and responses to the Loma Prieta earthquake.* Sacramento: Governor's Office of Emergency Services, State of California.

Source of Figures 5.8 and 5.9 in Chapter 5.

Bourque, L. B., Shoaf, K. I., & Nguyen, L. H. (1977). Survey research. *International Journal of Mass Emergencies and Disasters, 15, 71-101.*

Reports the basic methodology used, sample characteristics, and selected findings from the Northridge and Loma Prieta studies.

Brick, J. M., Waksberg, J., & Keeter, S. (1996). Using data on interruptions in telephone service as coverage adjustments. *Survey Methodology, 22, 185-197.*

Using data from the 1997 National Survey of America's Families, examines differences among respondents in nontelephone households, households with interruptions of telephone service, and those with full telephone coverage. The characteristics of children in households with interruptions are more similar to those in nontelephone households than to those in households with no interruptions.

Brick, J. M., Waksberg, J., Kulp, D., & Starer, A. (1995). Bias in list-assisted telephone samples. *Public Opinion Quarterly, 59, 218-235.*

Describes research on the coverage bias for a particular method of list-assisted sampling used in combination with the Waksberg-Mitofsky method. This article is one example of the extensive literature on random-digit dialing techniques of sample selection and, in particular, the Waksberg-Mitofsky method.

Brown, E. R. (Principal Investigator). (2002). California Health Interview Survey (CHIS). Center for Health Policy Research, University of California, Los Angeles, 10911 Weyburn Avenue, Suite 300, Los Angeles, CA 90024.

Source of information reported about the California Health Interview Survey's interviewing techniques in Chapter 1.

Catania, J. A., Binson, D., Canchola, J., Pollack, L. M., Hauck, W., & Coates, T. J. (1996). Effects of interviewer gender, interviewer choice, and item wording on responses to questions concerning sexual behavior. *Public Opinion Quarterly, 60,* 345-375.

Examines the influence of the gender of the interviewer, the use of questions that are supportive of what may be perceived to be nonnormative behavior, and increased respondent control on the quality of data on sexual topics. Findings suggest that males, compared with females, tend to be influenced by variations in item wording, interviewer gender, and respondent control across a wider range of sexual topics.

Conrad, F. G., & Schober, M. F. (2000). Clarifying question meaning in a household telephone survey. *Public Opinion Quarterly, 64,* 1-28.

Compares two interviewing techniques for clarifying factual questions in a national survey.

Council for Marketing and Opinion Research, Inc. (2001). *Results: Tracking response, cooperation, and refusal rates for the industry, April 12.* Retrieved November 2, 2001, from http://www.cmor.org

Source of information on response rates in market research reported in Chapter 1.

Council of American Survey Research Organizations. (1982). *On the definition of response rates.* Port Jefferson, NY: Author.

Early report on developing standard terminology and reporting mechanisms for response rates in surveys.

Derogatis, L. R., & Spencer, P. M. (1992). *The Brief Symptom Inventory (BSI): Administration, scoring and procedures manual-I.* Baltimore: Clinical Psychometric Research.

Provides a description of the construction of the Brief Symptom Inventory, its psychometric characteristics, and methods for scoring it.

Engelhart, R. (n.d.). *The Kish selection procedure.* Unpublished manuscript, University of California, Los Angeles, Survey Research Center.

Readable description of Kish tables and how they are used to select the designated respondent in a household.

Freeman, H. E., Kiecolt, K. J., Nicholls, W. I., & Shanks, W. L. (1982). Telephone sampling bias in surveying disability. *Public Opinion Quarterly, 46,* 392-407.

Reports on results of the California Disability Survey that indicate telephone interviews provide good estimates of subgroups of the disabled population,

information on current and anticipated areas of policy concern, and informa-
tion for geographic areas important in rehabilitation program planning.

Freeman, H. E., & Shanks, J. M. (1983). Foreword: Special issue on the emer-
gence of computer-assisted survey research. *Sociological Methods &
Research, 12,* 115-118.

*Description of the early development of computer-assisted telephone inter-
viewing at the University of California's Berkeley and Los Angeles campuses.*

Gaskell, G. D., O'Muircheartaigh, C. A., & Wright, D. B. (1994). Survey questions about the frequency of vaguely defined events: The effect of
response alternatives. *Public Opinion Quarterly, 58,* 241-254.

*Examines how different selections of response options influence the data
obtained.*

Gaskell, G. D., Wright, D. B., & O'Muircheartaigh, C. A. (2000). Telescoping of
landmark events: Implications for survey research. *Public Opinion
Quarterly, 64,* 77-89.

*Examines how forward and backward telescoping of landmark events differs
with characteristics of survey respondents and results in serious miscalcula-
tions of the dates of key events.*

Groves, R. M. (1989). *Survey errors and survey costs.* New York: John Wiley.

*Draws from the social science and statistical literature to examine survey
errors and the relationships among different types of survey errors. Presents
cost models that attempt to reduce various errors while making explicit the
consequences for data quality.*

Groves, R. M., Dillman, D. A., Eltinge, J. L., & Little, R. J. A. (Eds.). (2002).
Survey nonresponse. New York: John Wiley.

*Comprehensive book deliberately combines research that asks why nonre-
sponse occurs, how it might be reduced by survey design, and how data
should be analyzed in the presence of nonresponse. The editors suggest that
these three questions do not share the same research history, but it is becoming clear that they need to be blended in the future.*

Groves, R. M., & McGonagle, K. A. (2001). A theory-guided interviewer training protocol regarding survey participation. *Journal of Official Statistics, 17,*
249-265.

A theory of survey participation suggests that sample individuals engage in more thorough cognitive processing of the survey request when their concerns about the request are addressed by the interviewer. A training regimen was constructed that taught trainees to classify respondent concerns, using the respondents' terminology, into themes; trainees were taught facts to communicate regarding those concerns and were drilled in rapid, natural delivery of those facts. Two experimental tests of the training regimen showed increases in cooperation rates for interviewers who received training.

Gubrium, J. F., & Holstein, J. A. (Eds.). (2002). *Handbook of interview research: Context and method.* Thousand Oaks, CA: Sage.

Provides good coverage of the methodological issues surrounding interview practice, including its varied forms. Addresses concerns centered on distinctive respondents, special institutional applications, technical matters related to data processing, analytic strategies, and representational questions.

Hurtado, A. (1994). Does similarity breed respect? Interviewer evaluations of Mexican-descent respondents in a bilingual survey. *Public Opinion Quarterly, 58,* 77-95.

Reports on a study that examined Mexican-descent, Spanish/English bilingual interviewers' evaluations of Mexican-descent, Spanish/English bilingual Mexican respondents in a national survey. (It is widely assumed that interviewers should be matched to respondents on important social characteristics such as race.) Interviewers evaluated respondents who met conventional U.S. societal criteria of success (better educated, higher income, fair skinned, European looking, English speaking) as better able to understand and answer questions, and as more cooperative and interested in the interview.

Inkelas, M., Loux, L. A., Bourque, L. B., Widawski, M., & Nguyen, L. H. (2000). Dimensionality and reliability of the Civilian Mississippi Scale for PTSD in a postearthquake community. *Journal of Traumatic Stress, 13,* 149-167.

Describes some of the psychometric characteristics of the Civilian Mississippi Scale as used in the Loma Prieta study.

Jordan, L. A., Marcus, A. C., & Reeder, L. G. (1980). Response styles in telephone and household interviewing: A field experiment. *Public Opinion Quarterly, 44,* 210-222.

Early comparison of in-person and telephone interviewing found that demographic characteristics of those sampled did not differ, but that the telephone sample had more missing data for family income; more acquiescence, eva-

siveness, and extremeness response bias on attitude questions; and more responses to checklists.

Kalton, G. (1983). *Introduction to survey sampling.* Beverly Hills, CA: Sage.

Readable book on sampling procedures for surveys; accessible to nonstatisticians.

Keane, T. M., Caddell, J. M., & Taylor, K. L. (1988). Mississippi Scale for Combat-Related Posttraumatic Stress Disorder: Three studies in reliability and validity. *Journal of Consulting and Clinical Psychology, 56,* 85-90.

Describes early development of the Mississippi Scale for Combat-Related Posttraumatic Stress Disorder.

Keane, T. M., & Wolfe, J. (1990). Comorbidity in post-traumatic stress disorder: An analysis of community and clinical studies. *Journal of Applied Social Psychology, 20,* 1776-1788.

Early discussion of comorbidity between posttraumatic stress disorder and other psychological conditions.

Keeter, S. (1995). Estimating telephone noncoverage bias with a telephone survey. *Public Opinion Quarterly, 59,* 196-217.

Compares households reporting "intermittent" phone service with nontelephone households surveyed through in-person interviews.

Keeter, S., Miller, C., Kohut, A., Groves, R. M., & Presser, S. (2000). Consequences of reducing nonresponse in a national telephone survey. *Public Opinion Quarterly, 64,* 125-148.

Compares a standard survey conducted over a 5-day period that used a sample of adults who were home when the interviewer called and a rigorous survey conducted over an 8-week period that used random selection from among all adult household members. The authors conclude that the two surveys produced similar results.

Kish, L. (1965). *Survey sampling.* New York: John Wiley.

Classic book on designing samples for surveys.

Kish, L. (1987). *Statistical design for research.* New York: John Wiley.

Addresses basic aspects of research design that are central and common to economics, sociology, psychology, political science, health sciences, education, social welfare, and evaluation research.

Krosnick, J. A. (2002). The causes of no-opinion responses to attitude measures in surveys: They are rarely what they appear to be. In R. M. Groves, D. A. Dillman, J. L. Eltinge, & R. J. A. Little (Eds.), *Survey nonresponse* (pp. 87-100). New York: John Wiley.

Reviews research on including a "no opinion" option among the response alternatives for attitude and behavior questions. Concludes by recommending that a no-opinion option should usually not be provided.

Lauterbach, D., Vrana, S., King, D. W., & King, L. A. (1997). Psychometric properties of the civilian version of the Mississippi PTSD Scale. *Journal of Traumatic Stress, 10,* 499-513.

Describes psychometric characteristics of the Civilian Mississippi Scale as used in the National Vietnam Veterans Study.

Link, M. W., & Oldendick, R. W. (1999). Call screening: Is it really a problem for survey research? *Public Opinion Quarterly, 63,* 577-589.

Examines whether telephone answering machines and caller-ID services affect nonresponse, with mixed results.

Martin, E. (1999). Who knows who lives here? Within-household disagreements as a source of survey coverage error. *Public Opinion Quarterly, 63,* 220-236.

Examines how expanded roster cues and probes affect the identification of individuals with marginal or tenuous attachments to households.

Martin, E., Abreu, D., & Winters, F. (2001). Money and motive: Effects of incentives on panel attrition in the Survey of Income and Program Participation. *Journal of Official Statistics, 17,* 267-284.

Households in the U.S. Census Bureau's Survey of Income and Program Participation were randomly assigned to receive a debit card worth $20, a debit card worth $40, or no incentive. Incentives of $20 and $40 significantly improved conversion rates of prior noninterviews, with results more pronounced for certain demographic subgroups. Prior complaints about the survey's burden were not influenced by incentives.

Miller, P. V. (1984). Alternative question forms for attitude scale questions in telephone interviews. *Public Opinion Quarterly, 48,* 766-778.

Compares two ways of asking 7-point scale attitude questions in a national telephone health survey.

Ott, R. L. (1993). *An introduction to statistical methods and data analysis* (4th ed.). Belmont, CA: Duxbury.

Source of Figure 5.1 in Chapter 5.

Riopelle, D., Bourque, L. B., & Shoaf, K. I. (2001, March). *Survey of potential early warning system users: Trinet policy studies and planning activities in real-time earthquake early warning. Task 1 report.* Los Angeles: University of California, School of Public Health, Center for Public Health and Disaster Relief.

Reports the design and findings of the Trinet Study.

Saris, W. E. (1991). *Computer-assisted interviewing.* Newbury Park, CA: Sage.

Provides an overview of computer-assisted telephone interviewing, computer-assisted personal interviewing, computerized self-administered questionnaires, computer-assisted panel research, and touchtone data entry.

Simmons, T., & O'Neill, G. (2001). Table 2: Households and families for the United States, regions, and states, and for Puerto Rico: 1990 and 2000. In *Households and families: 2000, Census 2000 Brief C2KBR/01-8.* Retrieved January 21, 2002, from http://www.census.gov/prod/2001pubs/c2kbr01-8.pdf

Source of data on "unmarried partnership households" reported in Chapter 3.

Singer, E., Groves, R. M., & Corning, A. D. (1999). Differential incentives: Beliefs about practices, perceptions of equity, and effects on survey participation. *Public Opinion Quarterly, 63,* 251-260.

Examines the public's reactions to equity issues raised by the use of incentives and investigates the effects of different reactions on people's willingness to participate in surveys.

Singer, E., Van Hoewyk, J., & Maher, M. P. (2000). Experiments with incentives in telephone surveys. *Public Opinion Quarterly, 64,* 171-188.

Through a series of experiments, examines how prepaid versus promised incentives, advance letters, and advance letters with prepaid incentives affect response rates, response quality, sample composition, response bias, interviewer and respondent expectations, and costs.

State of California, Office of Statewide Health Planning and Development. (2001). *Hospital annual utilization data profile, 2000.* Retrieved January 25, 2002, from http://www.oshpd.state.ca.us/hid/infores/hospital/util/index.htm

Source of data on the number of acute care hospitals in Los Angeles County reported in Chapter 5.

Steeh, C., Kirgis, N., Cannon, B., & DeWitt, J. (2000). Are they really as bad as they seem? Nonresponse rates at the end of the twentieth century. *Journal of Official Statistics, 17,* 227-247.

Examines nonresponse in the 1990s for two RDD surveys, one national and the other at the state level, tracing changes in refusals, noncontacts, and other noninterviews.

Sudman, S. (1976). *Applied sampling.* New York: Academic Press.

Comprehensive discussion of sampling that does not require readers to have sophisticated statistical knowledge.

Survey Sampling, Inc. (1998a, May 23). *Calculating sample size.* Retrieved January 18, 2002, from http://www.surveysampling.com

Provides information for potential consumers about how Survey Sampling, Inc., calculates sample size.

Survey Sampling, Inc. (1998b, May 22-23). *Random digit samples, parts 1 and 2.* Retrieved January 18, 2002, from http://www.surveysampling.com

Provides brief descriptions of the range of RDD samples provided by Survey Sampling, Inc.

Survey Sampling, Inc. (1998c, May 23). *Summary of sample types.* Retrieved January 18, 2002, from http://www.surveysampling.com

Overview of available sample configurations.

Todorov, A. (2000). Context effect in national health surveys: Effects of preceding questions on reporting serious difficult seeing and legal blindness. *Public Opinion Quarterly, 64,* 65-76.

Demonstrates how the contexts within which questions occur, and particularly immediately prior to screening questions, influence prevalence estimates in health surveys.

Traugott, M. W., Groves, R. M., & Lepkowski, J. M. (1987). Dual frame designs to reduce nonresponse. *Public Opinion Research, 51,* 522-539.

Reports the results of a series of experiments designed to improve response rates. Methods examined include standard random-digit dialing, purchased lists of phone numbers, advance letters, and the use of names.

Turner, R. H., Nigg, J. M., & Paz, D. H. (1986). *Waiting for disaster: Earthquake watch in California.* Berkeley: University of California Press.

The core of questionnaires used in the Northridge and Loma Prieta surveys was adapted from a questionnaire originally developed for this study.

University of California, Los Angeles, Office for Students With Disabilities. (n.d.). *Annual report 2000-01.* Los Angeles: Author.

Source of data used in Chapter 5 for the example on constructing a disproportionately stratified sample.

UCLA Office of Academic Planning and Budget. (November 2001). Data retrieved from http://www.apb.ucla.edu

Source of data on fall 2001 undergraduate enrollment used for examples of simple random and stratified samples in Chapter 5.

U.S. Bureau of Labor Statistics. (1987, March). *Report of the Data Collection Task Force on the Demonstration Database.* Internal memorandum.

Early report on the need for standard definitions and complete reporting of response rates in surveys.

U.S. Bureau of the Census. (2000). QT-04. Profile of Selected Housing Characteristics: 2000. Data set: Census 2000 supplementary survey summary tables. Retrieved November 2, 2001, from http://factfinder.census. gov/servlet/QT...04000US06&qr_name=ACS_C2SS_EST_G00_QT04

Source of the 2000 Census data on telephone coverage in households reported in Chapter 1.

Waksberg, J. (1978). Sampling methods for random digit dialing. *Journal of the American Statistical Association, 73,* 40-46.

First description of the Waksberg-Mitofsky method for selection a random-digit dialing sample.

Wänke, M. (1996). Comparative judgments as a function of the direction of comparison versus word order. *Public Opinion Quarterly, 60,* 400-409.

Prior research suggests that comparative judgments in survey questions are influenced by the direction of the comparison, but findings are confounded by word order in that the subject usually is presented first and the referent second. This paper disentangles this confounding. Results suggest that the direction of comparison does influence responses, but that word order does not.

Glossary

Abstract term—A term that is complex and thus difficult for some people to understand. Sometimes surveyors cannot avoid using abstract terms in questionnaires, but whenever possible they should consider providing synonyms or definitions of the terms for respondents.

Acquiescence bias—The tendency of study participants to want to cooperate with and please researchers.

Adaptation of questions—The survey researcher's practice of using established sets of questions but changing them to make them more appropriate for the current study. Examples include translating questionnaires and using questions that were originally designed for self-administered questionnaires in a survey administered by interview. Researchers should be cautious in adapting questions. They must always give full credit to the persons who originally designed the questions and, when possible, consult with the designers when making decisions about adaptation.

Administration of questionnaires—The process by which questionnaires are distributed to and filled out by respondents. Questionnaires may be administered by interviewers as part of in-person or telephone surveys, or they may be filled out by respondents either in group settings (such as classrooms or workplaces) or as individuals.

Adoption of questions—The survey researcher's practice of using sets of questions that were developed by other researchers exactly as they were developed. When surveyors adopt questions, they must give full credit to the person or group who developed the questions.

Advance letter—A letter sent to a potential study participant that explains what the study is about, who is conducting the study, and how the data will be protected and used; indicates who will be contacting the potential respondent and when that contact will take place; and provides information about how the recipient of the letter can obtain further information.

Anonymous data—Data that, once collected, can never be connected to the person or organization that provided the information.

Answer categories (or response categories, or response choices)—The set of responses to a closed-ended question from which a respondent selects his or her answer(s).

Bias—The tendency for researchers to project their own perceptions, behaviors, and knowledge onto the participants in their studies. The presence of bias can affect a study in such a way that it does not obtain a complete picture of what is happening in a population. Researchers can reduce bias by using appropriate methods in designing and conducting their studies.

Bilingual—Having the ability to read, write, and speak two languages fluently.

Branching—A technique for varying the number of questions and the sequence in which questions are asked in the survey instrument through the use of skip patterns.

Branching allows the surveyor to tailor the questionnaire so that it can gather data from different respondents with different experiences.

Callback—A repeat attempt to reach a potential respondent by telephone when earlier calls have resulted in non-answers or busy signals, have reached answering machines, or have made contact with persons who are not eligible to participate in the study.

Ceiling effect—A special form of heaping in which the surveyor creates ordinal or interval response categories for closed-ended questions such that a substantial number of respondents select the highest category and the resultant variance in responses is restricted.

Closed-ended question—A question for which the respondent is provided with a series of alternative answers to choose among.

Cluster sample—A form of probability sample that is selected such that clusters within it represent the larger population. Cluster sampling is used more often in in-person surveys than in telephone or mail surveys.

Code frame—The series of variables with numeric codes for answers that the surveyor creates out of verbal data. The surveyor must create the code frame for answers to open-ended questions in order to be able to analyze the data with traditional statistical techniques.

Coding—The assignment of numbers to verbal data for purposes of entering the data into computer programs for analysis.

Cold calling—The telephone interviewing practice of calling potential respondents who are unaware of the study and who do not know the interviewer in order to establish whether or not they are eligible for the study and, if so, to interview them.

Computer-assisted telephone interviewing (CATI)—Survey interviewing conducted over the telephone in which the questionnaire is programmed into a computer along with information about the sample. The interviewer reads the questions to the respondent from a computer monitor and records the respondent's answers directly into the computer.

Confidentiality—Protection of a respondent's identity. To ensure confidentiality, survey researchers make sure that individual respondents cannot be identified within a data set, usually by stripping all identifiers (e.g., telephone numbers) out of the data file and reporting findings only in statistical groupings.

Content analysis—The process of developing code frames or structured numerical variables and response categories out of verbal data. Surveyors must perform content analysis to convert answers to open-ended questions into analyzable numeric data.

Control—The survey researcher's power to manage both who participates in the study and the order in which data are collected.

Convenience sample—A type of nonprobability sample made up of individuals the researcher finds to be readily available and willing to participate.

Data collection—The process of gathering information about individuals, groups, agencies, households, organizations, and so on. Data can be collected using questionnaires, through observations, or from records.

Data entry—The process of entering information from a coded questionnaire into a software package that stores the data in a file for subsequent analysis. Data entry is largely automatic when the data are collected using a CATI system.

Data reduction—The process of turning the verbal data collected during interviews into quantifiable data in a machine-readable format. Data reduction is largely automatic when data are collected using a CATI system.

Demographic data—Data that describe the characteristics of a person, household, or organization; demographics include information about age, gender, education, income, and racial and ethnic identity.

Designated respondent—The particular person within a household or institution who is eligible to be interviewed in a telephone survey. Surveyors instruct interviewers to use one of four methods for selecting the designated respondent in a household: Kish tables, Troldahl-Carter-Bryant tables, the Hagan and Collier method, and the last/next birthday method.

Double-barreled question—A single question that actually asks two questions rather than one.

Dual-frame sample—A sample selected from multiple sources, such as random-digit dialing and telephone directories.

Estimate of time (for questionnaire completion)—Approximation of the amount of time an average respondent should take to complete the questionnaire. One purpose for conducting pretests and pilot studies is to estimate how long respondents will take to complete questionnaires, so that modifications can be made if necessary. A potential respondent should be provided with a realistic estimate of the time it should take to complete the questionnaire.

Exhaustive response list—A list of alternative answers provided for a closed-ended question that includes answers that comfortably and appropriately represent all persons studied.

Exploratory study—A study in which the researcher is assessing whether a particular topic is worthy of research and whether research can feasibly be conducted on the topic.

Floor effect—A special form of heaping in which the surveyor creates ordinal or interval response categories for closed-ended questions such that a substantial number of respondents select the lowest category and the resultant variance in responses is restricted.

Font—A size and style of typeface used in a written document.

Formatting—The process of setting up a data collection instrument so that it can be easily understood by interviewers and respondents. Elements that surveyors need to consider in formatting include the use of space and consistency in the style of questions, instructions, and answer alternatives.

General instructions—Instructions given to the respondent that introduce the study and explain what it is about, who is sponsoring it, and how the data will be used. In telephone surveys, a respondent may receive general instructions in an advance letter or from the interviewer, who reads the instructions to the respondent before beginning the questionnaire.

Grid—A question format used for sequences of questions that have similar objectives. By using grids in questionnaires, surveyors can save space and link related data appropriately.

Hagan and Collier method—A method for selecting a designated respondent within a household in which the interviewer first asks to speak to either the oldest or youngest male in the household. If no such person exists, the interviewer then asks for the comparable female in the household.

Heaping—The creation of response categories for closed-ended questions in such a way that a plurality or majority of respondents select a single category and few respondents, if any, select other categories.

Illiteracy—The inability to read and write. In the United States it is estimated that 20% of the adult population is unable to read and write in English.

Implementation—The multistage process of preparing and administering a survey and processing the question- naires.

Incentives—Money, services, or goods provided to respon- dents in order to encourage their participation in a study.

In-person (or face-to-face) interviewing—Interviewing in which the interviewer and the respondent are in the same place, often the respondent's home, and can see each other.

Interviewer—A person who is hired and trained to interview respondents for a study.

Jargon—Specialized language that is usually associated with a particular professional group or work group. Acronyms are a form of jargon. Like slang, jargon should not be included in questionnaires.

Kish tables—A set of 12 tables used as part of a method for selecting a designated respondent within a household. The interviewer first lists all adults 18 and over who reside in the household and then uses the specific Kish table that has been preassigned to that interview to determine who is to be interviewed.

Language barrier—An obstacle to a potential respondent's participation in a study owing to the fact that he or she does not speak and/or read one of the languages in which the study is being conducted.

Last/next birthday method—A method for selecting a des- ignated respondent within a household in which the interviewer asks the person who answers the phone who in the household had the last birthday or will have the next birthday.

Letterhead—Stationery with a preprinted heading, address, and other information that identifies an organization. Printing correspondence with potential respondents on letterhead helps establish the legitimacy of a study and may increase some individuals' motivation to participate.

Literacy—The ability to read and write.

Literature search—The survey researcher's examination of published books and articles for reports on theories and prior studies concerning the researcher's topic of interest. Conducting a literature search is one of the first steps in developing a survey design and a questionnaire.

Logical ordering of questions—The organization of the questionnaire so that related questions are together and not mixed in with or interrupted by other topics.

Machine-readable—Readable by a computer. Data need to be set up in machine-readable form so that they can be entered into a computer for analysis.

Mailing—The coordinated sending of a questionnaire or advance letter through the mail such that all those individuals to whom the material is sent receive it at approximately the same time.

Motivation—The desire to participate in a study. The topic of a study often influences a person's motivation to participate, and the methods used in the design of a study also affect motivation. In an interview survey, the interviewers themselves can affect motivation.

Monitoring (of an interview)—A procedure in which a field supervisor listens in on all or part of an interview in order to assess the interviewer's ability. Such monitoring ensures that interviews are conducted as intended.

Mutually exclusive response list—A list of alternative answers to a closed-ended question in which all choices are clearly independent of one another, so that the respondent has no trouble selecting the response that best describes him or her.

Network sample—See **Snowball sample.**

Next birthday method—See **Last/next birthday method.**

Nonprobability sample—A sample that does not allow the researcher to estimate the likelihood of any given person, household, institution, or organization being selected for the sample.

Objectivity—Neutrality, or the careful avoidance of bias, in the way the researcher designs and administers the study.

Open-ended question—A question on a questionnaire that includes no preset list of possible answers for respondents to choose among.

Order effects—The influence that one set of questions (or answer categories) may have on the answers respondents provide to later sets of questions.

Paper-and-pencil administration—Administration of a questionnaire in which the data collected are recorded on a paper copy of a questionnaire or on a related answer sheet.

Partially open question—A question on an interviewer-administered questionnaire for which the researcher has developed a list of alternative answers but the list is not intended to be read to the respondent; rather, the list is intended for use by the interviewer in recording the respondent's answers.

Pilot study (or pilot test)—A full testing of all aspects of the study, including the selection of subjects and the full collection of all data. A pilot study is a "study in miniature."

Population—All of the individuals, households, institutions, or organizations that meet a certain criterion (e.g., live in California).

Precoding—The assignment of variable names to each question and numeric codes to each answer alternative before the questionnaire is actually administered, so that data can be entered into a computer efficiently as interviews are completed.

Pretesting—The process of testing parts of the questionnaire during questionnaire development, generally with a convenience sample of respondents who are thought to be the "most different" on the section of the questionnaire being tested (e.g., a researcher would pretest on both males and females, both older persons and younger persons, or the like). (Note that this is the primary meaning of the term *pretesting* as it is used in survey research; it should not be confused with the same term often used to mean the data collection that takes place before the administration of an intervention in an experiment or quasi-experiment.)

Primacy effect—The tendency of respondents, when answering closed-ended questions, to select the first answer heard or read rather than considering the full list of alternatives.

Probability sample—A sample for which the researcher can estimate how likely it is that each person, household, or other unit in the population will get into the sample.

Probe—The sequence of follow-up questions that an interviewer uses to make sure he or she has a full understanding of a respondent's answer to a question. Interviewers use probes particularly with open-ended questions.

Purposive sample—See **Quota sample.**

Questionnaire—An instrument containing a structured, standardized sequence of questions that is used in an interview or filled out by a participant in a study.

Quota sample (or purposive sample)—A type of nonprobability sample in which the researcher attempts to exert some control over how study participants are selected. For example, the researcher determines the numbers of males and females to be interviewed, how many persons of particular religious affiliations are to be interviewed, or the times, places, and days of the week when interviews are to be conducted.

Random-digit dialing (RDD) sample—A type of probability sample that is both unique to telephone surveys and probably the type used the most often. The population of telephone numbers is listed and the sample is drawn from this population using simple random sampling procedures. RDD samples may or may not be list-assisted (that is, created with the assistance of lists such as telephone directories to increase the efficiency of the sample).

Recency effect—The tendency of respondents, when answering closed-ended questions, to remember and select the answer they heard or read last rather than any of the prior alternatives.

Refusal—The act of refusing to participate in a survey study. Also used to refer to a person, household, or institution that refuses to participate in a study.

Refusal conversion—The process of persuading a potential respondent to be interviewed for a study after he or she has initially refused to participate.

Reliability—The reproducibility of the survey data. That is, data are considered to be reliable when the same distribution of characteristics, experiences, behaviors, or attitudes would be obtained in data collected at a different time, by a different data collector, or using a different methodology.

Residual "other" category—An unspecified option included in the answer categories provided in response to a closed-ended question. Including such a category is particularly valuable when the researcher is not sure that the list of alternatives provided is exhaustive.

Response rate—The proportion of people, households, or institutions that are selected for a study from whom or about which data are successfully collected.

Sample—The individuals, households, institutions, or organizations selected out of a population for study. There are three primary types of samples: probability, systematic, and nonprobability.

Sample frame—A list of individuals, households, institutions, organizations, or phone numbers that represents the population and from which the sample is selected.

Satisficing theory—A theory that states that respondents tend to answer questions by choosing the first satisfactory or acceptable response alternative offered rather than taking time to select optimal answers.

Sensitive topic—A topic that respondents may be reluctant to discuss with researchers. Sexual behaviors and illegal behaviors are among the topics generally thought to be sensitive.

Simple random sampling—A type of probability sampling in which the researcher uses a random numbers table or random numbers generator in a computer to select persons from the population or sample frame. In this form of sampling, the fact that a particular person is selected for the sample does not influence who the next person selected will be.

Skip instructions—Instructions within a question in a questionnaire that allow branching to occur and so enable data collection to be modified for respondents with different characteristics, experiences, knowledge, and attitudes.

Slang—Words and phrases developed within and used by particular groups. Slang sets the members of one group off from those of other groups and functions as a shorthand form of communication. Because not all respondents are likely to understand slang terms, surveyors should not include them in questionnaires.

Snowball (or network) sample—A type of nonprobability sample in which the first people interviewed are asked to provides names of other people or groups "like them." Researchers often use snowball sampling when the groups in which they are interested are difficult to identify or to locate, or when the subject under study involves illegal behaviors.

Specifications (or research specifications, or questionnaire specifications)—Complete documentation by the researcher of the purpose of the study, how the sample for the study was selected, how interviews should be conducted, where and why questions were included in the questionnaire, and how questions should be handled. Interviewer specifications are usually extracted out of the research specifications.

Sponsorship—Financial and other support provided by organizations or other groups for the conduct of a study.

Standard question battery—An existing set of questions that has been widely used in prior research studies.

Stratified sampling—A type of probability sampling in which the population or sample frame is first divided into sections, or strata, and then simple random sampling procedures are used to select the sample within each section.

Subjectivity—A form of bias in which the researcher perceives that respondents are "like" him or her, or that he or she "knows" what respondents think and do. Subjectivity is the opposite of objectivity.

Survey—A system for collecting data from a population or sample at one point in time where it is assumed that there is heterogeneity in personal characteristics, attitudes, knowledge, and behaviors across the population.

Telephone access—The extent to which a population of interest has telephones or access to telephones.

Telephone interviewing—A data collection method in which interviewers administer the survey instrument to respondents by telephone.

GLOSSARY

Tracking—The monitoring of data collection, including the work of the interviewers and the extent to which the sample is being used up or exhausted. Appropriate tracking may show that more interviewers need to be hired, that another sample replicate needs to be drawn, and so on.

Transitional instructions—Instructions for respondents that appear in the questionnaire where questions on one topic end and questions on another topic begin. Transitional instructions give respondents a chance to "catch their breath" and help them change the focus of their thinking.

Translation—The process of converting a questionnaire that was written in one language into another language. Generally, two translators are used: The first translator translates the questionnaire into the second language, and the second translator performs a back-translation—that is, translates the first translated version back into the original language.

Troldahl-Carter-Bryant (TCB) tables—Tables used as part of a method for selecting a designated respondent in a household. The interviewer asks how many persons there are in the household of a certain age, such as 18 and over, and then uses the TCB table preassigned to that interview to select the respondent.

Vague qualifier—A modifying term that may be interpreted differently by different people. Most adverbs can be considered vague qualifiers.

Validity—The degree to which the data being collected really represent the range of experiences, opinions, behaviors, and types of people present in the population being studied.

Ventilation question—An open-ended question used at the end of a questionnaire to allow respondents to tell the researcher what they liked about the interview, what they disliked about the interview, which questions were difficult to answer, which questions they did not understand, and what the researcher should have asked about but did not.

Verification of data—The process of entering some or all of the data from a questionnaire twice and comparing the two data files for discrepancies. When discrepancies are found, the original questionnaire must be examined and any errors in data entry must be corrected.

Verification of an interview—A process in which a field supervisor recalls a respondent and reconducts all or part of the interview in order to assess the quality of the interviewer's work.

Vertical format—A questionnaire format in which the alternative answers to closed-ended questions appear under each other rather than listed horizontally. The advantage of this format is that interviewers, respondents, and data entry personnel can see and differentiate among the various alternatives easily.

Waksberg-Mitofsky procedure—A type of list-assisted random-digit dialing sample that has been widely used and discussed in the research literature.

GLOSSARY

About the Authors

Linda B. Bourque, Ph.D., is Associate Director of the Center for Public Health and Disasters, Associate Director of the Southern California Injury Prevention Research Center, and Professor in the Department of Community Health Sciences in the School of Public Health at the University of California, Los Angeles, where she teaches courses in research design and survey methodology. She has conducted research on ophthalmic clinical trials, intentional and unintentional injury, and community perceptions of and responses to disasters. She is author or coauthor of 60 scientific articles and the books *Defining Rape* and *Processing Data: The Survey Example* (with Virginia Clark).

Eve P. Fielder, Dr.P.H., has more than 35 years' experience in survey research. Since her early work in market research, she has been involved in all phases of survey design and administration and has conducted hundreds of surveys, both commercial and academic. For the past 30 years, she has been with the Institute for Social Science Research at the University of California, Los Angeles, where she is Director of the Survey Research Center. She has also taught survey research methods at UCLA and at the University of Southern California. She has consulted on studies for numerous organizations and community service agencies and has a strong background in cross-cultural research.